THE FARAWAY COUNTRY
Writers of the Modern South

)

OTHER BOOKS BY LOUIS D. RUBIN, JR.

AUTHOR *The Golden Weather* [novel] (1961)

Thomas Wolfe: The Weather of His Youth (1955)

No Place on Earth: James Branch Cabell, Ellen Glasgow, and Richmond-in-Virginia (1959)

EDITOR *Southern Renascence* [with R. D. Jacobs] (1953)

The Lasting South [with J. J. Kilpatrick] (1957)

Teach the Freeman: The Correspondence of R. B. Hayes and the Slater Fund for Negro Education, 1881–1893 (1959)

The Idea of an American Novel [with J. R. Moore] (1961)

South: Modern Southern Literature in Its Cultural Setting [with R. D. Jacobs] (1961)

The Faraway Country

WRITERS OF THE MODERN SOUTH

BY LOUIS D. RUBIN, JR.

UNIVERSITY OF WASHINGTON PRESS
SEATTLE 1963

Copyright © 1963 by the University of Washington Press
Library of Congress Catalog Card Number 63-19632
Manufactured by Vail-Ballou Press, Inc., Binghamton, N.Y.
Printed in the United States of America
Designed by Adrian Wilson

To the memory of

HARRY MITCHELL RUBIN, JR.

1922–1957

"*After all everybody,*
that is everybody that writes, is interested in living
inside themselves in order to
tell what is inside themselves.
That is why writers
have to have two countries,
the one where they belong and
the one in which they live really.
The second one is romantic,
it is separate from themselves,
it is not real,
but it is really there."

GERTRUDE STEIN

Preface

These are essays about certain men and women who were born in the Southern States of the American Union, most of them at about the same time, and who have written novels, stories, and poems, many of which have to do with the experience of living in that region. Taken all together, the essays make up something of a unit, and constitute an exploration, tentative and incomplete though it may be, of the relationship between the books these men and women wrote and the life and times of the region.

The work of these writers, and of a number of other writers some of whom are at least equally distinguished, has caused the period in which they wrote to be known as the Southern Literary Renascence. That period is not yet over, and though some of these writers have died, others are still very much at work. Thus any conclusions about modern Southern writing can at best be advanced only very cautiously. I do not pretend, therefore, to have written any kind of thoroughgoing historical and critical study of modern Southern writing. Instead I have selected certain writers, and certain books, that have interested me and have seemed to be especially relevant to my principal concern, which is the ways in which the work of these writers is related to Southern experience.

The reader should bear in mind that this is a fairly special concern. Otherwise he is likely to draw from these essays a very narrow and restricted notion of what these writers have been doing, and what their novels and poems are about. I have not hesitated, for example, to concentrate on a single one of Robert Penn Warren's many novels, to the exclusion of all the others, and to deal with but one aspect of that novel: the kind of society symbolized within it, and its relationship to the attitude of one of the characters toward another character. The same is true, in varying degree, of each of the essays in this book. They represent an attempt to use literature in order to understand Southern life, and I hope that in so doing I have not done violence to either the literature or the life.

In dealing as I do with the South, and with Southern writers, it will be obvious that much of the material herein presented is by no means uniquely Southern. That is to say, much that is true of Southerners during the twentieth century is likewise true of other Americans, and indeed of people in general. To the reader who, noting this, might ask that I account for my right to refer to the experience and the work of these writers as Southern, I can reply only that this is in no way an inclusive study of all aspects of the Southern Renascence, and that elsewhere I have several times addressed myself to just this question, particularly in an essay entitled "Southern Literature: The Historical Image," included in a collection of essays entitled *South: Modern Southern Literature in Its Cultural Setting,* edited by Robert D. Jacobs and myself. In that essay, and in certain other writings, I have sought to deal with the complex question of the South's historical experience within the Union, the impact of the

Civil War, the resulting intensification of certain attitudes and institutions, the delayed impact of industrialism on Southern life and the consequent explosive nature of the pent-up violence attendant to its arrival, the crucial role of the Negro as index and cause of Southern attitudes, and so on. In these essays I content myself with assuming the particularity of the experience, with the hope that the reader will not hold me responsible for demonstrating once again what I several times have attempted to prove to the best of my ability.

The essays that follow may be said to cover three generations of Southern writing. After the introductory essay, which is a general statement of theme, there is a commentary on a book by a writer who died almost a decade before most of the work of the major modern Southern writers began appearing, but a book that, I think, can be said to symbolize the transition from the genteel Southern literary tradition of the nineteenth century to the bold modernists of post-World-War-I times. At this point there might properly have been included an essay on James Branch Cabell and Ellen Glasgow, but since I have already published both a full-length book and an essay on these two early moderns, I could see no justification for traveling once again over such familiar ground. The succeeding essays, save the last, deal with four novelists and a group of poets who represent the literary generation that came into prominence in the 1920's and 1930's, and whose work in effect constitutes today the foremost achievement of the Southern Renascence. My choices are admittedly idiosyncratic; I have included some writers and writings that I admire, and have omitted certain others whose work I admire just as much—Andrew Lytle, Katherine Anne Porter, Carson McCullers. There is no particular reason for this; it is simply that for this book of essays, I have picked and chosen from among

writers and works that illustrate themes and concerns I
thought relevant to my inquiry. The final essay deals with
a writer of another and later generation, that coming
after the Second World War, and my attempt has been
to show how this man's work represents several note-
worthy changes in the character of modern Southern
writing which I think may indicate some important ad-
justments in recent Southern attitudes. I might have with
almost equal appropriateness chosen any of a number
of other younger Southern writers to illustrate these
changes, but it seemed to me that William Styron's fiction
was especially well suited to my purposes.

The cumulative result of these essays, I hope, is a
demonstration, through the work of a group of writers,
of the thesis developed in the first essay, which is that
Southern literature is of a culture, and that a culture
exists in time, and that changes in that culture are mirrored in its literature. At the same time, however, I hope
that I have made it plain that literature is a work of the
imagination, and therefore that any attempt at a literal,
one-for-one equation of poetry and fiction with the details of the life from which they grow must inevitably
be a distortion of the culture and the literature. The
process of alchemy that we call art will not admit of
easy sociological analysis, and the only road toward understanding and using literature to analyze culture must
be through the work of art itself.

There must someday be a thoroughgoing critical history written of twentieth-century Southern literature.
Whether the time is already at hand when someone can
undertake such a history I do not know. I can speak
only for myself; I know that for me that day has not
yet come. Too many of the major figures are still active and flourishing for me to attempt to view their
lives and their work as a unit, and to relate that unit to

the still turbulent life and times of the region. In the post-script to this collection I advance a few very tentative judgments, but any further than this I am not prepared to go, for I view modern Southern literature and the Southern Literary Renascence as something still very much alive and changing. To seek to embalm it as literary history just now would appear to me to be presumptuous, to say the least. That eventually this must be done, and that the work of the writers of the modern South must inevitably constitute a long and distinguished chapter in the history of American letters, one absolutely essential to the understanding of that history, I have no doubt. If my own inquiries should prove to be of some future use in the writing of such a chapter, I should be quite pleased.

Ten years ago I was fortunate enough to receive a fellowship from the editors of the *Sewanee Review*. These essays grew directly out of the responsibilities I accepted with that fellowship. For this and numerous other kindnesses I should like to record my grateful appreciation to the editors, in particular Monroe K. Spears and Andrew Nelson Lytle. In 1956 I received a John Simon Guggenheim Memorial Fellowship which encouraged me to continue the investigations that these essays represent, and to the kindness of the officers of that esteemed foundation I am most indebted.

I am sure that Robert D. Jacobs will recognize many of the ideas in this book, especially those having to do with William Faulkner, as his own, however I may have maimed them. The same is true of C. Vann Woodward; it was as his student, more than a decade ago, that I undertook to write an essay that led to my interest in the central concerns of this book. For the longtime interest and encouragement of Donald R. Ellegood I am indebted beyond repayment. I am glad to say, too, that I have been one among many writers who have experienced the kindness and the encouragement of Hiram Haydn. Especially in the revision of these essays I have relied heavily on the good judgment of C. Hugh Holman. During the writing of these essays I was fortunate for much of the time to have had as my colleague at Hollins College John W. Aldridge, on whose critical insights I drew liberally. And finally but by no means least of all, I am grateful to many of my students at Hollins College on whom I tried out some of these ideas, in particular the Misses and then-Misses Sally Durham, Jane Winston Carpenter, Katherine Paul Letcher, Nelle Carter, Anne-Claude Piguet, Shannon Ravenel, Elizabeth Forsythe, Elizabeth Rutherford Seydel, Jean Nicholson Meyer, Axson Evans Brown, Jane Lyell Stephens, Audrey Lucille Taylor, Eleanora de Branges, Elizabeth A. Gummey, Anna Montague Sevier, Güneli Tamkoç, Hila Caulley, Jean M. Simpson, Terry Herrin, Leta F. Austin, Jon Monroe Ellison, and Jane Gentry; and Mr. Richard Benvenuto.

Essays and portions of essays included in this collection appeared originally in the following publications, and I wish to acknowledge with thanks permission to reprint them:

Virginia Quarterly Review, for "The South and the Faraway Country," XXXVII, No. 3 (Summer, 1962), 444–59, and "The Road to Yoknapatawpha," XXXV, No. 1 (Winter, 1959), 119–32.

Sewanee Review, for a portion of "William Styron: Notes on a Southern Writer in Our Time," entitled "An Artist in Bonds," LXIX, No. 1 (Winter, 1961), 174–79.

New York Review, for a portion of "The Golden Apples of the Sun," entitled "Virgie Rainey and the Golden Apples of the Sun," I, No. 1 (Spring, 1958), 10–15.

Contents

THE FARAWAY COUNTRY
Writers of the Modern South

1

THE SOUTH
AND THE
FARAWAY COUNTRY

In Mark Twain's *The Adventures of Tom Sawyer*, there is an image that occurs at frequent points, and provides for the fictional activities of Tom and his cronies a kind of dimension that is very important to the way in which we read the novel. The image is of Cardiff Hill, "beyond the village and above it, . . . green with vegetation, . . . just far away enough to seem a Delectable Land, dreamy, reposeful, and inviting." Again and again Mark Twain gives us this motif. It serves to throw the events of the novel against a backdrop of nature and time, contrasting the sharp realism of the dialogue and the lively, often violent action with an underlying sense of never-never-land experience, so that the time and the place become an Eden-like country, long ago and far away, very much like a dream.

Mark Twain, as we know, left the town of Hannibal, Missouri, when a young man. Yet the source and subject of his best art remained the time and place of his youth, the town on the Mississippi River before the railroads came. The remembered life of that small community, the people he had known there while growing up, provided him with the fictional country that housed two American classics. Scoff though Mark Twain did at many features of Southern life, his literary imagination was always more small-town Southern than he cared to admit. Though his Western books gave him his first reputation, the Twain we read today is primarily the man who wrote of life in a little Southwestern river town, a town more Southern than Western in its patterns and attitudes.

In many ways, I think, Mark Twain is the prototype of the Southern writers of our own time. Like them he grew up in a small, contained community, and like them he was propelled by his art and his times far beyond that community. Westward and then eastward he went, into the busy life of post-Civil-War industrial America. By the accident of American history the country of northern Missouri was not allowed to remain sleepy, Southern, and contained; indeed, the economic and political forces that destroyed agrarian America were already at work during his boyhood.

Only in the Confederate South was the industrialization of America arrested, by the military and economic defeat of the War, and communities like Mark Twain's Hannibal allowed to exist for another half-century. Not until the twentieth century did the South feel importantly the effects of the industrialization that was changing the face of American life. Then it too produced distinguished writers whose art mirrored the transition from one kind of life to another. In the novels and poems of the writers of the modern South we also catch sight of the kind of community life, "dreamy, reposeful and inviting," that Cardiff Hill typifies in the Twain novels, furnishing a background against which the most violent and unromantic activities can take place, serving to place all that activity in a rich context of time and change, time flowing like the great river that moved past Hannibal, carrying Huck Finn and Nigger Jim along with it, suspended as it were outside chronology, apart from the human activity taking place on the shore.

To understand the literature of the South of our own time, it is essential to keep in mind the small-town, small-city origins of the writers who created it. They grew up at a time when the fabric of Southern community life as it had existed for many decades was beginning to break up before the forces of the twentieth century. As writers they are themselves symbols, I think, of that disintegration. The communities in which they were born were just beginning to change from being small, contained, settled towns, in which agriculture was the chief occupation, in which all was fixed and ordered, and everyone knew everyone else, and who he was, and who and what his family was, and in which life seemed to hold few surprises. The Southern community had been self-sufficient, an entity in itself, with a mostly homogenous population, relatively orderly and fixed in its daily patterns.

The young Southerner of good family who had gone off to college was expected to and did come back to his community after graduation to assume his role in community life. Intellectual activity, such as it was, was also a community affair; the intellectual was not cut off from his society. He *belonged*. He was not, in fact, what we would call an intellectual at all, for the very term presupposes a primary allegiance to ideas, to the life of the mind, as against everyday preoccupation in a world of things. There was a literary tradition in the South, but it was always subordinate to the general patterns of community life, and did not exact the kind of intensity and singleminded devotion that we associate with important artistic attainment. "Southerners," Ellen Glasgow recalled, "did not publish, did not write, did not read."

And while this is an exaggeration, it is quite true that belles lettres played a very subordinate role in Southern society. The Southern writer of the late nineteenth century—you will find his work in that dreary shelf of books entitled *The Library of Southern Literature*—was judge, physician, lawyer, businessman, clergyman, journalist, and so forth. He was part of his community; his neighbors read his poems and stories; he did not consider that his literary activity set him importantly apart from ordinary community life.

Nor did it in truth do so; and to the detriment of that literature. For it was not a literature of great intensity, and did not come from the kind of spiritual detachment that develops long-range perspectives on human activity so as to expose its underlying values and meanings. Able as the Southern writer was to confront his own personality within the limits of community life, he did not need to move very far outside the values of that community in order to define reality. For him, reality and everyday life were one and the same, and his literature was part of the life he engaged in as a citizen. Only an occasional misfit, such as Poe, was unable to discover his ultimate reality in everyday life and was thus forced to create it for himself through his art. The typical Southern author of the nineteenth and the early twentieth centuries was not an exile, either spiritually or geographically, from his community; and so Southern literature before World War I is mostly genteel and respectable, dealing primarily with surfaces, the product of minds for whom the particulars of community life provided all the spiritual and moral nourishment and order they needed in order to exist as human beings.

But in the twentieth century, after the First World War, the South did begin to produce memorable literature, stories and poems of great moral and spiritual intensity, of tremendous intellectual depth. And unlike his precursors, the twentieth-century Southern writer has not also served as judge, physician, lawyer, clergyman, journalist, and so forth; he has not been able to find his spiritual sustenance and order within community life itself, to play his full role as citizen. Insofar as he has been a writer he has also been an intellectual, an artist, largely cut off from the daily existence of his fellow Southerners, whether he continues to live in the South or not. He has outgrown the dimensions of his community. The version of reality it afforded him has not been sufficient for him; he has had to create it for himself in his stories and poems.

For the Southern community as it used to be has broken down, and the twentieth century has come in. The settled, fixed patterns of town life have been violently disrupted. Not only have towns become cities, and cities, metropolises, but the moral order of the older South, the old notions of certainty and belief, have ceased to suffice as a sufficient explanation and an adequate basis for daily experience. I speak not only of religion, but of attitudes toward the values of the community, toward history, toward society. The future novelist or poet, growing up in the South in the 1900's and 1910's, did not find, as his father and grandfather had been able to find, sufficient emotional scope within the life of the community. He went off to college, but what he learned, instead of preparing him for community life, only intensified the separation between him and his origins, and after graduation he did not return home. He went elsewhere to live and to write, and if he did come back later on, it was not in the way that his father and grandfather came back. In important respects he remained separated from his neighbors, living in his own private country, creating his own private Yoknapatawpha counties and Altamonts so as to discover through his art the order and meaning that "real life" no longer afforded him.

The Southern writers who created the memorable literature of our own time almost all went North at one time or the other. It was as if the change in the Southern community, and in the role possible to young men and women like themselves within it, propelled them out of the South in search of more congenial surroundings. Early in Thomas Wolfe's *The Web and the Rock* there is a moment when George Webber dreams of the metropolis of the North. "And at the end, forever at the end of all the fabled earth," Wolfe wrote, "there hung the golden vision of the city, itself more fertile, richer, more full of joy and bounty than the earth it rested on. Far-off and shining, it rose upward in his vision from an opalescent mist, upborne and sustained as lightly as a cloud, yet firm and soaring with full golden light." To the young North Carolinian, the city was the place of fulfillment, of achievement. There *escape* was possible —from the South, from the settled, fixed community where there were prescribed limits and boundaries to what he could be, where nothing was unknown, where he, his family, and all the other inhabitants occupied their accustomed and proper places. By contrast, in the legendary metropolis life was not conscribed and bounded, opportunities for fulfillment were numerous, and a young man was supposedly judged by what he could *do*.

But when the young Southerner got to the city and took up his residence there, what he found was very different from what he had imagined. The youthful dream of the metropolis soon changed, often as not to a nightmare. The huge impersonality of city life, the frantic pace, the swarming crowds, the feeling of being no more than a cipher in the "vast manswarm," proved

not to be so enchanting a replacement for the limitations
of provincial life back home. The city began to seem
merely big and ugly. The novels of the modern Southern
writers contain numerous descriptions of young Southerners adrift in the metropolis—Quentin Compson of
Faulkner's *The Sound and the Fury* makes his way aimlessly about Cambridge, Massachusetts; Peyton Loftis of
William Styron's *Lie Down in Darkness* wanders about
New York; the Wolfean heroes stalk the canyons of the
metropolis; Eugene MacLain of Eudora Welty's *The
Golden Apples* walks through the mists of San Francisco.
All of them are Southern; all are far from home, filled
with the same sense of bewilderment at their estrangement from the community of their origins.

Allen Tate's poem "The Subway" vividly expresses
something of what they found in the city, and how they
reacted to it. Composed while Tate lived in New York
City in the late 1920's, it speaks of the subway as a place
"where ogives burst a red / Reverberance of hail upon
the dead / Thunder like an exploding crucible," of feeling as if one were being "hurled religiously / Into the
iron forestries of hell," and of being "dazed, while the
worldless heavens bulge and reel / In the cold revery of
an idiot."

Most of the Southern writers did not remain in the
metropolis. Of the important figures, only Wolfe stayed
on; this is understandable when one considers that only
Wolfe possessed the kind of romantic temperament that
enabled him to accept and even revel in a completely
solitary social existence. Much of Wolfe's writing, though
comparatively little of his best work, consists of a personal exploration of the varieties of loneliness possible in
the city; he gloried in playing the role, as he put it, of
"God's lonely man." As for the others, they all went
back home, though by no means all of them stayed there.

The return home, and what the Southerner finds there, is much less often remarked in Southern writing, however, than the sojourn in the metropolis. What the Southerner who comes back home speedily discovered was that though one might very well take up his physical residence in the old community, he could not in some important ways go home again. For what he learned in the metropolis confirmed him in his inability to accept the conditions of Southern life any more. He could not look upon things that as a child he had accepted without question, without being struck by their insufficiency. It was perhaps this that had sent him northward in the first place, but at the time he had not realized it; or if he had sensed it, had forgotten about it while away. Now he came back, to find that the happy homeland of his memory was not so idyllic any more—and, he was forced to admit to himself, never had been. While living away he had known a strong sentimental attachment to his home community and its ways. But he found that he could not put down his roots again, for the soil was too thin. For better or for worse he had become confirmed in perspectives, interests, attitudes that set him apart from his neighbors in the old community.

The homeplace had changed too. It was no longer the community it had been, and he perhaps realized it with particular force, for he had been away for awhile and had not been a part of the transaction as it took place. He had read about what was happening back home, but he did not believe it. Now he saw it was true.

So the Southerner engaged in becoming a writer departed again—whether he departed literally or figuratively does not matter. He may very well have stayed on, and so far as he and his fellow townsfolk were concerned, he may be said to have been living "in" the South. But he was not a part of the community any

longer; not really, not even if he pretended to himself
that he was. His standards were different, his attitudes
toward the common Southern experience were different.
He may have become very "Southern"—but in a quite
self-conscious way, as if playing a game with himself.
For one cannot really be self-consciously Southern; they
are antithetical attitudes. One cannot be mentally detached from the Southern community while physically
a part of it, and be fully a member of that community.
The essence of membership in the old Southern community was the sense of belonging, of being able to define one's place, one's attitudes, one's identity as a man,
through one's role in that community's life. When the
community ceased to provide that anchor and definition,
then in an important sense it no longer existed.

An incident in the career of Robert Penn Warren furnishes an illustration of this. When in the late 1920's some
members of the group of Southern poets known as the
Nashville Fugitives conceived the idea for a volume of
essays defending the traditional Southern rural way of
life and opposing the industrialism that was making such
inroads in their section, Warren was a student at Oxford
in England. For the book, Warren undertook a study
of the Negro's place in the South. His essay, entitled
"The Briar Patch," was an articulate defense of racial segregation.

Almost thirty years later, in 1958, Warren published
another analysis of the Negro's role in the region. Entitled *Segregation*, it constituted almost a complete re-
versal of his earlier position. Somewhat later Warren was
interviewed by the editors of *The Paris Review*, and one
of the questions asked was about this change in his attitude toward the race issue. Warren explained that when
he had written the essay in 1930, he was conscious of

"some sort of discomfort in it, some sense of evasion." He was "trying to prove something" in the essay, in contrast with the fiction that he was just beginning then to write, in which he was "trying to find out something, see something, feel something."

The real change in his attitude toward the Negro issue, he went on to say in the interview, came not while he was at Oxford, but when he went back home several years later. "In a little while," he recalled, "I realized I simply couldn't have written that essay again. I guess trying to write fiction made me realize that. If you are seriously trying to write fiction you can't allow yourself as much evasion as in trying to write essays."

So long as Warren was away from the South, he could view the Negro issue in the traditional Southern way. But when he came home, he realized that he could not see the Negro's status as something involving an idyllic relationship between benevolent white folks and devoted darkies. So long as he had been in England and elsewhere, he had been quite prepared to do so, to sentimentalize the matter. But when he came home with his new experience—in his case it was the writing of fiction—and settled down to live in his home region again, he realized the extent of his divergence from the old Southern modes of thought. Then, and not until then, did Southern ways of approaching an important human problem seem unrealistic and inadequate. What Warren discovered, in effect, was that he too could not go home again.

Warren came back to the South from England shortly after 1930, but he did not go back to his hometown in Kentucky. Instead he taught at various universities, notably at Louisiana State in Baton Rouge where he was an editor of *The Southern Review*. And though Warren continued to write about the South, both then and during

his later sojourn in Minnesota and Connecticut, it cannot
be said that he was ever again part of the pattern of the
small-town Southern community life. Similarly his fellow Fugitive Allen Tate came back to the South, but
not to small-town Southern life. Another eminent Fugitive, John Crowe Ransom, came back after the First
World War to teach at Vanderbilt University, remaining there until 1937, when he went to Kenyon College
in Ohio to settle down.

To examine the careers of the other Southern writers
is only to confirm the observation. Andrew Lytle found
that one could not be both farmer and writer; for many
years he lived in the not-very-Southern university community of Gainesville, Florida, and now he teaches at
the University of the South. Eudora Welty has found
Jackson, Mississippi, a comfortable place in which to
live, but the dissection of the Southern community in
The Golden Apples could not have been written by anyone without a tremendous sense of detachment from that
community. Katherine Anne Porter has not resided in
the South for years; neither has Carson McCullers nor
Caroline Gordon. Even Donald Davidson, who in his
political writings has strongly promulgated the traditional Southern position on segregation and other controversial issues, has in his prose and poetry conducted an
extended rebuke to his native region for its desertion of
what he considers its historical heritage and attitude.

Not even William Faulkner, a self-confessed "farmer"
who wrote all of his major work while back home in
Oxford, Misissippi, can really be said to have fully "come
home again" after his stay in the cities of New York and
New Orleans. He lived "in" Oxford, to be sure, with occasional forays to Hollywood, but no one will contend
that his novels were written as a part of his role as citizen
in that Southern community. They are the product rather

of his spiritual detachment from the community, and represent an intense scrutiny of the moral and human dimensions of that community's past, by one who could no longer accept the everyday values of community life. What most of Faulkner's fellow Missisippians thought of the relationship of his literary art to his role as citizen can be characterized in the verdict that the editor of the Jackson *Daily News* pronounced when informed that his fellow Mississippian had been awarded the Nobel Prize for literature: "He is a propagandist of degradation and properly belongs in the privy school of literature."

The Southern writers could not "go home," whether physically they did so or not, because the South to which they thought they were returning did not exist any more. It was the South of their childhood, the South of a time when they had not yet recognized within themselves the intense aesthetic perceptions that gradually set them apart from their neighbors and sent them northward in the first place. Indeed, the original journey away had not been a deliberate act of removal, so much as the recognition and confirmation of a separation that had already been taking place. They had grown away from their neighbors, because even in the South of their childhood the community was no longer able, as for their parents and grandparents it had been able once, to provide the emotional and intellectual stimulation that would have permitted them fully to exist within the community. They were twentieth-century Southerners, of two countries now instead of one. The real South, for them, was not the geographical region, but the country within their minds, the artistic image they had created and put into their stories and poems. Not Asheville but Altamont was the real South for Thomas Wolfe. Not Clark County, Kentucky, but an imaginary country where "tasseling corn, / Fat beans, grapes sweeter than muscadine /

Rot on the vine" was Allen Tate's South. "In that land we were born," Tate's poem "The Mediterranean" concludes; but that land existed, I think, in his poems and his mind and heart. And in the poems and novels of the modern Southern writers, one might add, it will, like Cardiff Hill in *Tom Sawyer,* continue to exist for a long time to come.

I doubt that any imaginative writer writes primarily "about" a particular time or place when he sets his fiction or poetry in a recognizable locale or era. The term "historical novel" is a misnomer when used to describe a good novel, as is the term "local color," now thankfully extinct. Leo Tolstoy did not write "about" Russia, nor William Faulkner "about" Mississippi. Instead, both men used geography and history to embody countries of their own, in which the characters and scenes could act out fables designed to show what it meant to be alive and human. In the artistic image the people, places, and events become transformed into characters and scenes, the extent of their fidelity to real life varying from writer to writer. A writer creates out of his experience. When sometimes that experience is closely bound up with the details of memory and observation, we say he writes "about" certain historical times and places. But topically the novels of William Faulkner and Robert Penn Warren, or even Wolfe's for that matter, may no more properly be tied to the everyday South than those of Ernest Hemingway to Oak Park, Illinois. What the writer importantly draws from his background are certain attitudes toward language and toward experience, and these he can never escape. We discern important and recognizable influences of such things in his books, so that we can speak legitimately of "Southern fiction" or "the Russian novel." But it is the attitudes, not the topical subject matter, that make possible this identification. The process by which they become art is not local or regional, and cannot be limited to any time or place. Literature is by nature a universalizing process; the raw material of particular experience is transformed into knowledge of human life, and is made to embody the artist's perception of what being human means. The reader of a Faulkner novel may learn something about life in Mississippi, but he is certain to learn about what human experience can be like, whether in Mississippi or Boston or Stockholm. Otherwise there would be little purpose in reading Faulkner's novels. *The Sound and the Fury*, far from signifying nothing, has a great deal to say, but only a small part of it about Oxford, Mississippi.

Thomas Wolfe, in describing his autobiographical protagonist's return to Altamont for the first time in seven years, wrote: "Eugene was back in space and color and in time, the weather of his youth was round him, he was home again." Space and color and time are apt words to describe the way in which Wolfe wrote of life in Altamont, but the "home" to which Eugene Gant returned was not the flesh-and-blood-and-brick Asheville where Thomas Wolfe was born, but an imaginary place and time directly related to Asheville only in certain factual particulars. These particulars served the purpose of "grounding" or "anchoring" Wolfe's fiction, giving him points of reference from which he could pyramid his own created community of fiction. He tells us what some of these points of reference were: an old iron railroad trestle, a horse moving down a street, a dialogue between passersby, a watch given him by his brother, an episode recounted by his mother, the ringing of a church bell, the sound of workmen going home to lunch, the whistle of a freight locomotive south of town. From such things he constructed his novel. I suspect that everything in *Look Homeward, Angel* is given logic and organization by these particulars, which in themselves exist in no order or logic recognizable to others familiar with them in "real life." The order and logic are imaginative, related to "real life" in Asheville at numerous intervals, but governed by no desire or necessity to remain faithful to everyday experience in Asheville. Asheville is merely *used* to help make up Altamont; though one is impossible without the other, the relationship may be likened to the one existing between the model the artist chooses, and the painting he creates. (Would anyone think to attribute Rembrandt's genius as a painter to the fact that Saskia served as his model, even though one might very well be able to recognize Saskia from looking at the painting? Rather it was the detachment with which Rembrandt was able to view his model, the qualities that painter rather than model provided, that just as much as the affection of painter for subject give the Saskia paintings their artistic worth.)

In a similar way, I think, the Southern writers are "detached" from the everyday South, whether they live in it or apart from it. They are linked to it by certain attitudes, experiences, events, scenes, people who exist or did exist in the Southern community, and are part both of the writer's and the community's experiences—(Rembrandt, after all, was married to Saskia). But what such things mean to the writer and to the community is vastly different. For the community they are part of "real life"; for the writer they are ordering devices for his imagination. The citizens of Asheville no doubt were greatly puzzled by what Thomas Wolfe made of the old fountain in the town square. For them it was a water fountain; for Wolfe it became a tremendous symbol for the flow of time.

When did it become such a symbol? Not, I venture to say, as Thomas Wolfe walked across the square to his father's monument shop while a boy. Rather, it was as he thought of it later, as his imagination grasped the sensible memory of the fountain and wove it into the fabric of the novel he was writing. When he wrote the novel he was in point of time and place far away from Asheville; he was living in Altamont.

If, however, the actuality from which the symbol derives is transcended in the work of art, this is not to say that the life of the work of art is without its ultimate relevance to so-called "real life." What the artist does, what the Southern writer has done with the South, is to give to his experience a logic and order greater and more accessible than that of "real life." He fashions his own country because, I think, of his desire to effect an order greater than the one everyday life can provide for his experience. When "real life" as he knows it fails to furnish on its own terms a sufficiently coherent and ordered view of experience, the writer creates his own. The life of Faulkner's Yoknapatawpha has a moral logic greater than the life of Misissippi, and if we can read it imaginatively we can grasp some of the logic. It is not the logic of everyday life, but it is life clarified and interpreted in the universal light of human experience. It is thus more "accurate" than "real life," because the particularities are given an overt moral structure not apparent in day-to-day experience. In this way Faulkner can tell us "about" Mississippi, or Wolfe "about" Asheville.

When a time and place produce important literature, as the South of our own time has produced it, it is a

sign, I think, that great change is under way in the time
and place. For change is disruptive, disorderly; the old
order gives way, a new order strives to establish itself.
At this point the issue is dramatized by its writers, not
in its immediate events but in its underlying structure, as
they seek to discover and give order to what is really
going on. In that sense Yoknapatawpha *is* Oxford, and
Altamont *is* Asheville, but an Oxford or an Asheville
that can be only very imperfectly recognized by its inhabitants. It cannot be recognized because it is too general, too ordered, and reveals so much more (and of
"real" experience so much less) than Oxford or Asheville. Yoknapatawpha is not Mississippi alone; in its human dimensions it is also Atlanta, London, Thebes. But
the inhabitants of Mississippi see only the particularities
of life in Oxford; they do not see London and Thebes.
Faulkner did, and he saw them *in* and *through* Oxford,
Mississippi.

The old South did not produce many great writers
because it did not detach its artists sufficiently from community life, as New England did detach them, making
them go in search of greater order than that afforded
through the community. The nature and hold of the
Southern community provided, however innocently, a
sufficiently complex emotional, intellectual, and aesthetic
order to accommodate all its members. That such an
order was not sufficiently viable and durable is not the
question; to its participants it seemed so at the time.
When it ceased to be adequate, major writers came into
existence in the South, leaving the community, returning
to it, but seeking in their art the moral order no longer
present for them in the community itself.

It was no coincidence that the South's literary renascence has come in the twentieth century, when the region was changing from a settled, contained community

into its modern role. Small-town life was breaking up; communities were losing their older tidiness and changing into vast cities. What several generations had known as certainty became uncertainty and flux. The patterns of community life, once seeming so orderly, were distorted and disarranged. And the process still goes on. The inhabitants attempt to fit the old patterns to the new developments, but with less and less success. Old attitudes hang on, to be sure, anachronistically, doggedly, forcing modifications in the response to the new demands. What will finally emerge in the South is anyone's guess.

Not that the average Southerner is often conscious of this confusion; he goes about his business, meeting each day's crises as they occur. The attitudes created in him by his regional heritage remain, and are modified slowly. It is the writers, rather, who sense what is happening, who search for order in "real life" and fail to find it, and so create their own order in their art. To the everyday life of the South they give dimensions not perceptible to those who are busy living in it all the time. In their attitudes and perspectives as artists they are detached, isolated, bound to "real life" only by certain opinions, as it were, that serve to support their art.

They live in another country. It is not the country in which they were born, nor the country to which they once fled, nor yet the South to which they came back. Like Mark Twain's Mississippi River community, it is the country of fiction. There they may see the meaning of things in time, for as they write they step outside of everyday life toward a timeless perspective in which a fountain splashing in the town square becomes a sign of change, a Confederate cemetery a symbol of man caught in time, a rotting mansion in the Mississippi wilderness the emblem of what human beings in a time and place aspired to be, and what they became.

2

THE ROAD TO YOKNAPATAWPHA:
George W. Cable and
John March, Southerner

Realism in Southern literature is supposed to have started with Ellen Glasgow. Before her, the typical Southern novelist was someone such as James Lane Allen, Thomas Nelson Page, or Augusta Evans Wilson, whose view of Southern life was of something involving happy darkies, noble old colonels, moonlight on columned mansions, and happy times "before de wah." To be sure, this view of Southern literature is somewhat oversimplified, but it is undeniable that, with the exception of the subliterature of the humorists, very little of the actual day-by-day experience of Southern life got into its literature. Miss Glasgow showed the way, writing what for her time were quite daring accounts of "real" Southern life. She was justly proud of her role in opening up new areas of experience in fiction; and if what followed proved much too strong even for her sensibilities, she must nevertheless be accounted as the first really important modern Southern novelist.

Why was Southern literature prior to Ellen Glasgow so notably bloodless and melodramatic? Elsewhere in this essay I shall speculate on the reasons. They have to do with the nature of the Southern community, the impact of the Civil War, the delayed arrival of industrialization, and so forth. Whatever the reasons, Southern society was not prepared, in the years before 1900, to have someone write about it realistically. There was no place in the community for such a writer. And if a writer came along who wished to write about the life he saw all around him, he faced difficulties not only from his home folks, but from the very nature of the American literary scene in the closing years of the nineteenth century.

What happened to the writer who sought, in the post–Civil-War South, to look at everyday Southern experience through eyes unclouded by romantic haze? We can find out what happened to him by examining a book by such a writer, George Washington Cable. The book is *John March, Southerner*, published in 1895, and nowadays all but forgotten. Yet its pages contain examples of literary realism, unmatched for frankness by any of his contemporaries, scenes and characters that seem more closely akin to the milieu of William Faulkner than to anything else written in Cable's own day and time.

For more than a half-century students of Southern literature have cited Cable as a monstrous example of what happens to novelists who succumb to the urge to preach. The standard version is that Cable failed to produce any books approaching the artistic attainment of his early stories of Creole life in Louisiana because his growing concern for Negro rights distorted his literary judgment. He ceased to write fiction and began composing tracts.

The novel in which the didactic finally overwhelmed the aesthetic is usually considered to be *John March, Southerner*. Jay B. Hubbell, foremost of the historians of Southern literature, echoes the verdict about the book when he declares that "it is the work of a reformer rather than an artist." This was precisely the reaction of Cable's editor, the celebrated Richard Watson Gilder, when he first read the manuscript in the summer of 1890. "I could weep for disappointment," he wrote Cable. "Instead of a return *to* literature, [it is] an attempt to fetch everything into literature save & except literature itself . . . *Beware of the Fate of Tolstoi.*" Edmund Wilson, in an exciting revaluation of Cable, has recently, and for somewhat different reasons, made the same criticism of the novel. Gilder, asserts Wilson, "was quite right in declaring that there was no literature in 'John March,' and that its salutary purpose is irritating."

The doctrine is sound enough. Didacticism can indeed spoil art, and frequently does. And Cable's work did decline in the years after *John March* was published. But unfortunately for the doctrine of antididacticism, when applied to *John March, Southerner* it is simply not true. For whatever that novel's faults may be, preaching is not among them. And what Gilder and Wilson both consider didacticism is the best thing about the novel—which despite its shortcomings is an extremely interesting novel, in my opinion the most important novel that George Washington Cable ever wrote.

It is good to have literary critics such as Wilson discussing Cable once again. If he is not a major American novelist, at any rate he wrote several quite good books that have been unjustly abandoned to the writers of literary history for too many decades. When in 1955 Richard Chase published an essay on *The Grandissimes* in the *Kenyon Review*, it was the first time in years that a critic of much reputation had paid any attention to Cable's existence. Our better scholars had not overlooked him, though, and in 1956 Professor Arlin Turner published a perceptive biography; and this work, though not primarily concerned with literary criticism, seems to have had the effect of getting Edmund Wilson interested in the Louisiana novelist once again.

As a critic, Edmund Wilson's merits and demerits are well known. Chief among his assets, perhaps, is his good taste, together with the courage to make that taste known. One of those rare critics who creates fashions instead of following them, Wilson has time and time again come up with essays giving serious attention to neglected authors, with the result that others are reminded of their existence and a spate of new editions and revaluations of their work follows.

But if Wilson is audacious in good causes, he is also frequently right for the wrong reasons. His taste is often better than his analysis—*Axel's Castle* is a prime example. What often happens, therefore, is that other critics, who but for Wilson's groundbreaking essays never would have thought to write about a particular subject, find that his conclusions are right in general but often very much awry in the particulars. Wilson on George Washington Cable is a case in point, it seems to me. While Wilson is quite correct when he declares that Cable possessed both "a remarkable literary gift" and "a kind of all-around intellectual competence that was unusual in that period in men of letters in the United States," he has failed to perceive exactly what that gift was, and has relegated Cable's most ambitious and most interesting novel to a very subordinate place in the Cable canon. For it seems to me that *John March, Southerner* is emphatically not "completely synthetic," as Wilson would have it, and that it is by no means true that "neither characters nor situations can be accepted by the reader as real."

John March, Southerner was written during the years 1890–93. Cable had left Louisiana five years before, to settle in Northampton, Massachusetts. His literary career in his native city had been one of ups and downs. First he had been highly admired and praised and then his stock began to tumble, until, by the time he departed for good, he was *persona non grata* among most of his fellow citizens. He had risen to prominence suddenly with publication of the stories in *Old Creole Days*. This had been followed by *The Grandissimes*, which both Wilson and Chase consider his best novel; *Madame Delphine*, a long story about the quadroons; *The Creoles of Louisiana*, a book of sketches of life in New Orleans and environs; and *Dr. Sevier*, a second novel. What had at first seemed pleasant local color, a little irksome perhaps to the old Creole families but hardly a source of much irritation to most New Orleaneans, had increasingly become an airing of subjects and attitudes repugnant to good Southerners. Cable had attacked Southern views on racial "purity" in *The Grandissimes*, and in *Dr. Sevier* he had not only portrayed New Orleans prison conditions in a most uncomplimentary manner, but had also suggested that the South had been morally in the wrong when it seceded from the Union. During the 1880's Cable's production of fiction fell off sharply, and the lecture platform and the magazine essay became his chief sources of income. In 1885 he outraged everyone by bringing out in book form the essay entitled *The Silent South*, along with other pieces in which he openly advocated an end to racial segregation in schools and elsewhere, and urged the white South to review its attitude toward the Negro. For his troubles he was branded a traitor to his region, accused of selling out his integrity for Northern magazine gold, and called a plagiarist in the bargain. His removal to Northampton was followed several years later by *Bonaventure*, one of his least important works. Thereafter he was silent as a novelist until *John March,* which was not published until 1895. Thus the novel represented a return on Cable's part to major fiction, after some years of platform activities and social agitation. The displeasure that Richard Watson Gilder expressed over what he considered the didacticism of the novel, after Cable showed him the opening chapters, was undoubtedly a deep disappointment to the novelist. Certainly, as Turner shows, it had the effect of ending what for some years had been a close friendship between the two men.

But before we accept Gilder's appraisal of the novel, it would be well to inquire just what he meant by accusing Cable of injecting everything except literature into the story. To do this, we must examine the status of American society during the late 1880's and early 1890's.

The period was one in which American attitudes toward the Negro freedman were undergoing a marked shift. During the War and the early years of Reconstruction, the Negro's desire for social betterment had enjoyed considerable favor among Northern public opinion. But gradually the idealism waned, as the problems of Reconstruction intensified, and the public showed a growing weariness with the Negro's plight. There were other issues now, and rebellion and the slavery conspiracy as political slogans became less and less potent. Furthermore, there was growing economic unrest in the rural areas and the cities, and Northeastern business interests seemed more seriously menaced by agrarian revolt than by once-rebellious Confederates in the South. And in the Southern states themselves, the Bourbon-dominated Redeemer governments were threatened by the rural elements. The Redeemers had in most instances wrested political control from the Negro, but they had not dared to discriminate against him too openly in education and welfare expenditures. Indeed, they had found that his vote could be controlled and used to hold down the bid for power of the rural, "white" counties of the upcountry. This was the period, too, of the New South, with its frenzied industrial and commercial activity. Agrarian agitation was accompanied by strong resentment of Bourbon favoritism to railroads and industry, as well as by rural whites' open hatred of the Negro and hostility to the use of Negro votes.

So that in the South, two related processes were going on. The upcountry, with its strong anti-Negro attitudes, was making itself increasingly important; while the Bourbons, fearing that their economic activities were imperiled by the agrarian elements, were searching for a device to allay upcountry hostility. What happened was something of a compromise, whereby the Bourbons went along with open anti-Negro moves while the farmers eased up on their hostility to business and commercial issues. There was no outright agreement to this effect, and the process varied in duration and intensity from state to state. But the upcountry was kept within the Democratic party, and the Democratic party became increasingly anti-Negro. The result was a host of Jim Crow laws, widespread discrimination in allocation of education funds, and steadily worsening conditions for the Negro.

Thus the South's attitude toward the Negro hardened, and the Northeast was willing to accede in Southern views on the Negro issue in order to keep the former Confederate states from uniting with Western agrarian reformers in hostility to Northeastern financial and commercial interests. Conservative people in both the North and the South found economic issues more pressing than the question of Negro rights, and there was a general willingness to let such matters slide.

Like many another Northern intellectual, Richard Watson Gilder mirrored this disenchantment. As Turner remarks, he had "gone largely over to the view that peace and prosperity would be best served in the South by withholding civil rights from the Negroes." And thus the controversial essays that Cable kept submitting to him for *The Century* magazine were rejected one after another.

When Gilder received the opening chapters of *John March, Southerner*, therefore, he was hardly likely to view with favor anything touching on the rights of the Negro in the South, the evils attendant on industrial and commercial expansion in the South, and the problems inherent therein.

Of what, then, consists the "didacticism" of the novel, the attempt to fetch extraneous matters into literary composition? In Turner's words, it consisted of "all the vexing problems of the post-War South: public education, segregation in public activities, including the churches, Negro suffrage, mob violence, corruption in government and the embezzlement of public funds, immigration, outside capital, natural resources." It consisted, in other words, of the subject matter of the novel. But need merely the *use* of such subject matter necessarily constitute preaching? Certainly in the twentieth-century novels of such Southern writers as William Faulkner and Robert Penn Warren it does not. Didacticism is not a question of subject matter, but of the author's attitude toward the subject matter. The issue is not whether Cable used controversial subject matter, but whether he used it as fiction or as propaganda. As Turner notes, "Gilder's judgment . . . is misleading, for the book does not argue these questions directly or dogmatically, and no specific solutions are offered."

So if Turner is right, as I believe he is, then Gilder objected to Cable's choice of unpleasant subject matter, not to the use he made of it. Gilder simply *did not want such matters treated at all;* their very presence in a novel about the South, he felt, constituted preaching. He did not want the South portrayed in such fashion; he wanted "literature," by which he meant moonlight, magnolias, and piquant Creoles. "My letter about the book must have disappointed you," he wrote Cable after receiving no reply to his first letter. "I trust I did not hurt you. I wrote in great disappointment myself, for I had great hopes of the next book to follow Bonaventure the Beautiful." Gilder had greatly admired those tales of picturesque Acadians; "Your fierce editor is very light on you this time, is he not?" he had written several years before, after reading one of them. "Well it is a beautiful story and will belong to literature. There is only one Cable." Quaint customs, delightful patois, simple virtues, humble religious folk; these were the proper subject matter for books about the South, and not race riots, corruption, industrial stress and strain. Such depressing subject matter was not only painful, it would not sell. The Century Company did not publish *John March, Southerner;* it was brought out by Scribner's.

What is the picture of the South that so pained Gilder, and seems to Edmund Wilson even today to be so "completely synthetic"? First of all, the novel is *not* laid in New Orleans, and no soft-voiced Creoles stroll through richly accented pages to soften the satire with their engaging ways. "The locale of the novel is entirely a notebook product," Wilson declares, "the result of a visit to a small town in Georgia."

But the choice of locale was not so haphazard as Wilson's words seem to imply. Rather, Cable chose northern Georgia deliberately, after much looking around. For this book was to be Cable's final say on the South, and to place it in Louisiana amid the careless, bantering Creoles would be to confuse the issue. Their very presence would set up a demand for the customary concomitants— those elements that had constituted *Old Creole Days* and *Bonaventure* and had gentled the satire of *The Grandissimes* and *Dr. Sevier*. The new book was to be Cable's attempt, as we shall see, to show the South as it was, not through the usual haze of local color. In the country of the Etowah and Kennesaw Mountain was the real South, with all its post-Reconstruction problems. Better to arouse no associations of the merely picturesque this time; these would interfere with the realism that Cable intended for the novel. The original and more accurate title was "Johnny Reb."

The novel takes place in a town called Suez. It opens as the War concludes, and John March is a small child perched behind his father riding on horseback. John grows up during the Reconstruction, comes to manhood as the white South regains control and the New South gets under way. Before the book closes it encompasses land speculation, race riots, duels, political deals, Negro suffrage and education, industrialism, and various other activities all too typical of the South during the latter part of the nineteenth century.

The student of Southern history will have no difficulty recognizing the milieu of the novel; it is described in C. Vann Woodward's *Origins of the New South*, Francis Butler Simkins' *A History of the South*, and various of the other reputable historical accounts of Southern life after the Civil War. Not the historian but the reader of postbellum, local-color novels is likely to be shocked by this book, because the customary literary picture of this period is that afforded in the work of Thomas Nelson Page. The devotee of "local color," accustomed to magnolia and verbena, with gentlemanly Yankees come down to wed shy Southern belles and thus heal the sectional schism, does not expect to encounter realism when the post-Civil-War South is being pictured.

For despite his romantic trappings, Cable is a realist. In certain ways he is much more of a realist than Ellen Glasgow, of whom it was said that in her work realism first crossed the Potomac, going North. Cable is realistic because his fictional world is eminently believable. He knows more about motivation, psychology, characterization in depth than Miss Glasgow learned until her later novels; perhaps more than she was ever to learn. There is not the dreadful high seriousness about her people that so spoils the earlier Glasgow novels, the absolute humorlessness that may permit some caricature but never any spoofing. Cable never sees life as a mortifying ordeal for the poor sensitive souls of this world, as Miss Glasgow did so persistently.

Let us examine a few portraits from among the gallery of characters with whom Cable peopled *John March*. Their counterparts will not again be encountered in Southern fiction this side of William Faulkner. John March's mother, for example, is an hilariously funny and pathetic creature. A Southern female poetess of a type so often encountered, she writes verse for the newspapers, seeks a Northern publisher, is fair game for any designing man, and is not only an abominable poetaster but a hypochondriac and self-pitier worthy, in a lighter vein, of Mrs. Compson in *The Sound and the Fury*. In short, she is an exquisite satire on the Flower of Southern Matronhood, United Daughters of the Confederacy style. No doubt Cable was plagued aplenty by this type; his revenge is consummate.

Of another sort is Cornelius Leggett, Negro entrepreneur and scoundrel. Leggett too is used for purposes of comedy, with some dialect humor in the best Thomas

Nelson Page tradition. More importantly, however, Leggett is not only picturesque but he is also a corrupt Negro politician, a lustful, immoral man, a blackmailer, and—paradoxically—a skillful advocate of Negro education and better opportunities for the freedman. He is an unusual creature, indeed, because in Southern fiction before the coming of Lucas Beauchamp, darkies are usually either good or knavish, but seldom are they both unsavory and, in spite of themselves, on the right side. Yet people are often that way, even if fictional Negroes in the pre-Faulknerian Southern novel are not.

Edmund Wilson sees Leggett as having been placed in the novel in order to show that Cable did not "idealize the Negro and invariably . . . sympathize with men of mixed blood," as his enemies claimed. Possibly, and yet it is perfectly obvious that Leggett, ignorant and weak, can rise from his bemirement only with help, and vaguely realizes this. How different he is from the kind and pleasant darky who knew his place, as good Negroes of the novels were sure to do, as well as from the martyred saint of the abolitionist novels such as those by Judge Albion Tourgee. Cable, his foes declared, wrote about the Negro in terms couched to please the North, not as the Negro really was. But the Negro of *John March, Southerner* seems closer to many of the race's post-War leaders than anyone else managed to come during Cable's time. Now, seventy-five years after *The Silent South*, one wonders who saw the most when he looked about him, Cable the renegade, with eyes supposedly blinded by Yankee gold, or the good Southerners who knew the darky as he "really" was?

The villain of Cable's novel is Major Garnet, certainly no ordinary stock Southern character of the long Victorian twilight. Cable made this Confederate hero an unprincipled opportunist, willing to mouth all the favorite slogans of his period to gain his own ends. Garnet is a man of power and respect in the community of Suez, president of a college, minister of the gospel—and also land speculator, conniver at fraud, and finally adulterer with his friend's wife. Villains did not come easy to Cable; he was always too keenly aware of human frailty. His picture of Major Garnet is not that of a thoroughly hateful man; for, despite Garnet's crimes, he is too human to go completely without the reader's sympathy. At the end of the novel, when most villains of the Major's type might be expected to have met death or the jail cell, we learn that the Major has decamped with his mistress, taken to the lecture circuit, and earns a living preaching throughout the South. How much more likely a fate, if less poetically just.

Another character drawn to realistic dimensions is Jeff-Jack Ravenel, newspaper editor and friend of John March. For this Confederate hero of indubitable ancestry and record is also a political time-server, who uses his journalistic influence for causes other than those of the highest public service. He is a man whose instincts are basically good, but whose intelligence is not directed toward any sort of an unprejudiced, critical examination of the shibboleths of his time and place. Professor Turner suggests that he represents too many young Southerners as Cable saw them, and one does have the feeling about men such as Jeff-Jack that they are entirely too willing to drift along, manipulating the status quo for their own advantage. Whatever else is true of Jeff-Jack, however, he is emphatically not a stereotyped Southern knight of the post-War period. He is a man of mixed motives and several sides. And he is thoroughly believable as a person.

Jeff-Jack and Major Garnet do not complete the roster of Confederate heroes. There is also General Halli-

day. Again Cable's handling of peerless leaders is un-
conventional. The General collaborates with the Reconstruction government, deals with Negro freedmen—
and even so gets elected to Congress. In the novels of
local color, Confederate heroes never did such things,
but in real life, similar careers were by no means unusual.
As Francis Pendleton Gaines has remarked, Cable was
not really in the plantation tradition of Southern fiction;
surely he was not when it came to depicting Confederate
heroes in *John March, Southerner*. They seem more like
William Faulkner's ex-Confederates, inclined to be both
heroes and practical businessmen and politicians.

General Halliday has a daughter, the beautiful Miss
Fannie, and she too displays some very untraditional
traits. For Miss Fannie, an authentic Southern belle with
all the proper accoutrements, marries Jeff-Jack Ravenel
with the full knowledge that in so doing she is making a
fairly unhappy marriage, that she is wedding a time-
server of less than complete integrity, and that she is doing so because she too prefers security to principle. If
ever there was a realist about marriage, it is Miss Fannie,
a far cry from Ellen Glasgow's high-minded, firm-
purposed Southern heroines.

In this array of supporting characters there is the
essential element of realism, the recognition that people
tend to act from a variety of motives and seldom out of
pure idealism or equally unalloyed avarice and villainy.
Such characterization not only makes for believable characters; it is an essential part of Cable's art. He habitually
approaches people as human beings, not as heroes and
villains.

Cable's secondary characters are vastly more successful
than are his romantic hero and heroine. For John March
and especially Miss Barbara Garnet tend to be entirely
too idealistic and too immune to the weaknesses of the

flesh. The fault, however, is not due to any didacticism on Cable's part, but to his reliance upon the conventional romantic plot structure of the day. On the level of love plot, *John March, Southerner* is not realistic. It is the habitual romance of a genteel era in which heroes and heroines were pure in heart and lived happily ever after. There are the usual coincidences, overheard conversations, and dark secrets which become illuminated at the very end to save the day for virtue, in proper *deus ex machina* fashion. The hero learns at the close, for example, that because of a mistake in property deed recordings he is actually the true owner of the villain's lands. He assures his beloved, who also just happens to be the villain's daughter, that he does not want the lands, nay, would not under any circumstances consider taking them; but all ends happily when they decide to marry and combine their holdings.

There is no use pretending, therefore, that Cable was not in many respects—in those that are obvious and on the surface—a conventional romancer, who knew the formula and was paid for using it. For the sake of his present-day reputation he knew it all too well when he came to write *John March, Southerner*. The love plot clashes painfully with the Faulknerian realism of setting and tone. In the Creole novels the line of demarcation was less obvious. The technique had been realistic, but the subject matter picturesque and remote. In *John March* the realism is not gauzed over by the charming Creoles, and the contrast is painful. "Oh! Oh! Oh! men are so rough some times!" declares Cable at the close, as his hero and heroine embrace. Thomas Nelson Page and Augusta Evans Wilson would not have had it happen otherwise. It was not the love plot that annoyed Richard Watson Gilder.

For all of Cable's lack of originality with his love

story, it still must be said that he sometimes manages to get his hero and heroine, and particularly John March, into some rather odd situations. Midway through the novel John swears that he will continue to love Miss Fannie Halliday even after her marriage. This is hardly shocking, but a certain irony is added to the declaration when after the wedding John finds himself on the same northward-bound train as the newly married couple, and Jeff-Jack is so intoxicated that his young spouse has locked him out of the bridal compartment. Nor does a later episode, in which John escorts Jeff-Jack's bride back home on the Pullman while the groom goes off to Washington, seem exactly proper, either, and General Halliday is considerably exasperated at John for helping out. Cable by no means was averse to making comedy out of such situations, with their veiled but always implied hint of the sensual. Jay B. Hubbell rightly remarks Cable's "susceptibility to the voluptuous." In a later novel, *The Cavalier*, Cable was to go even farther in skating on the thin surface of convention. In *John March* the characters disport themselves quite properly, of course, and John's thoughts are of the highest. But the humor of the situation, if not obvious to the participants, cannot fail to be obvious to the reader. At such moments Cable seems to be poking fun at his romantic plot even while developing it further.

Despite his reformist tendencies, Cable's attitude toward the frailties of the flesh in his fiction was peculiarly Latin-like. He seemed to recognize and even to delight in the inevitability of human shortcomings, and to be quite convinced that people are often complex creatures whose motivations can become considerably mixed. It was as if he had absorbed some of the easy compliance of the Creoles he so often portrayed. Cable and Henry James were close friends; and some of Cable's scenes in

John March are more reminiscent of James than of anyone else.

Although John March becomes a stereotyped swain whenever Miss Barbara Garnet enters the scene, what happens in *John March, Southerner* is not essentially romantic, but realistic. If we discount the love story—and we *can* do so, for though it is sometimes painfully with us, it is not the chief interest of the novel—we have left a subtle account of a young Southerner who learns to accept the life in which he finds himself for what it is, neither a tragedy nor a roseate utopia. John March's development in the novel is from innocence to awareness. He begins as an innocent young idealist who will not take sufficient account of the mixed motives and essentially compromised existence of those around him. As the story unfolds he passes from a naïve, uncritical optimism to an equally unrealistic disgust with the more sordid aspects of human conduct, and finally to a realization that he must accept people and things for what they are, and work toward his goals in terms of practical realities. At the end he is a wiser, sounder man, ready to deal with events as they come along.

Always, however, there is the love story. Edmund Wilson is quite right when he emphasizes the debilitating effect of the demands made by Gilder and Cable's Northern publishers for romantic stereotypes. "The slow strangulation of Cable as an artist and a serious writer is surely one of the most gruesome episodes in American literary history," he declares. In particular is this debilitation evident in *John March, Southerner*, despite Wilson's failure to recognize that in this novel, more than in any other, the clash of the two approaches can be seen. The novel is realistic in setting and event, in subject matter, and most importantly, in the dominant tone; yet superimposed on this realistic texture is a plot structure in the old style. Cable creates the milieu of Faulkner and affixes to it a story in the manner of Augusta Evans Wilson.

He is, in short, a transition figure, belonging neither in one world nor the other. His plotting harks back to Mrs. Wilson, to John Esten Cooke, to the thick syrup of the genteel age. His subject matter, his attitude, and his method look forward to the literary renascence of the twentieth century. *John March, Southerner* marks an epoch in the development of the literary consciousness in the South. Cable has learned as an artist to look around him at reality, to see the kind of reality that a Flaubert, a Faulkner, a Thackeray even, could see. Like the Southern writers of the post-World-War-I era, he could see things in various hues, colors, shapes, facets, and not seek to extract from experience the merely useful. Witness this passage from *John March:*

> The day was brisk. Ox-wagons from Clearwater, mule-teams from Blackland, bull-carts from Sandstone, were everywhere. Cotton bales were being tumbled, torn, sampled, and weighed; products of the truck-patch and door-yard, and spoils of the forest, were changing hands. Flakes of cotton blew about under the wheels and among the reclining oxen. In the cold upper blue the buzzards circled, breasted the wind, or turned and scudded down it. From chimney tops the smoke darted hither and yon, and went to shreds in the cedars and evergreen oaks.

Or again,

> The Garnets' wheels bickered down the town's southern edge and out upon a low slope of yellow, deep-gullied sand and clay that scarce kept on a few weeds to hide its nakedness while gathering old duds and cans.

Erskine Caldwell could pen no more realistic, even naturalistic portrayal of Georgia. Cable could not look out at the South around him and see only magnolias and shaded verandas. He could not view the South as something that must be gilded, championed, extolled patriotically, either to outlanders or, at least as importantly, to Southerners themselves. For Cable's artistic world was too real to be anything less than searched out, explored. In this respect he was kin to members of the generation of the 1920's and 1930's, those who saw the South not in slavish worship but appalled fascination. When he thought his region ugly, he pointed it out; his art would not permit a partial picture. He was no less the Southerner for not confusing loyalty with adulation. In John March's words,

> I spent a year in Europe coaxing men to leave their mother-country for better wages than this. Of course, that was all right. But it brought one thing to my notice: that when our value is not mere wages, it isn't every man who's got the unqualified right to pick up and pull out whenever he gets ready. Look out that window. There's the college where for five years I got my education—at half price!—and with money borrowed here in Suez! Look out this one. Mr. Fair, right down there in those streets truth and justice are lying wounded and half-dead, and the public conscience is being drugged! We Southerners, Fair, don't believe one man's as good as another; we think one man in his right place is worth a thousand who can't fill it. My place is here!—No! let me finish; I'm not fatigued at all! How I'm to meet this issue God only knows, but who'll even try to do it if I don't?

But that is rhetoric, of course; it does not ring true. It is romantic, sentimental, excessive. John March talks not like a man, but like a plaster saint, and the author's earnestness obtrudes awkwardly through the transparent words. This is not Cable the realistic artist speaking, but Cable the romancer.

For the real division in George Washington Cable is not between the novelist and the social reformer, as contemporary critics thought, but between realist and romancer. As realistic artist, Cable looked at his world with truthful eyes and created his fiction from the undiluted, unstylized world about him. As romancer, he tried to accommodate this vision with the stereotype of the popular literary formula. Because the artistic conventions of his day would not allow him to create fiction out of the harsher realities, he wrote the Creole stories, and saved his social criticism, his perception of the injustice, the ugliness, the hypocrisy for the lecture platform and the magazine essay. He wrote *The Silent South*. Then finally he gave up, and tried for once and for all to use in fiction the knowledge and insight that his realistic eyes provided him, and he wrote *John March, Southerner*. It was his farewell to the South. But it failed, because of the demands of the nineteenth century, its editors, and its public. They were not yet ready for realism.

For this was the heydey of local color, when Southern novelists were supposed to be quaint and to create fiction out of colorful Creoles and warm-voiced planters, with slaves who said "massa" and heroes whose hearts beat strong because always pure. He could not look around him and describe what he saw. His fellow townsfolk would not abide his candor; his Northern editors and readers feared his taste for unpleasantness. In the 1920's Faulkner could shovel coal in a power plant at night and write *As I Lay Dying* during the day. In New York there would be an editor to recognize its worth, a publisher to print it, and eventually a public to admire it in his lifetime. Cable had no such editor, no such publisher. The public for reading *John March* had not yet been created. And besides, it was a time when the man of letters did not live alone; he was supposed to be an influence in the community, and poets and novelists addressed themselves, or so they thought, to an audience of general readers. Such an audience wanted more Barbara Garnets, not Cornelius Leggetts.

Cable never saw the conflict. He sailed into the controversy over civil rights for the Negro, hoping to change the minds of his fellow Southerners. Yet Negro rights as such did not chiefly concern him, though he thought they did. He was seeking the right to be realistic about his region. The Negro was the symbol, but what was at stake was not only whether he could describe Negroes as being less than idyllic or less than depraved, but whether he could write of compromised politicians, opportunistic Confederate heroes, infested prisons, the whole world of everyday existence. Accept the usual dichotomy of Happy Darky or Uppity Nigger, and Cable must perforce accept the vision of the oleander-scented South, the perceptual limits of Thomas Nelson Page. And that was precisely what he could not do.

Fifty years later William Faulkner faced no such choice. His picture of his native land was every bit as harsh as the one seen by Cable, and harsher, because Faulkner saw things from the viewpoint of tragedy rather than irony. But by Faulkner's time there was no thought, either in his own mind or that of his publishers, that his books could or should be the everyday fare of his Mississippi neighbors. By the 1920's the young writer of vision and integrity was by nature removed from the temptation of popularity.

For Cable, who came two generations too soon, the chasm between entertainment for clubwomen and tired businessmen and straightforward use of the full artistic imagination for the imagination's sake alone did not seem so broad. He thought it was possible to be honest and popular at the same time; he was expected to be popular. But the realistic artist in Cable could not be popular, and the realistic artist was dominant—for a while at least. The artist saw Cornelius Leggett and Jeff-Jack Ravenel. The man of letters in the community tried to justify the realistic artist by trying to show why the vision *should* be popular. He failed. A half-century later he would not even have tried to make the effort.

And so Cable left the South, retreated to Northampton, and after a few years tried once more. He wrote *John March*, seeking in it to compromise a dilemma the existence of which he perhaps only dimly perceived. When this novel too failed of success, he turned to other subjects. He became a romancer pure and simple. He lived by his pen, and if realism was not in demand he would give it up. He tried to divide his perceptions into two parts: he wrote formula novels, and engaged in reform movements and projects for public uplift. He laid aside for good the realistic vision that neither accepted nor rejected the ideals of the marketplace. In realism there was no place at all for such oversimplifications. Cable had not the financial independence to do what James did, and turn his back on popularity; nor the nerve to do what Herman Melville did, and earn his bread in other ways while writing to please himself alone. He had been too popular; he could not let it go.

Before he gave up trying, he wrote one book, *John March, Southerner*, in which despite its romantic trappings he was able to show his native region in the rich daylight of reality. Two generations later the same vision would provide the substance that distinguished writers would use to create a new literature, the lineaments of which Cable, before anyone else, first imperfectly sketched.

3

CHRONICLES OF YOKNAPATAWPHA: The Dynasties of William Faulkner

> *"And now we're going to talk about love."*
> Shrevelin McCannon in *Absalom, Absalom!*

In the Modern Library edition of William Faulkner's *Absalom, Absalom!* is a map of a mythical county named Yoknapatawpha. Lying between the Tallahatchie and the Yoknapatawpha rivers, this county is bisected by the railroad line built by Colonel John Sartoris, described in *The Unvanquished.* At the center is the town of Jefferson, with the Confederate monument at the square by the left side of which it was necessary to drive the idiot Benjy Compson in *The Sound and the Fury*—if Benjy passed the monument on the right, he would bellow in terror at the strangeness. Close by is the courthouse where Temple Drake testified at Goodwin's trial in *Sanctuary.* Outside of town is the mansion owned by Miss Joanna Burden, the spinster who was killed by Joe Christmas in *Light in August.* At a point just north of Jefferson is the spot where old Bayard Sartoris died in young Bayard's car in *Sartoris.* To the northwest, twelve miles out of town, is the mansion of Sutpen's Hundred, where Thomas Sutpen strove to establish his dynasty in *Absalom, Absalom!*—not far away is the fishing camp where he was beheaded by the tenant farmer

Wash Jones. Southwest is Frenchmen's Bend, where Flem Snopes got his start in his drive for affluence in *The Hamlet*. A short distance from there is the place where the bridge was washed away, preventing the Bundren family in *As I Lay Dying* from crossing over the river.

Here, in this ordered and delineated square of make-believe countryside, is the scene of all the novels of Yoknapatawpha, the fictional chronicle of men in a time and place that is the modern South's most enduring literary monument. It is perhaps the best known county in the South; its fame is worldwide. Two thousand and four hundred square miles in area, with a population of 6,298 whites, 9,313 Negroes, its sole owner and proprietor was William Faulkner.

The relationship of Yoknapatawpha County to La Fayette County, Mississippi, and that of its county seat, Jefferson, to the town of Oxford, Mississippi, where William Faulkner grew up and lived, has been frequently debated. The violent events that take place in Yoknapatawpha, and that have given it such prominence, have seemed to some of Faulkner's fellow Mississippians to be a libel on the state of Mississippi and on the South. "Some of Faulkner's writings are about as popular in his home county as a dead skunk would be in a sleeping bag," according to John B. Cullen, one of his fellow Oxford residents. "Outsiders read Faulkner's books," he says, "and think the people of our county are all ignorant heathen. Not all of us are."

Yet that same commentator, in his *Old Times in the Faulkner Country*, describes numerous happenings that gave Faulkner some of the inspiration for the events of his novels. In one instance he tells of the lynching of a Negro murderer, in which Cullen himself participated, that seems very similar to the situation in *Light in August*. There is a significant difference, however. The lynched

Negro in real life was a drunken murderer. The lynched Negro of the novel, Joe Christmas, is that; but he is also a doomed mortal searching for meaning in a chaotic world. His act of murder is not the result of a drunken impulse but is the last, despairing act of a tormented man, putatively tainted with Negro blood, who has spent his life trying to fight his way through a world where all is black and white, but who can find certainty for himself only in violent death. Thus Joe Christmas' struggle, instead of being a sordid and meaningless act of violence, is deeply moral, for it is an allegory of the soul seeking to determine what it is and how to define itself.

This is the kind of ultimate issue that the citizenry of La Fayette County, Mississippi, seldom confront in such recognizable and direct terms. The citizens of Yoknapatawpha, by contrast, face such problems constantly. Therein lies the difference between Yoknapatawpha and La Fayette, between Jefferson and Oxford; for the fictional chronicle has been given the high order of tragedy or comedy by an artist whose vision discovered the problems of many men and times in the daily doings of his fellow townsmen. Little wonder, then, that the citizens of Faulkner's homeland feel resentment and uneasiness at the Yoknapatawpha novels; they do not recognize themselves in such ultimate proportions. Life for them is not so stark, so cataclysmic in its dimensions; if it were they might not be able to endure it at all. Happily, they can go about the business of real life without having to view it as either comedy or tragedy, which for them it is not. But thanks to Faulkner, it is for us.

One of the reasons life in Yoknapatawpha is hardly recognizable to citizens in La Fayette is that Yoknapatawpha is imbued with a tremendous consciousness of time and history, so that the doings of its inhabitants are part of an historical procession in which the generations come and go; and the activities of men and women in the community are seen as part of the workings of time and change. Viewed as a whole, the chronicle of Yoknapatawpha takes place over a stretch of almost two hundred years of American and Southern history, beginning when the first settlers came into the Mississippi wilderness and set up the trading post of Jefferson, and ending with the downfall of the Old South and the rise of the modern-day community. One novel links with another; the characters of one appear in another; family names, the lines and shapes of community life, continue from generation to generation, in good times and bad, in war and peace, tragedy and comedy. There are highlights and there are low points; the saga is not uniformly successful, and the meaning of what is going on is by no means always consistent from novel to novel. But taken together, it is a single chronicle, a *roman fleuve*, of a sort unparalleled in American fiction, worthy of comparison with the novels of Balzac, Trollope, and other such extended accounts of generations of men in human time. The role of each character, when viewed against the backdrop of the full saga, is placed squarely in time and history, so that each figure in the chronicle exists in the present, is the product of the past, and bears implications for the future. As a character in one novel remarks, "The past is never dead, it's not even past."

Far from being private and special in meaning, the doings of the people of the novels have an historical significance. "The South," remarks a Canadian youth in *Absalom, Absalom!* "The South. Jesus. No wonder you folks all outlive yourselves by years and years and years." So they do, and the action of one man in one time determines the response of another many years after the first has died. Yet the country outlasts both. Yoknapatawpha

County becomes the constant, with its fields, rivers, farmland and homes remaining anchored in time, while the lives of the men and women inhabiting the land come and go.

It is a time continuum that Faulkner is after. The typical form of the Yoknapatawpha novels, which seems at first so puzzling to the reader and then falls momentously and often catastrophically into place as the novel progresses, is that of a single consciousness. Frequently it is not linked to any one character, yet it is the product of a fixed, centered viewpoint, a perceiving eye and mind, which takes in the actions and conjectures the thoughts of men and women in time. This "center of consciousness" is always at work speculating, recapitulating, and finally pronouncing the meaning of what has happened, seen at last as a whole, completed action. Sometimes, as in *Absalom, Absalom!*, the center of consciousness can be identified with a single observer, who in that novel is Quentin Compson. At other times, though, as in *The Sound and the Fury*, none of the participants themselves can be credited with the role of being the single, encompassing percipient; rather it is we as readers who are made, not merely through narration but through a complex process of identification and conjecture, to furnish the focus of consciousness in which what has happened can be resolved and given order and meaning. In a strange and quite original way, Faulkner forces the reader to become an actual participant in the consciousness of the drama; the reader plays his role, just as the characters do, is made to learn and to speculate and actually to take part. Not content with manipulating his people and their actions, Faulkner requires our own engagement in the story. Only in this way can the story give up its meaning—through our actual participation, our dramatic involvement, so that what is taking place applies not only to the characters, but to an aspect of our own consciousness as well. In such novels as *The Sound and the Fury* and *Absalom, Absalom!* Faulkner uses the stream-of-consciousness technique, pioneered by James Joyce, in a way that Joyce never attempted—to bring the reader himself into the narrative as a focus of experiencing and perceiving. By withholding information, revealing it at certain times and in certain ways, conjecturing and hinting, suggesting and teasing, he introduces the reader into the actual story, makes the stream of consciousness that of our own consciousness. In *Absalom, Absalom!* we almost *become* Quentin Compson, not merely through sympathetic identification with his motivations but through genuine participation in the functioning of his imagination. In *The Sound and the Fury* we are not made to become any of the characters themselves, but to serve as a center of perception necessary to the revelation of the novel. No wonder reading a Faulkner novel can be such an exhausting performance! Not content with telling us what has happened, he has made us play a role in it! As a technical feat it is without parallel in modern literature.

What is gained by such a method? Nothing more or less than the fictional experience of time itself. We are enabled to perceive, as no character in a novel, no matter how sentient, could possibly perceive, the convergence of past into present, the impact of one existence upon another, that constitutes some of the complexity of human experience as unfolded in time. We see the generations rise and fall, we see the actions of people in one time and place affecting those of others in other times and places, and thus we are enabled to participate in the historical continuum in place and time that is Yoknapatawpha County. It becomes our County, our experience; Faulkner, through a marvelous virtuosity of technique, gives it to us. It enables him to tell a story with a kind of psychological realism that is the very essence of actuality. And we share, not only the experience, but the motives and the judgment as well.

The Yoknapatawpha chronicle, in its main story line, encompasses three progressions. First there is the settling of Yoknapatawpha and its movement to power and then to catastrophe during the nineteenth century. Second, there is the post-Civil-War decline and fall of the great landed families of Yoknapatawpha as the century ends and the twentieth century comes in. Finally there is the South of our own century, in which new families take over the holdings and the power of the old aristocracy. Related to this development is another involving the problems of the Negroes and the poor whites. Seen as one tremendous action in time, the whole drama is a chronicle of human history in which the forces of continuity and change contend with one another. The numerous problems of definition, values, morality, and community that beset men in a time of transition are dramatized and explored.

Faulkner's notion of history is one involving the sum total of various "little" experiences. Human beings act out their lives under various circumstances and conditions, and their humanity is tested by each new development. The historical circumstances may change, placing men and women in various situations and requiring various responses of them in those situations to survive. The one essential quality that everyone must display, no matter what the occasion, is *humanity;* and conversely, the one crime of which no man must ever be guilty is *inhumanity*. Callous disregard for one's fellowmen, the use of human beings as if they were animals, failure to behave with human dignity—each is a crime, censurable in Time, and history is the working out of these individual transgressions and the subsuming of them into its stream. When in his Nobel Prize speech Faulkner spoke of "love and honor and pity and pride and compassion and sacrifice" as the eternal verities by which men live, and to which the novelist must cleave, he was describing the central thesis of his own fiction, not making a general remark about Life and Art. Faulkner seeks to show the contemporaneity, as well as the timelessness, of the basic human emotions. The South for him is the scene, the environmental and historical circumstance, in which the humanity of his characters is tested. The various "problems" of the South that figure so vitally in his fiction—slavery, the Civil War, the Negro (both from the standpoints of the white Southerner and the Negro himself), the decline of the plantation aristocracy, the coming of the commercial ethic to Yoknapatawpha County—are made into occasions for such tests, trying the characters in order to discover their worth as human beings. It is as if each such "problem" called into question the ability of humans to live up to their code of values, to exhibit "love and honor and pity and pride and compassion and sacrifice" in their lives. The South is thus the stage for Faulkner's great human drama, the story of the attempt by human beings to translate these abstract moral values into concrete behavior.

Faulkner's great novel of the nineteenth-century South is *Absalom, Absalom!* The story of a man named Thomas Sutpen and his attempt to found a dynasty in the wilderness of Yoknapatawpha early in the nineteenth century, it is a sweeping parable of the South's own hopes and its fate. Sutpen came to Mississippi from the West Indies, though originally he was from western Virginia. Through incredible heroism during a slave revolt in Haiti he had won family and fortune, only to find that the wife he had thought Spanish was in reality part Negro. Since in Sutpen's time and place this would prohibit him from establishing the dynasty he had in mind, he left wife and infant son, taking only some slaves, and came to Yoknapatawpha in the then-unsettled Southwestern frontier. By great perseverance and almost super-human energy he builds a mansion, establishes a plantation, and then wins the hand of the daughter of a Jefferson storekeeper. A son and daughter are born; the dynastic plans seem to be working well. Then his son Henry goes off to college and returns home with a friend, a young man from New Orleans named Charles Bon, who soon becomes engaged to be married to his daughter Judith. At that point Sutpen suddenly sees his dynasty in danger, for he insists that Charles is his own son, by the woman he had married and abandoned in Haiti.

Then the Civil War intervenes; Charles Bon and Henry Sutpen go off together to fight, Sutpen becomes colonel of a regiment in Virginia, and his wife dies. All somehow hope that the War will resolve their difficulties for them, but at the end Charles and Henry ride back to Sutpen's Hundred in Mississippi, and Henry kills Charles to prevent him from marrying his sister Judith.

When Sutpen comes back, he prepares to begin all over again. He becomes engaged to his dead wife's younger sister, Rosa Coldfield, but the engagement is broken when he proposes that they sleep together and marry only if their child is a male. Now Sutpen, who has abandoned his attempt to restore his plantation and has set up a crossroads store, fathers a child on the granddaughter of an illiterate tenant and hanger-on, Wash Jones. When it turns out to be a girl, Sutpen taunts Wash Jones into killing him. Jones picks up a rusty scythe, beheads his liege lord, kills his granddaughter and her child, then walks into a fusillade of bullets from Sutpen's neighbors.

Only Judith Sutpen and Clytie, another daughter of Sutpen's by a slave woman, are left. They send to New Orleans, bring back Charles Bon's son by a quadroon woman to live with them. The son marries a Negress. He and Judith die in an epidemic; now only Clytie and the idiot mulatto Jim Bond, son of Charles's son and the Negress, remain. At the close of the saga Henry Sutpen comes home to die; and when an ambulance is sent from the town to take him to a hospital, Clytie sets fire to the rotting old mansion. The last of Sutpen's dynasty goes up in flames. The idiot Jim Bond alone is left, to howl pathetically off in the woods near the ruins.

The story is not told in any such straightforward chronological sequence as that, however. Instead it is pieced together, a little information at a time, by Quentin Compson, who hears accounts from Rosa Coldfield and from his own father, whose father in turn was Sutpen's friend. Not until the last do we learn, as Quentin learns, exactly why Henry Sutpen killed Charles Bon. The entire experience is one in which Quentin, and the reader with him, discovers what caused Thomas Sutpen's dynastic ambitions to crumble; this involves the recreation of Sutpen's past and the realization of the kind of man he was, and the kind of a time and place it was that could make his life and death possible.

Sutpen's crime was that he was innocent, ignorant of what constituted human responsibility, motivation, experience. He lived outside his society, attempted to use it only to further his ends. Everything existed for his design, an abstract scheme in which the human beings who of necessity figured in it were considered as so many pawns. In his rise and fall Sutpen seems to symbolize the South and its tragic error in attempting to build its civilization on the enslavement of human beings. "It's because she wants it told," Quentin thinks as

Miss Rosa Coldfield relates her story, "so that people whom she will never see and whose names she will never hear and who have never heard her name nor seen her face will read it and know at last why God let us lose the War: that only through the blood of our men and the tears of our women could He stay this demon and efface his name and lineage from the earth."

A man of great strength and tremendous will, Thomas Sutpen worked heroically at his labors; it is finally time that stops him, in the guise of the old man with the rusty scythe. The one ingredient utterly absent from his makeup was the one that might have made all his efforts meaningful: the capacity for genuine love and compassion. His desertion of his first wife, coldly, calculatedly, because her Negro blood would spoil his design; his failure, later on, to acknowledge Charles Bon's kinship, for the same reason—both actions are those of a man whose mind cannot comprehend human affection. Just so, the South, in its attempt to perpetuate the institution of slavery, might be said to have been doomed to failure because the economics of the slavery system cancelled out its compassion for fellow humans. Sutpen tried to build his dynasty on the shifting sands of opportunism and on the sweat of the bondsman; and in the end the denial of his blood son's humanity, the rejection of Charles because he had Negro blood, wrecked his design and left Sutpen's Hundred a rotting mansion in the wilderness.

The fall of Sutpen is the fall of a civilization, one doomed from its very start and yet possessing stature and the possibility for heroism, making a valiant effort to persevere on the earth by overcoming human limitations. Nor is Sutpen's rise and fall applicable in its meaning to the nineteenth-century South alone; for Sutpen's true antagonist was the antagonist of all men, the limitations of the mortality out of which he was constructed. His rise and fall take place along lines reminiscent of Greek tragedy, and surely Thomas Sutpen is guilty of that *hubris* that the Greeks accounted so grievous a human flaw.

By telling the story of *Absalom, Absalom!* the way he does, Faulkner forces us to participate in the chronicle, so that like Quentin Compson we feel it bearing down upon us, all around us, influencing our own present state of mind. Quentin is what he is—we learn much more about him in *The Sound and the Fury*—because of his past, which is the past of his family and his region. And Sutpen's career seems greatly significant to Quentin, intricately bound in with that past. "I am older at twenty than a lot of people who have died," he tells his roommate toward the end of the story.

In *The Sound and the Fury* Quentin is but one of several members of the Compson family, one of the great landed dynasties of the South, which has now come upon evil times. The novel recounts the final disintegration of the Compsons. Formerly they had been governors and generals, had owned square miles of Mississippi soil, furnished the leadership for the community. But in keeping with the downfall of the Old South their stature and role have diminished; until in the twentieth century, when the events of the novel take place, the family is a decayed, fiberless shell of its former glory.

Most of the action of the novel occurs during three April days in 1928, but the meaning of the doings of those three days is dependent upon the past, especially a day in June of 1910. There are four Compson children; Quentin; his sister Candace, known as Caddy; Benjy, formerly Maury, an idiot; and Jason, youngest and the most venal and vicious of the lot. On April 7, 1928, the time of the first section, Quentin is long-since dead, and his sister Caddy has been exiled from the family for many years. Caddy's daughter, Miss Quentin, runs off with a carnival employee, taking a large sum of money from Jason's strongbox. We are not, however, made aware of this at all during our reading of the first section; the day is seen through the eyes and simple memory of the idiot Benjy, who remembers at random, and through the logic of free association, various events of a much earlier day when both Quentin and Caddy were still part of the family. Through Benjy's mirrorlike mind we learn what kind of persons the Compsons are; and, almost without realizing it, we receive descriptions of certain actions of which the significance is revealed only later, as minds more intelligent than Benjy's react to them.

During the course of the novel Quentin's father drinks himself to death, Quentin's sister Candace becomes pregnant by one youth and marries another, Quentin finishes a year at Harvard and then commits suicide by drowning, Candace's child comes to live with the family and finally runs away; and Jason grows up and works in a hardware store, steals his niece's money, then has it stolen back by her. It is a story of moral and spiritual collapse. The father's days are spent in drink and futility. The mother is a self-pitying hypochondriac who can provide neither love nor guidance for her children, and whose selfishness brings grief to all. Caddy is a tortured, driven girl who seeks in sexual promiscuity a substitute for the love she is denied from her parents. Quentin himself can find no logic or purpose for his life, and is obsessed by useless, abstract notions of family honor and role, until at the last he can gain peace only in death. Caddy's daughter, Miss Quentin, is so tormented by Jason's cruelty and venality and the lack of her absent mother's love that she decamps with the carnival worker. Benjy, the idiot, is finally gelded and placed in an institution. Of all the Compsons, only Jason survives in Yoknapatawpha County, and the price he pays for survival in the modern world is to lose all attributes of honor, virtue, and kindness, and to become a vicious, materialistic scoundrel.

Again, however, the collapse of the Compson dynasty is presented not in chronological fashion, but in such a way as actually to make us part of the action of the three days in April, 1928, when Miss Quentin decamps and all hope dies for the Compsons. During the Benjy sequence we see events without grasping their separateness or meaning. In the Quentin sequence that follows, we go back to 1910 and learn what drove Quentin to suicide; here the communication is tortured, disjointed, oppressively cerebral. Then we go forward to the day before Miss Quentin departs, into Jason's mind. Through his bitter, malicious version of experience, many of the events we glimpsed through the previous episodes come into focus, as well as the moral degradation they represent. Finally, through the Negro servant Dilsey and Jason again, but this time seen externally and objectively, we watch the tragedy working out to its close, the disintegration of the Compson family, the conclusion of sound and fury. The leadership of Yoknapatawpha County is no more; its lands have all been sold, its precepts of honor and pride forgotten, and only the sordid present remains, personified in Jason, a member of the Compson family only in name.

It is Quentin, I think, who is the key figure in the tragedy, for his life symbolizes what has gone wrong. No wonder that it was he in *Absalom, Absalom!* who pieced together the story of Thomas Sutpen; for to Quentin such men as Sutpen represent the impossible burden of the past, towering, in the very enormity of their guilt and their heroism, above the diffused, disordered bondages of the present. "We see dimly people," Quentin's father had remarked in *Absalom, Absalom!*, "the people in whose living blood and seed we ourselves lay dormant and waiting, in this shadowy attenuation of time possessing now heroic proportions, performing their acts of simple passion and simple violence, impervious to time and inexplicable." Thomas Sutpen's story, in its stark, tragic outlines, contrasts keenly with Quentin's own plight in *The Sound and the Fury*. Sutpen was ruthless, inhuman—and of great stature and dignity. Quentin can discover in his own life and time no such occasion for terrible simplicity, no such direct and heroic possibility for action. The hour for immediate, uncomplex response has gone. His private situation is one of confusion, disorder; the old notions of behavior, the old responses to events and occasions, have degenerated into hollow slogans and abstract postures. He clings forlornly to notions of honor and virtue, which to him have become mere fetishes, unsupported by the needs and conditions of his own circumstance; and when finally their appalling inappropriateness and inadequacy become apparent to him, he chooses suicide as the only way out.

Quentin, and Quentin alone, could have staved off the collapse of the Compson family. It is the breakdown inside him of the family ideals of love, honor, and responsibility that removes from the family its one possible source of stability and strength, of love unmarred by weakness and self-deception, that might have held them all together had Quentin been a different kind of person than he was. The ascendancy of Jason's low cunning, the flight into oblivion of Caddy, the hopeless struggle of Miss Quentin for love and affection, are possible because of what took place on June 2, 1910, when Quentin chose death over continued struggle against the futility of his time. With Quentin's demise, the Compson heritage, which had lasted for almost one hundred years, is doomed. And the failure of Quentin, of course, is the product of the failure of those who came before him.

To fill the vacuum in the community caused by the fall of the Compsons, and of their counterparts the Sartorises in other Faulkner novels, there arises a new race of men, the Snopeses. They are folk of weasel-like craftiness, materialistic, suspicious of all save their own, without scruple or code. It is a Snopes that Jason Compson has become in all but name by the close of *The Sound and the Fury*, for in Yoknapatawpha County it has almost become necessary to be a Snopes in order to survive. The Snopeses, whose saga is told in the trilogy comprised by *The Hamlet*, *The Town*, and *The Mansion*, are descended from Ab Snopes, who sold stolen horses to both sides during the Civil War; their ascendancy to power in Yoknapatawpha coincides with the collapse of the old ideals and the notions of role and leadership. Chief among the Snopeses is Flem, who gains control of much of the settlement of Frenchmen's Bend in *The Hamlet*, then goes to Jefferson and takes over. Flem is Faulkner's prize villain. He is ruthless, cunning—and he is sterile, for a true Snopes cannot reproduce himself. The emotion of love is utterly unknown to him. The Snopeses trade sharply and dishonestly; they will stoop to any depth to gain their ends, for unlike the Compsons and the Sartorises they have no standards of ethical behavior to conform to at all. Flem Snopes always stays within the law; he cannot be beaten that way; but there is no kind of trickery, no deal too despicable, that he will not employ to secure his ends.

Snopeses are not the stuff from which high tragedy is made; they do not possess stature enough for great drama. They are rodentlike creatures who swarm over the county of Yoknapatawpha. Unhindered by idealistic scruples or consciousness of role, through sheer persistence they gain control of the land. Theirs are the virtues that pay off in twentieth-century Yoknapatawpha life—thoroughgoing materialism, avarice, cleverness. Their rise to power becomes a kind of low comedy, in which the reader is wryly amused at their slyness and disgusted at their viciousness. The success of their mean cunning is contrasted with the failure of the now useless idealism of the Compsons; it is as if Faulkner were saying that honor, courage, pride, pity, love were outmoded attributes in the twentieth-century South, and that animal shrewdness and avarice were all that mattered now. When Flem Snopes finally falls, in *The Mansion*, it is at the hands of another Snopes, but the implied moral, that Snopesism is ultimately self-defeating, is dramatically unconvincing.

To read so pessimistic a conclusion from the Yoknapatawpha saga, however, is to forget that Faulkner was not composing a history of the South, and to misread the moral dimensions of the time continuum he set up in his fiction. The basic element of the time scheme of the Faulkner novels is the fact that no arbitrary distinction can be attempted between past and present, for the present contains the past and derives its meaning from it. Thus the omnipresent need for honor, justice, and love that makes up the central moral preoccupation of the novels is not confined to a past day; the need for those qualities is shown as existing more than ever in the present. Thomas Sutpen does not function purely as a symbol of the flaw in pre-Civil-War Southern society. The moral of his life, which is that an abstract quest for power and status conducted without regard for human love and decency must fail, is true for him in his day, and for us in ours. What Sutpen ignores, places no value on, is human love; it is the one essential quality lacking in him; its absence and his failure to allow for it in his dealings with men and women bring his great design down to defeat. He uses human beings for his selfish purposes; attempting to work out his design without love, he uncovers forces greater and more tenacious even than his own strength, and he is destroyed. Similarly the collapse of the Compsons and the rise of the Snopeses constitute treatises on the inescapable need for the ideals of love, duty, and justice in human affairs, if man is to achieve anything in his life beyond the predatory status of wild beasts. His are not naturalistic tragedies of environment; there exists always, for all Faulkner's creatures, the element of *choice*.

In Faulkner's other two most important novels, human love is again the inescapable requirement. In *Light in August* its absence in the life of Joe Christmas brings tragedy. In *As I Lay Dying* its presence, for all its warped and twisted quality, redeems the Bundren family.

Light in August, which some consider Faulkner's greatest work of fiction, is the story of a mulatto, Joe Christmas. The illegitimate son of a poor-white girl and a circus roustabout, reputedly (though by no means certainly) a Negro, Joe is reared in an orphanage, where his playmates taunt him with accusations of "Nigger," and where he inadvertently witnesses an attendant's liaison with an interne. He is unaware of what he has seen, and was in the attendant's room stealing some toothpaste to eat. To his lasting confusion, he is rewarded not with punishment for the theft but with a bribe. Later he is adopted by a rigorously Calvinistic farm couple, receives punishment by his foster father instead of compassion, and weak indulgence by his foster mother instead of firm guidance. He takes up with a whore, strikes down his foster father when surprised by him at a dance, is beaten by the whore's companions, and then flees. For years he wanders, fighting, gambling, living in various guises, now white, now black, until in his thirty-third year he comes back to Mississippi. He takes up residence in a shack behind an old house in the woods near Jefferson, owned by Joanna Burden, a Northern-born white woman of stern Calvinist upbringing and violent, hitherto repressed sexual desire. He works at a sawmill, sells moonshine whiskey, and at night sleeps with the woman. Finally she enters change of life, loses her capacity for physical desire, and begins praying for Joe's soul. This act, like all acts of possession and kindness, enrages him; he kills her, is hunted by a posse, gives himself up, flees from jail as a lynch mob gathers, and is shot to death and castrated.

The novel is filled with violence, and Christmas is at its center. His struggle is against all human ties, against all love and dependence. Tortured by doubt as to whether he is white or Negro, he wars with society to see whether he can do without its very existence. He will not acknowledge brotherhood, friendship, love. He will not participate, he will not serve. Like God, he will be independent. He is forced into violence to test his freedom; finally the only test left is death, and he goes back to Jefferson and destruction. In Faulkner's world, only God can be independent.

The love that was denied Christmas and that Christmas in turn denied, makes his struggle inevitable and gives to his life the motivated violence of a protest against society and humanity. In his destructive pride Joe Christmas attains tragic proportions, the proportions of the Antichrist. In *Light in August* Faulkner examines Southern Calvinism, Southern racism; and in the excess of the one and the inhumanity of the other he portrays the denial of the love that holds human life together. Without love, without compassion, there is only violence, disorder, tragedy.

As I Lay Dying, a considerably less violent work, is centered on a family, the Bundrens, who live in the Frenchmen's Bend country of Yoknapatawpha County. The Bundrens are outside the cycle of decline and fall of the major families of Yoknapatawpha; they are poor dirt farmers working for a meager existence in the hill country. Like the Negroes of the County, families such as the Bundrens engage in no titanic battles with time; they only endure, living on the land, aspiring to little more than subsistence. As the novel opens the mother, Addie Bundren, is about to die. Her eldest son, Cash, is building her coffin for her. Addie dies, and in obedience to her wish, the coffin is loaded onto a wagon and the Bundren family sets out for Jefferson to bury her. The trip, which consumes many days, is a bizarre journey with numerous vicissitudes. Each of the Bundrens has private reasons for wanting to take the body to Jefferson, and many things both comic and pathetic occur before the mother is finally lowered into her grave. The novel is related in a series of short internal monologues, in which we observe the journey through the eyes of the father, the five children, and others. There is even one sequence in which the mother's thoughts as she lay dying are revealed; it is a key passage, for Addie Bundren's attitudes toward her various children explain and determine the children's own personalities. Again the attempt is at a time continuum; the focal point of consciousness includes the thoughts of various characters, but is outside of and beyond them. Just as in *The Sound and the Fury*, we are forced into our own participation as the central consciousness of the novel, so that events happen around us.

Much of *As I Lay Dying* is low comedy, a travesty on family love, similar to Erskine Caldwell's tales of the Southeastern tobacco land. Unlike Caldwell's people, however, the Bundrens come through as genuine human beings, who for all their squalor and even depravity are capable of integrity and even nobility far beyond the animalistic behavior of the *Tobacco Road* folk. The wretchedness and squalor of their lives is not unmixed with a kind of heroism, so that the journey to bury Addie Bundren both burlesques human devotion and affirms it. In their own way all of them love the mother; even the incredibly lazy and selfish father is faithful, if very much in his own fashion and for his own reasons, to his wife's wish. Each of the Bundrens—father, mother, daughter, sons—lives in his own private experience, but the family as a unit is strong enough to persist and endure in its purpose, though one of them goes mad in the process. We can finally discover no meaning for their cohesion and their purposiveness except love, a grotesque, appalling kind of love in many ways, but love nonetheless.

The whole chronicle of Yoknapatawpha, of which I have discussed only what I consider some of the major novels, is in one sense a treatise on the central importance of love and compassion for one's fellowman. It is a failure in love that brings down the Compsons in *The Sound and the Fury:* the father's love for his children does not include firm moral precept; the mother's love is only for herself; Quentin's love for his sister is self-love for an abstract concept of Compson honor; Caddy seeks love in sexual promiscuity; Jason survives without love, but at the price of all for which the name Compson has stood. In *Light in August* Joe Christmas receives punishment without understanding, love without firmness or guidance, and, lacking a standard of human value, he attempts unsuccessfully to live in defiance of all human ties. In *The Hamlet* and the other volumes of the Snopes trilogy Flem Snopes exists without any capacity for love, and his life is sterile and barren. Thomas Sutpen fails in *Absalom, Absalom!* because his grand design is conceived without love. *Intruder in the Dust* ends in triumph because Chick Mallison's loyalty to his friend Lucas Beauchamp proves stronger than prejudice and hatred. Love, however travestied and distorted, holds the Bundrens together in *As I Lay Dying*. The convict's compassion for a fellow human being enables him to win a moral victory in *The Wild Palms*. Temple Drake's promiscuity and selfishness bring tragedy in *Sanctuary*. And so on. In each of its many modes, the Faulknerian world is based on human love, with the dignity and justice that it makes possible in society, and the tragedy that arises out of its violation. The necessity for love is the one constant in all the novels and stories. Those truly capable of love can face their experience with courage and purpose, and if they fail, they go down honorably. Without love there can only be lust, animalism, futility. With love, human beings can attain their full stature as men.

Isn't it odd that this Mississippi novelist, whose works have carried a highly sophisticated literary technique forward to its farthest reaches, whose fiction shows so profound an insight into the deepest psychological recesses of human behavior, should have ended up reiterating what is after all one of the oldest and most elementary moral truths? That this man who has written so shockingly about so many appallingly shocking things, should turn out to be so uncompromising, so unswerving a moralist? One thinks of that other great twentieth-century literary moralist, the Frenchman Marcel Proust. The fictional milieus of Proust and Faulkner are as different as two milieus can be, and yet each of these authors has shown how, through the torment of man's passions and the fires of his hatred and vanity, man can and must learn the compassion that is the product of the love of life and of one's fellow men. What has been said of Proust might with equal appropriateness be said of Faulkner: that in his moral zeal he exhibits the fervor and faith of an Old Testament prophet. How very shortsighted and shallow are those who have written of Faulkner as if he were a writer of cheap, "dirty books," as if he pandered to filth and obscenity. Criticism of Faulkner's "immorality" and "sensationalism," I am convinced, is the result of ignorance. To those who know his work, he appears the most moral and idealistic of writers.

What is the relationship, one might sometimes wonder, between William Faulkner's art and the state of Mississippi? It is surely not simply geographical. I have already suggested that the reason Faulkner's version of experience is not acceptable to many of his fellow Mississippians is that he depicts it in the kind of ultimate dimension of tragedy, a dimension not apparent to those who are busy living the life that he writes about. People do not customarily see their lives as a moral drama of the soul's own bitter travail, nor do they see themselves as living in history. All the same, one must insist, that is precisely what life was for Faulkner as an artist. And it is the function of his art to delineate the lines of meaning that lie concealed in the confusion of everyday life. John Crowe Ransom has used the term "concrete universal" to describe the nature of poetry, and this definition is no less appropriate for fiction. The novel is not merely life; it is life, as has been said, *charged with purpose*. When Faulkner wrote about life in Yoknapatawpha County, he made explicit and obvious a meaning and a morality that in La Fayette County life remains implicit and diffused. He saw human beings as actors in a great historical morality play, and he was sometimes very distressed over their failure to play their roles. Since the human beings Faulkner knew most about lived in Mississippi, it was their life that he chose to depict. Who, after all, had a better right to do so?

All this, however, does not answer the question of what there is about life in Mississippi that caused a William Faulkner. What was there in his environment that helped make him the great literary artist that he was?

Some would contend that there is *nothing* causal in the relationship, that Faulkner might just as readily have been born in New Jersey, or Iowa, or anywhere for that matter. What is remarkable about Faulkner is his genius; and genius is not a matter of environment. Now without doubt it is precisely his genius that made him the great novelist that he was, and merely to be born in Mississippi is not sufficient to make a man into an important writer.

Even so, it seems to me, it is not true that *no* relationship existed between the high art of William Faulkner and the circumstances of his environment. Were Faulkner's novels merely isolated phenomena, it would be one thing. The truth is that William Faulkner was but the best and most talented of a *whole group of writers*, including other distinguished artists, all born and reared in the selfsame state of Mississippi at approximately the same time. Not only are there Faulkner and Eudora Welty, but there are Stark Young, Shelby Foote, Elizabeth Spencer, Tennessee Williams, Hubert Creekmore, Ben Ames Williams, and James Street, to mention only the best known of a sizable number of writers. There is nothing quite like that roster anywhere else in twentieth-century American writing; to deny that some relationship exists between the art and the time and place is to fly in the face of impressive coincidence. The phenomenon of these writers all coming along at about the same period, all of them natives of a state hitherto not especially noted for its cultural achievements, must inevitably send one searching for an explanation in the life out of which their art evolved.

It has been suggested, not entirely facetiously, that the reason people in Mississippi grow up to write books is that there is no one for them to talk to down there. No doubt it is true that, as compared with life in large metropolitan areas, a young person of artistic sensibilities growing to maturity in a predominantly rural and "backward" region might be driven in on himself, so to speak; consequently he might tend to develop the kind of intense self-awareness that we think of as one of the conditions of literary achievement. However, if this by itself were enough, we might expect that the state of Montana, say, should likewise have produced some major American writers in our time. To my knowledge it has thus far failed to do so.

Mississippi, however, is *not* Montana. It is not, and during Faulkner's boyhood it was not, a sparsely settled, semifrontier area. Instead it is a place in which sharply etched patterns of social life, even though they came abruptly and not until the 1840's, had been securely implanted ever since the time of the Civil War. There grew up an inherited tradition of caste and of class leadership, in which social and cultural life (such as it was) were closely bound in with a religious orthodoxy that seemingly provided for its members an absolute anchor in time and place, a set, ordained relationship to the cosmos. And it is true that Mississippi was, and even today largely remains, fiercely rural, with the conservatism that life with a direct dependence on the land often involves. This is the picture of an ordered and orderly society, and such I think Mississippi aspired to be.

Yet if we examine the history of that state, we are struck by the disorder as well. Within two decades of its settlement it was ravaged by opposing armies. During the Reconstruction it was the scene of the most violent political disputes, and in subsequent decades it was a center of Populist agitation. From the outset its record in race relations has been one of much violence. It was the Mississippi Plan that showed the South how to disfranchise the Negro freedman. Year after year Mississippi led the South in lynching bees. In our own time the South has again and again been embarrassed by the zeal, extending to all manner of brutality and lynching, with which Mississippi has promulgated the "separate but equal" doctrine. It was Mississippi that produced the late Senator Bilbo, and the late Congressman Rankin, and before them, Governor Vardaman. Mississippi leads the nation in illiteracy, in brutality toward its Negro people—and in major novelists!

I am proposing that nowhere else in the South has the tension between tradition and change, between moral precept and animal instinct, between wealth and poverty, between order and disorder, between black and white, between aristocracy and redneck, been so sharply drawn, and so dramatically revelatory. For the worst abuses of the sharecropper system, for the most lordly of plantation dynasties, for the most vicious aspects of the race question, for the highest illiteracy rate, for the most beautiful examples of antebellum town architecture, for the most tranquil kind of pastoral existence, for the worst abuses of popular democracy and demagoguery in action, for the most dogged, tenacious stand of the old feudal *mores* in the face of twentieth-century industrial civilization, there is no place like Mississippi.

And if, as I have suggested elsewhere, the changeover from one way of life to another, the transition from a fixed society to the fluid, modern community, the breakdown of the old rural pattern and the rise of the industrial ethic, can dislodge the potential writer from his community, send him away from it and then back to it, cause him to examine his life with the artistic detachment that is born of spiritual estrangement and yet with the compassion that comes of kinship, have we not gone far toward accounting for the phenomenon of William Faulkner?

No, we have not "accounted" for it. Nothing can account for it, except a frank avowal of his genius. One would be hard put to find an explanation in the facts of Mississippi life for the astounding things that Faulkner does with the stream-of-consciousness technique, for example. But we have, I think, noted some of the social and cultural impetus that can help a man to become a novelist.

If art rises out of and is a product of a culture, then Faulkner's art must be seen as growing out of the culture of his region and his state, and we must recognize that the society in which Faulkner was reared helped to teach him to measure men in the way he has done. Mississippi it was, with its tensions, its contradictions, its passions, brutalities, heroisms, triumphs, shames, that spiritually nurtured the high art of William Faulkner.

Surely it cannot be denied that Faulkner's novels are directly concerned with the actual events of Mississippi life. The decline and fall of old landed dynasties, the conflicts of Negroes and whites, the rise of the rednecks; lynchings, rapes, floods, murders, and so forth—surely these *involve* life as it is lived in Mississippi. They are not *typical* of life in Mississippi; but then, what tragic poet has ever described typical people and typical situations? Faulkner's milieu is not, and never has been, the realistic portrayal of everyday life. Eudora Welty is far more satisfactory in that respect. No one with any intelligence (perhaps I should except Jean Paul Sartre) would think to read a Faulkner novel as a faithful account of daily existence in the South. Such matters are obvious, I am sure, to the intelligent reader, and such a reader no doubt would deem it of little value to devote any concern in a literary essay to what the man in the street, particularly the Mississippi man in the street, might think of William Faulkner. And he would be correct. But I am writing of Faulkner and his relationship to the South, and one cannot think of a region apart from its citizens. Faulkner has been affected as a novelist, and his art became in part what it is, *because* of his estrangement from the values of those average citizens. He did not write as a representative member of his community; he did not write for his fellow Mississippians; and, in short, the very sensibilities that made him into a novelist are precisely those that isolated him from the community.

I am not contending that it could or should be otherwise. Besides, one would be willing to pay a good deal for any kind of estrangement that resulted in *The Sound and the Fury*. But the point is that in the South the nature of the community during Faulkner's early years was such that it exerted a considerable pull on him to belong to it and to accept its standards, and the process of his divergence therefore, whether consciously or unconsciously, involved much conflict and tension. One does not give up membership in a community without a struggle. Yet the situation of the South in Faulkner's time, as I noted in the opening essay in this book, was such that it did cause its artists to become estranged from it, and the two-way pull between the social community and the private artistic sensibility produced some very dramatic literary results. It helped give us not only Faulkner's novels but the poetry and fiction of all the modern Southern writers.

They are writers of the changing South, the cultural fruits of a tremendous human drama that has shaken a region's social, cultural, economic, and political life to its core. The South has been in transition. The process of upheaval has jarred loose a number of talented artists, who have searched through the confusion and the change for sight of the ordering pinions that can give meaning to their experience. Their art constitutes this search. For Faulkner, what he saw and felt about his time and place assumed the mighty guise of tragedy, and the lineaments of the life he knew was given the essential dignity and importance of the tragic vision. In such a vision the elemental, rockbound human qualities, in their simplicity and their grandeur, shine through.

2

THOMAS WOLFE:
Time and the South

Thomas Wolfe was born in Asheville, North Carolina, in 1900. His origins and upbringing were squarely lower middle class. All the other writers of the modern South came from families that were among the cultural leaders of the community, the Southern squirearchy, with its antebellum roots. Not so Wolfe; his father was a stone-mason from Pennsylvania, a man who worked with his hands and was proud of it—though, as his son several times reminds us, he always wore a starched collar and tie on the job, with an apron pulled up over his good clothes to protect them from the dust. His mother's people, the Westalls, were a numerous mountain family; many of its members had come down to the town at about the time of the Civil War. They were "new people," and had no strong ties with the pre-War Southern aristocracy. Some of them grew quite wealthy during the late nineteenth and early twentieth centuries. Thomas Wolfe was the first member of his immediate family to go to college; he wanted to go to the University of Virginia or to Vanderbilt—it is interesting to speculate on what might have happened had he been sent to the latter school —but his father insisted that he attend the state university in Chapel Hill.

72

When we look at Eugene Gant's childhood as pictured in *Look Homeward, Angel,* what is most striking about it is its cultural impoverishment. There were a few books in the house—of poems, the obvious ones, for his father liked to declaim sentimental verse—but of literary and artistic interest there was almost none, save perhaps his sister's ambition to be a successful popular singer. A scene in *Look Homeward, Angel* describes how Eugene Gant, inspired by the tercentenary of the death of William Shakespeare, affixes a portrait of the poet to the wall, scrawling under it Ben Jonson's words, "My Shakespeare, rise!" He is tortured about it thereafter by the family: "Will My Shakespeare pass the biscuits?" and so forth. Despite the humor, however, an element of pathos is apparent in the episode. It shows us something of the kind of understanding a young man of Wolfe's temperament and interests must have received from his family.

Mrs. Wolfe ran a boardinghouse, a sprawling, cheaply constructed affair with bare, calcimined walls and poorly lighted halls. Jonathan Daniels describes how Wolfe's body lay in state in the boardinghouse after his death in 1938. The coffin, he writes,

> filled half the front room, which was hall also, of the old boarding-house. Above it there were long cracks in the yellow plaster ceiling. He was home.
> "Those melancholy cracks in the yellow plaster looking down at him!" the woman who was his friend said. "I know he fled from those cracks, and there he lay helpless while they triumphed over him."

The observation was an apt one; Wolfe's childhood was a time of much ugliness, and sometimes the depiction of Altamont that we read in *Look Homeward, Angel* is as bleak, as barren, as unlovely as any description in the work of the Midwestern naturalistic novelists such as

Dreiser and Anderson. Eugene Gant's career, no less than Thomas Wolfe's, was a search for loveliness, for aesthetic joy. He dreamed of the shining city beyond the mountains, where all would be radiant and beautiful. In 1923 he wrote from Harvard to his mother, about the plays he was going to write:

> What I shall try to get into [people's] dusty, little pint-measure minds is that a full belly, a good automobile, paved streets, and so on, do not make them one whit better or finer,—that there is beauty in this world,—beauty even in this wilderness of ugliness and provincialism that is at present our country, beauty and spirit which will make us men instead of cheap Board of Trade Boosters, and blatant pamphleteers. . . .

The life that Eugene Gant knows as he grows up, from his childhood to the moment when he prepares to leave Altamont for the golden city, involves drunkenness, violence, drabness, pain, penury, death. His recoil from the ugliness of so much of his environment is into himself; by his twelfth year, we are told, he has learned to "project mechanically, before the world, an acceptable counterfeit of himself which would protect him from intrusion." He is sent out early to earn money, first by selling magazines, then by delivering newspapers in the early morning on the Niggertown route. His mother is preoccupied with real estate; his father, grown old and sick, engages in periodic violent drinking bouts from which he staggers home, reeling and cursing.

Sent to a private school, Eugene comes under the protection of the wife of the principal, who mothers him and reads poetry to him. It is an oasis of beauty in a wilderness of drabness and pain: "Against the bleak horror of [the boardinghouse], against the dark road of pain and death down which the great limbs of Gant had already begun to slope, against all the loneliness and imprisonment of his own life which had gnawed him like hunger, these years at Leonard's bloomed like golden apples." At school he reads Wordsworth, Burns, Shakespeare, Jonson; meanwhile his father is dying, his brother Ben growing more aloof and bitter each year, his sister Helen off singing in theaters somewhere.

Yet set against the cultural impoverishment of family life and the town, the barrenness of the boardinghouse, is the outdoor world, the mountains that ringed Altamont, nature, the seasons. This aspect, largely missing in the novels of the Midwestern naturalists, is abundantly present in Wolfe. Frequent episodes are given over to the description of natural beauty, the coming and going of the seasons in the Carolina mountains: "Spring lay abroad through all the garden of this world. Beyond the hills the land bayed out to other hills, to golden cities, to rich meadows, to deep forests, to the sea. Forever and ever." In nature, and through his imagination, Eugene escaped from "the dim fly-specked lights, the wretched progress about the house in search of warmth, Eliza untidily wrapped in an old sweater, a dirty muffler, a cast-off man's coat." In the twenty-fourth chapter of *Look Homeward, Angel,* Eugene walks downtown. It is a humorous chapter, quite unlike the bleak naturalistic depictions of wretched prairie towns by Dreiser, Anderson, and Lewis. The portrait is done not in harshness and viciousness, but in affection and joy for the people and places seen and known. We must not forget this when we discuss Wolfe's attitude toward the community in which he grew up: there is attraction and revulsion, pleasure and pain, and their often contradictory mixture is essential to an understanding of Wolfe.

Look Homeward, Angel is a chronicle novel, describing the first twenty years of Eugene Gant's life. It is dominated by the passing of time. Old Gant is dying;

the family is falling apart; Eugene is growing up. Everywhere is the massive fact of change. The Gants are always in a state of turmoil. Eliza sets up a separate establishment at the boardinghouse, busies herself with real estate. Early in the novel Grover dies; much later on Ben too dies. Helen marries and leaves. Eugene goes off to college. Of stability and certainty there are almost none. The only fixed element is Eugene's own consciousness, and that too changes and expands as he becomes an adolescent and discovers sex, desire, art. Even as a child he had stared at a baby picture of himself, and "turned away sick with fear and the effort to touch, retain, grasp himself for only a moment." The novel is a series of episodes strung out in time: almost every chapter of *Look Homeward, Angel* contains in its first paragraph a reference to the flight of time and the coming and going of the seasons.

Occasionally the characters observe themselves caught in time, and can only look with awe and fear at what they see. Old Gant sells the stone angel of his youth to adorn a prostitute's grave, then steps out onto the porch of his monument shop. For an instant all life in the town square below seems suspended, "and Gant felt himself alone move deathward in a world of seemings. . . ." At the very close of the novel, when Ben has died and Eugene has completed college and is preparing to depart for the North, he stands on the porch of the shop exactly as Old Gant had done, and converses with the ghostly shade of Ben. The fountain in the square is suddenly motionless, frozen in time. The stone animals of the monuments get up and walk. All that he has seen and known parades before Eugene's unbelieving eyes. Then, in the climactic moment of the novel, he sees, coming along past the fountain carrying his load of newspapers, "himself —his son, his body, his lost and virgin flesh." His own childhood self passes by, the self lost in time, vanished down the years. Eugene calls to him. "His voice strangled in his throat; the boy had gone, leaving the memory of his bewitched and listening face turned to the hidden world. O lost!" So swiftly has it all happened, almost without his knowing it; he has grown to manhood, and whatever he once was is lost and unrecapturable. Time, chronology, change; these are the only reality he knows. Then the fountain begins splashing again, and the novel is concluded.

There are two narrative progressions in *Look Homeward, Angel.* Eugene, as we have noted, is born within the community, grows up, and prepares to leave. His father comes to the community from the outer world, becomes increasingly trapped within it, struggles vainly to escape, grows old and sick, will soon die there. This dual movement, into and away from Altamont, constitutes the structure of the novel. W. O. Gant is the frustrated mortal, the lonely American never acquiescent in his lot, who wanders from childhood onward, drifting to Altamont by chance, taking up residence there, marrying a woman he does not love deeply, fathering children, growing old and sick, and finally waiting to die. As a boy he had learned stonecutting; he wanted to carve an angel, but his skill was sufficient only for lettering monuments. He keeps a stone angel on the porch of his shop, curses it, reviles it; it is a reminder of what he wanted to do and be. Finally he sells it to adorn the grave of a prostitute. *Look Homeward, Angel* is subtitled "A story of the buried life," and Old Gant's life is buried, hidden under the debris of the years. "Where now? Where after? Where then?" Wolfe asks after Gant sells the statue and watches the town square grow still.

Important though W. O. Gant's journey is, *Look Homeward, Angel* is his son Eugene's book. It is seen through his consciousness. We do not need the foreword "To the Reader" to tell us that the point of view is that of Eugene looking backward. The meaning and unity of all the events in the novel lie in their impact on Eugene, not only the Eugene who grows up in the book, but the Eugene who is remembering it all. Eugene is the youngest son of W. O. and Eliza; as his father grows old, he grows to manhood. His early years are filled with conflict—between his father and mother; between the claims of the Woodson Street home his father owns and the boardinghouse his mother buys and operates; between Altamont's small-town ways and its ambitions to become a metropolis; between the conservative instincts of the society and the boomtown atmosphere of everyday life; between his own artistic leanings and the thoroughly middle-class attitudes toward such interests held by his family and the townsfolk.

As the novel develops, so does Eugene's gradual estrangement from family and community. The death of Ben culminates the process of Eugene's alienation from the family. His developing aesthetic and intellectual interests, his revulsion from trade and business, his growing ambition separate him from his fellow townsmen. Hatred of the ugliness and pettiness of small-town life causes him to withdraw into his own consciousness; after Ben is gone his isolation is almost complete. The Eugene who looks not townward but toward the distant hills at the conclusion of the novel is done with life in Altamont; his gaze is on the shining city, the promise of artistic achievement. He will avoid the entombment within the town that his father suffered, the emotional suffocation that was Ben's lot, for unlike them he will be saved by his genius, by the miracle of his art. (That his best art would be the recreation of life in the same town is an interesting irony, and not unimportant to what the town meant for Wolfe.)

The midway point in the process of alienation, it seems to me, is the part of the twenty-fourth chapter, mentioned previously, that describes Eugene as he leaves Leonard's school with his friend George Graves and walks into the city. Laughing and bantering as he goes, Eugene sees the people, places, and events of Altamont life as in a moment of stasis, before his own vision has become so subjective that it will permit him to see things only as they affect his private identity. It is a matchless portrayal of a small city's downtown area, one neither distorted by adult prejudgments nor overly simplified by a child's naïveté. Afterward Eugene will discover sex, and love, and death, and art, and never again will he be able to look at Altamont with so much objectivity as he does on that day. It is the halfway mark; before it comes, Eugene is a small child, still largely unseeing; afterward he is a preoccupied, self-centered adolescent, caught up in his moods and desires. Just once, in this chapter, Altamont is seen whole. Thereafter Eugene is growing away from it too rapidly to look at it for what it is.

At the close of *Look Homeward, Angel,* Wolfe's autobiographical protagonist is about to leave for the city; not for New York—his rendezvous with the greatest of American metropolises is to come later—but for Boston, and graduate study at Harvard University. Wolfe's stay there is recounted in the opening chapters of *Of Time and the River.* His ambition is to become a great playwright, and not surprisingly he soon finds the drama workshop of Professor James Graves Hatcher (George Pierce Baker) an insubstantial, artificial affair. When the New York producers who have been considering his play reject it, he stages an epic alcoholic bout while back home with his family, then departs for New York, the "enfabled rock."

New York is where Art is to be found, promise made good, love, romance, discovered, fame attained. All that has been desired supposedly will come true in the city, which in Wolfe's work takes on the mystical vision of an impossibly rich and glorious land of fulfillment. In one of his many gastronomic metaphors, Wolfe has Eugene address himself to the city and declare his desire "to devour you, golden fruit of power and love and happiness; to consume you to your sources, river and spire and rock, down to your iron roots; to entomb within our flesh forever the huge substance of your billion-footed pavements, the intolerable web and memory of dark million-visaged time." With growing excitement he races northward on the train, plunges into the streets of the metropolis, begins his life there.

Soon, however, as Wolfe is quick to point out, the golden city loses its sheen, the fabulous towers become cold and menacing, and Eugene and his creator grow to hate their minute, impoverished, laborious existence as one of the city's many millions. "What have we taken from you, protean and phantasmal shape of time?" Wolfe asks the metropolis on Eugene's behalf; "What have we remembered of your million images, of your billion weavings out of accident and number, of the mindless fury of your dateless days, the brutal stupefaction of your thousand streets and pavements? What have we seen and known that is ours forever?" He answers the query himself:

> Gigantic city, we have taken nothing—not even a handful of your trampled dust—we have made no image on your iron breast and left not even the print of a heel upon your stony-hearted pavements. The possession of

all things, even the air we breathed, was held from us,
and the river of life and time flowed through the grasp
of our hands forever, and we held nothing for our hunger and desire except the proud and trembling moments,
one by one.

Eugene rejects the metropolis; in the process he has
become George Webber, a somewhat more sullen and
socially conscious protagonist who nevertheless is almost
as autobiographical as his predecessor. He—George-
Eugene-Thomas—has experienced loneliness, love, fame,
success, and finds them all barren, as forsaken and as un-
tenable as he had once found Altamont (and its suc-
cessor, Libya Hill). What the Wolfean protagonist finally attains, however, is not the social conscience that
is supposedly George Webber's by the end of *You Can't
Go Home Again,* so much as the entire isolation of the
self. All that remains to him is the immediate response
to various aspects of his experience as they impinge upon
the consciousness of the protagonist, but these aspects
possess no meaning except in the way they register upon
the protagonist's own identity. By this I mean that for
the mature George Webber the world is entirely subjective, and not only that, but entirely solipsistic. In
other words, it exists only as it affects him. This is not
what Wolfe *says* about George and the world; he says
precisely the opposite. But dramatically, fictionally, it
is what we as readers *see.* The scenes, episodes, events
described by Wolfe in his fiction after *Look Homeward,
Angel* are given unity and meaning only in that they
occur to the same person; of themselves they contain
little or no structure or form. Nor do they, in truth,
change the Wolfean protagonist very much. He is much
the same person at the end of *You Can't Go Home Again*
as he is when he leaves for the city after *Look Homeward, Angel*—a little more sober and heavy-handed, per-

haps, a little less fervent, but not really very changed. Whatever meaning finally emerges in Eugene-George-Thomas's life is no more (or less) than the knowledge that he exists, that life changes, that eventually he too will die. The rejected order of Altamont has been succeeded by no greater order, no more genial, more golden community; once Altamont has been put aside, as it has been by the time of Ben's death, only the private self remains.

Wolfe is a writer, after *Look Homeward, Angel,* of fragments. Some are glittering, some are sensuous, some are sordid, but they are not joined in any order. The only unity is vague and for the most part rhetorical; again and again Wolfe resorts to the device of simply saying that they are "all" part of "something," but he does not know what the "something" is that they "all" constitute. "*All* the vision of the magic earth," he says, and "*all* the grime and sweat and violence of the city," just as it is "the *whole* wrought fabric of life in the city," and "*all* that we know is that having everything we yet hold nothing," and "*all* these memories of his father's life" and "*all* the noises, rhythms, sounds and variations of the train" and "*all* man's living memory of morning, youth and magic"—there are long catalogs, and more often great, adjectival outbursts of agony and ecstasy, especially throughout *Of Time and the River* (from which the preceding phrases were selected at random), but there is no more organization, no more meaning or unity than that of simple accumulation. *Of Time and the River* is fragmentary, becoming increasingly so as it goes on, and eventually we realize that nothing is going to "happen," that as we read we receive only so many episodes, adding up to no more than their cumulative accretion. And even *The Web and the Rock,* the love story that constitutes the closest approximation to a plot provided by Wolfe after the first novel, leaves George Webber essentially unchanged, unaffected by what has happened to him.

The extent to which Wolfe's work, after *Look Homeward, Angel,* is composed of such fragments is hardly recognized, I think, by most of his readers. The fact is that he did not give direction or unity to any of his books after the first. He toiled over the various parts of *Of Time and the River* for years, until suddenly his editor, Maxwell Perkins, sent it to the printer while Wolfe was out of town. Had it not been for Perkins' insistence that *Look Homeward, Angel* be followed by another big book, the episodes in *Of Time and the River* might have appeared in more fragmentary form—and perhaps to their advantage. Wolfe's last two novels, published after his death, were even less the product of a single imagined pattern; indeed, they were given their status as novels primarily by Edward Aswell, Wolfe's second editor, who joined them together, provided transitional passages, and titled them. The contents of the last two volumes were by no means composed as portions of a unified narrative; many of the better episodes were first published separately, and are read best that way. It is no more than accurate to say that Wolfe completed only one long novel, *Look Homeward, Angel;* and a host of short novels, novelle, stories, and sketches. Their published appearance in the form of long novels was not his doing—which is not to say that he would not have acquiesced in their presentation in that form, as he did with *Of Time and the River.* But he did not compose in that fashion; he had in mind only a vague plan into which everything was supposed to fit. Whether he would ever have worked it out coherently cannot be determined. Perkins decided that Wolfe would never do it, and he gathered together the material that constitutes *Of Time and the River* and sent it to the printer, after changing the entire narrative from the first to the third person! The extent to which Wolfe's later decision to leave Perkins and Scribner's was due to his secret knowledge (despite his and Perkins' public disclaimers) that it was not *his* book is hard to say. At the suggestion of Professor C. Hugh Holman I have read over the published correspondence of the period of the famous break, and it seems to me that no other explanation is really credible.

If Wolfe had insufficient control over the publication of *Of Time and the River*, *The Web and the Rock* and *You Can't Go Home Again* were even less the books he intended them to be. In February of 1938 Wolfe wrote a long synopsis of "the book" to his new editor, Edward Aswell. That summer he went westward on a trip. He left Aswell an enormous quantity of manuscript with which Aswell was to familarize himself while Wolfe was away. Wolfe fully expected that the rewriting and organizing would require at least another full year. But he was never to have the chance. In Seattle he came down with the illness that caused his death in September of 1938. After Wolfe's death, Aswell went to work, grouping and collecting. To guide him he had only a long but sketchy outline which Wolfe had left with him. He drew not only upon the manuscript, but on Wolfe's letters, notes, and other materials. Some of the manuscript dated back to the days of *Look Homeward, Angel;* some had been written just before Wolfe's last trip. For one sequence Aswell actually used part of the synopsis in the letter of February 14, which had never been posted and was discovered only after Wolfe's death.

There is no doubt that Aswell labored devotedly and tirelessly to edit all the material into coherent form. But the fact remains that it was *not* the form that Wolfe gave it, and there is no telling what might have evolved had he been around to spend the year of rewriting he planned. And it seems to me that it is, finally, something of a disservice to Wolfe to have brought out his posthumous work in the way that it was done. He is presented as the author of four full-length novels, when in fact he wrote only two novels by himself (if one counts *Of Time and the River*) and a great mass of shorter materials that he intended to fashion into novel form, but did not live to accomplish. To publish material as if it were a novel arouses certain expectations on the reader's part which, when not fulfilled, result in a disappointment that interferes with his appreciation of what actually was written. Wolfe's reputation, it seems to me, would have been far better served had the manuscripts he left been edited and published as a group of short novels. It is quite true that Wolfe intended for them to be part of a longer work, but since he did not live to do the rewriting and editing this would have entailed, it was not the task of an editor do it for him, no matter how close his friendship with Wolfe.

What I am saying, in effect, is that I should much rather have read three or four short novels, for their own sake, than the same material as combined and edited into *You Can't Go Home Again*. It seems to me that a considerable task remains for Wolfe scholars to do: a close textual study of the manuscript left by Wolfe when he died, including all that placed by Wolfe's editor into novel form, leading to the preparation of a definitive published text. I should like to know, for example, the dates of composition for each episode. I should also like to know the extent to which Wolfe's editor cut and edited his material. Was any of the Eugene Gant ma-

terial edited to read "George Webber" by Mr. Aswell?
Did Aswell himself actually write many of the transition
passages between episodes? If so, which ones?

I am perhaps being unfair to Aswell; certainly his
labors on behalf of his dead friend were selfless and
devoted. It is true, too, that had Wolfe been offered the
choice, he might well have approved of Aswell's doing
what he did. Yet I question, not Aswell's intentions,
which were of the best, but his judgment. The fact cannot be gainsaid that the two final novels were presented
as if Wolfe wrote them that way, when he did not do
any such thing, and that he left only the most sketchy
of plans for his book. It will not do to maintain, as Aswell
did in his account of the editing of the posthumous material, that Wolfe "did not know whether in the end it
would make one book or a dozen, and he didn't much
care. That seemed to him the publisher's problem, and
he was right about it. What went into each volume was
largely a matter of convenience and practicability."
What Wolfe and his editor, acting in concert, might
have done with finished material is one thing; but this
was unfinished material, written over the course of almost a decade, involving at least three different protagonists. ". . . My very strong hunch at present," Wolfe
wrote to Aswell shortly before leaving for the West,
"is that it may be best to allow me to proceed with my
work without any great assistance until I have brought
it to a further stage of development and completion."
To present such material as Wolfe's finished work, and
in a form purported to be the one that Wolfe intended
for it, is to give a very misleading impression of Wolfe's
literary work after *Of Time and the River*.

If I have labored this matter of texts and editions,
it is because I feel that there is an almost universal mis-

understanding about the nature of those last two novels, and thus about Wolfe's work as a whole. Most readers of Wolfe's fiction with whose views I am acquainted believe that Thomas Wolfe wrote two novels and left behind the manuscripts of two others, which his editor subsequently tied up and published. *He did no such thing.* All that he left behind were *fragments.* After *Of Time and the River* he never wrote another novel. And this is important to realize for what it means about Wolfe's imagination. The act of creating and forming a novel involves giving a meaning to the material, seeing it as a whole unified action. The truth is that once Wolfe left Altamont and the community of his childhood he was, as an artist, unable to give any meaning to his experience except that it had happened. *Of Time and the River* starts off as if headed for somewhere, but it never gets there. Wolfe's art was essentially one of recall, and in such a process only the life of his childhood fell into orderly place and direction. Altamont he saw whole, as a place with real people living in it who belonged there, in which he, as a child, had his role into which for a time at least he fitted, and in which his father, his mother, his family each had their positions. Looking back at his childhood, he saw it as a growing away from the town, a mounting alienation from a community that became, so far as his judgment was involved, increasingly less orderly and meaningful; so that at the end Eugene Gant stands on the porch of the marble shop, and is awed by the way that what he has known and understood has vanished in time. Then he turns away toward the city.

Significantly, I think, Wolfe is the only one of the major Southern novelists whose fiction, after his first book, is no longer set primarily or even importantly in the community of his origins. The forces that propelled him away from Asheville were so intense, so relentless, that once he had described the process of alienation he could not return there artistically. He never came home again, physically or spiritually, save for short visits. The only meaning he could discover for Asheville was, finally, that of change. It is time and change that give direction and order to Altamont; and since time is inevitably a process of loss, there remained at last only death and memory. No wonder Wolfe is the most eloquent writer about death of his generation! It was the only surety he could deduce from what he had known—life briefly is, and then it ends.

He was caught up in the process of time, fascinated by it; like his friend Scott Fitzgerald he saw himself as a creature of time and change, but unlike Fitzgerald he was never detached about it, never able as an artist to see himself as a limited and finite participant in the spectacle. As an artist he was, as it were, the very eye of time itself, recording and experiencing it. He was bound utterly to it, unable, for purposes of fiction, to separate himself from the actual force and direction of the experience that he underwent as boy and man. Fitzgerald had the same vision of himself in time, but between Fitzgerald the artist and Fitzgerald the man in time there was a great—and for the man a tragic—difference. In Wolfe no such division existed; the art suffered accordingly, for only when the conditions of the experience itself, and not the implied meaning of the experience, possessed a discoverable unity and direction was Wolfe able to give wholeness to his fiction. *Look Homeward, Angel* is the story of Wolfe's growth from birth to young manhood; it has the cohesion of the novel of growth, the developing self-consciousness of the individual. Eugene comes to realize his isolation, his separation from his family and community; this is the progression of *Look*

Homeward, Angel. He did not have to discover that meaning; it is manifestly and physically there.

A Yoknapatawpha County, a continuing community such as Faulkner created, was impossible for Wolfe, because he could not separate himself from his experience and use it. The milieu of Faulkner's childhood furnishes the texture for a number of novels, each possessing the form of individual works of art. Faulkner could select from what he knew and use it for his own purposes as a novelist. Wolfe could not pick and choose from his experience, for it was not real enough, when viewed apart from its personal impact on him, to permit him to convert and manipulate it. Altamont exists as part of Wolfe's consciousness, and since his experience of Altamont had been one of change, progressive alienation, death, that was all that Altamont could mean for him. Apart from that process he could not take the milieu with sufficient seriousness to give it a meaning of its own in other novels.

Wolfe's reputation as a novelist, it seems to me, will rest primarily on *Look Homeward, Angel,* and, to a considerably lesser extent, *Of Time and the River.* Nothing Wolfe wrote afterward has anything like the appeal of the Eugene Gant material. Eugene is romantic, extravagant, self-indulgent, histrionic—and he is one of the great characters of modern American fiction. So, for that matter, are the other Gants; taken together they are a remarkable fictional family. The intensity that Wolfe brought to Eugene and his family goes along with the dramatization of fully realized characters functioning in a vivid, believable social situation. Eugene is autobiographical and ardent; in *Look Homeward, Angel* Wolfe dramatized himself and his milieu with consummate skill.

As he grew older, Wolfe came to realize Eugene Gant's limitations. In the winter before his death he wrote to Edward Aswell that "the value of the Eugene Gant type of character is his personal and romantic uniqueness, causing conflict with the world around him; in this sense, the Eugene Gant type of character becomes a kind of romantic self-justification, and the greatest weakness of the Eugene Gant type of character lies in this fact." He went on to say that in his new novel there must be "no trace of Eugene Gant-i-ness in the character of the protagonist; and since there is no longer a trace of Eugene Gant-i-ness in the mind and spirit of the creator, the problem should be a technical one rather than a spiritual or emotional one."

When one reads a statement such as this, the only thing to do is to look at the writing Wolfe was doing in his last years, to see whether what he says is true. We do not know for sure which portions of the posthumously published material were written at which periods in his life, though it is obvious that much of the middle portion of *The Web and the Rock* is, in content and attitude, a direct continuation of *Of Time and the River*, with only the names changed. By contrast, the early portions of *The Web and the Rock*, and perhaps the closing chapters too, obviously were composed much later. The same is manifestly true of much of *You Can't Go Home Again;* in most instances we can tell from dates of periodical publication and from references in Wolfe's published correspondence. Was Wolfe, then, correct in his claim that in the later material "there is no longer a trace of Eugene Gant-i-ness in the mind and spirit of the creator"?

The answer is, No. There is little evidence, insofar as Wolfe's fictional imagination was concerned, that he ever managed to get far outside of the sense of "per-

sonal and romantic uniqueness," of "romantic self-justification," that he rightly associates with Eugene Gant.
He *says* that such associations were not true of him any
longer; obviously he did make a militant attempt to leave
romantic subjectivity and write socially conscious, po-
litically conscious fiction. But as a novelist he continued
to see his experience with the same kind of personal
absorption, the self-justification, the thoroughly egocentric valuation of the world that characterized the earlier
novels. There is, to be sure, somewhat less romantic rap-
ture; his protagonist no longer goes about uttering wild
"goat cries"; but Monk Webber's view of the "real
world" is just as egocentric as Eugene Gant's ever was,
and he takes himself just as seriously as Eugene ever did.
Wolfe could not write fiction otherwise than in terms
of himself. Unlike Fitzgerald, he could never look at his
"real-life" self with sufficient irony to create a consciously romantic, innocent character. He views his adult
experience precisely the way he viewed childhood and
adolescent experience, and as fiction it works not nearly
so well—as indeed one might expect.

Eugene Gant is first a child, then a youth, and finally
a very young man. In *Look Homeward, Angel* the romantic intensity of his self-justification and self-import-
ance is more attractive than not. But by the time we get
halfway through *Of Time and the River* it has long since
begun to wear thin. A good rule of thumb in the Wolfe
novels is that the closer in age the protagonist is to
Thomas Wolfe, the less believable he is as a created,
fictional character. The only perspective Wolfe ever
seems to have gained on his material as a novelist is that
of temporal distance. That is to say, as long as he is
reasonably older than his protagonist, he is able to dis-
tinguish between the protagonist's values as a fictional
character and his own as a novelist. But once this auto-

biographical distance is gone, he has no perspective from which to evaluate the character's motivations and actions except those of the character himself. For the character is always himself.

He could never write otherwise. Toward the end of his life he turned back to the country of his origins. In his long novel there was to be a first section, a prologue, that was to be about his mother's people and their place in the mountain country. Nine chapters of the prologue, published posthumously as *The Hills Beyond*, were completed at the time of his death, and we can read them and watch the same process happening as before. What begins as an objective chronicle of mountain forebears soon comes to center more and more in the consciousness of young Edward Joyner, in spite of the fact that Edward is supposed to be only an ancestor of the true protagonist. Wolfe's father appears on the scene, in a fictional guise only slightly different from that of W. O. Gant in *Look Homeward, Angel*, and soon the "prison walls of self" close around young Edward, until the last chapter Wolfe wrote is very close to the same kind of subjective, private meditation that we associate with Eugene Gant. It may be that had Wolfe lived he could have forced the narrative focus back outside of Edward's mind and gone on to finish the prologue, but it is impossible to say. When the fragment closes, Wolfe seems close to the point where he began and ended in all his other fiction—himself.

In this respect Wolfe's fiction is importantly different from that of almost all his fellow Southern authors. With all the others, the fictional is usually third-dimensional, external; there is little or no authorial intrusion into the independence of the characters. We almost never have the feeling, when reading the fiction of Faulkner, Warren, Welty, and the others, that the author is dramatizing not only the character, but himself as well. There is an achieved anonymity about most novels by the contemporary Southern writers, and for that matter about their poems as well; we never sense that the authors are imposing their personal, "real-life" values upon the fiction, artificially and from without. They seem as artists to be able to step away from the book, to give it an objective representation, an independence, whereby the meaning is inherent in the fiction. Faulkner, for example, is never limited to his own personal preoccupations; he can give his novel whatever meaning the developing fictional situation requires. Not so Wolfe; the emotions of the central character, the evaluation of the experience being described, are always the author's "real-life" feelings about a "real-life" situation. Wolfe never knew the meaning of artistic anonymity, so far as his own work was concerned. He is always *subjective;* he can never go out beyond himself to create life independent of its impact on the autobiographical protagonist.

In *Look Homeward, Angel,* that kind of approach to the central character, Eugene Gant, was highly appropriate to the demands of the characterization, for Eugene *is* an egocentric child. We expect him to consider himself a unique person, to view the world entirely through his own responses. "Romantic self-justification" on the part of the author works, so far as Eugene is concerned; and the intensity of Wolfe's sense of isolation from the world gave Eugene Gant a believable intenseness about everything he did and thought. Besides, Wolfe the adult author was removed from Eugene the adolescent character by the physical fact of age; an adult is writing about a boy, and is thus able to perceive some of the limitations of the character's view of his experience. And not only that; there is also the fact that the members of his family, whom he used as models, are not merely reflections of

Wolfe's personal needs, as almost all the characters drawn from his adult life are. He saw the Gants as individuals and could write about them in their own right, not as they affected him alone.

When, however, Wolfe wrote about Eugene the man, and George Webber the man, that perspective was missing. An adult author is writing about an adult character; and, because he is Wolfe, he cannot perceive any difference between the character's attitude toward his experience and the meaning of the experience itself. All he knows is what the character feels, and all the character feels is what Wolfe felt. We have to accept completely and without reservation the character's subjective version of "real life," or else the character appears ridiculous; and to do this we have to identify ourselves with the character. And the character's view of himself and his life is *very* romantic. If, then, the reader cannot take just as romantic, as egocentric a view toward the character's experience as the character himself takes, the author's fictional imitation of "real life" will not be very convincing.

This is what is wrong with most of the fiction after *Look Homeward, Angel.* In *The Web and the Rock* he writes as follows:

> What is it that a young man wants? What is the central source of that wild fury that boils up in him, that goads and drives and lashes him, that explodes his energies and strews his purpose to the wind of a thousand instant and chaotic impulses? The older and more assured people of the world, who have learned to work without waste and error, think they know the reason for the chaos and confusion of a young man's life. They have learned the thing at hand, and learned to follow their single way through all the million shifting hues and tones and cadences of living, to thread neatly with unperturbed heart their single thread through that huge laby-

rinth of shifting forms and intersecting energies that make up life—and they say, therefore, that the reason for a young man's confusion, lack of purpose, and erratic living is because he has not "found himself."

In this, the older and more certain people may be right by their own standard of appraisal, but, in this judgment on the life of youth, they have really pronounced a sterner and more cruel judgment on themselves. For when they say that some young man has not yet "found himself," they are really saying that he has not lost himself as they. For men will often say that they have "found themselves" when they have really been worn down into a groove by the brutal and compulsive force of circumstance. They speak of their life's salvation when all that they have done is blindly follow through an accidental way. They have forgotten their life's purpose, and all the faith, hope, and immortal confidence of a boy. They have forgotten that below all the apparent waste, loss, chaos, and disorder of a young man's life there is really a central purpose and a single faith which they themselves have lost.

There, it seems to me, is the real issue. For Wolfe is asserting in this passage what I think he passionately believed all his days, for all his disclaimers of continued "Gant-i-ness": that the youthful romantic view of the world is the *true* view. The world is a place of boundless possibilities, endless opportunities; and the proper response to the world is one involving just such wild, romantic fury and ecstasy. Note that he speaks of the "*apparent* waste, loss, chaos, and disorder"; he does not really concede that the romantic attitude is in the least chaotic and disorderly. Persons who "follow their single way," who seek to "work without waste and error," who have "learned the thing at hand," are those who have lost their life's purpose and faith, whom experience has "worn down into a groove." It is not, in other words, the work, but the "feeling" about it that counts. This is an

entirely subjective attitude toward experience; reality
exists not in the experience of life itself, but in the way
one feels about it. Life is "that huge labyrinth of shifting
forms and intersecting energies," and to attempt to come
to grips with life by setting out along any particular approach or "thread" is to lose oneself. For life is best understood by abandoning oneself to its "chaos and confusion," not by searching for order and purpose. Indeed,
the only way to achieve order and purpose is through an
ardent embracing of disorder without trying to understand it. In that case, therefore, any order must consist
of the individual's perception of disorder. Thus order
and meaning are entirely personal and subjective.

That Wolfe believed this as an artist, whatever he
may have said as a man, is very clear. The "real world"
is only what it meant to Eugene Gant or George Webber.
And what it meant to them is the way they *felt* about it.
The intensity of feeling, not the truth of the thing felt,
is what matters. This is why, I think, Wolfe is the writer
for so many younger readers. Not only does Wolfe
glory in the ecstasy of his feelings; he tells his readers
that nothing matters except feeling. The ability to chan-
nel, to direct one's emotions, to set them in motion toward action and accomplishment, is not important.

The evaluation Wolfe attaches to the adult Eugene
Gant's and Monk Webber's attitude toward the world
and to their place in it is precisely that of many of
Wolfe's most enthusiastic admirers. For them, as for
Wolfe, it is a Brave New World. The reader who cannot, however, judge things as he did when, like Monk
Webber, he was twenty-three years old, is too often
likely to find the adult Eugene and Monk more than a
little silly. The younger reader prefers *Of Time and
the River*. The older reader will probably prefer *Look
Homeward, Angel*. There is no reconciling the two view-

points. Of the two viewpoints, one might say that one of them is more mature than the other. If one happens to be twenty-three years old, however, he will doubtless admit no such thing.

But Wolfe was *not* twenty-three years old when he wrote his novels. How can we account, therefore, for the tenacity with which he held on to such a perspective, for the intense self-justification, the colossal subjectivity that characterize him as man and writer? What caused him to see his experience so completely in terms of himself, to remain imprisoned within his own feelings, so to speak, so that, try as he might, he could never break away from what he termed his "Eugene Gant-i-ness"?

It would be foolhardy indeed to hope to single out an explanation. The creator of Eugene Gant was a very complex person, and, just as with Faulkner, one must finally halt before the phenomenon of genius. And whatever else we may think of him, Wolfe possessed a large supply of the quality we call "genius."

All the same, I want to speculate a little about Wolfe and his relationship to his culture. I have already noted that almost alone of the Southern writers of his generation, Wolfe came not from the gentry, but out of a solid lower-middle-class background. And I have noted, too, that there was a singular barrenness, an absence of cultural and aesthetic richness, about his childhood; the ugliness of much of his early experience, the aesthetic and cultural impoverishment, is strikingly evident in his description of life in the Gant household. Now if we compare Wolfe's childhood with that of other Southern writers of his generation, we will see that every one of the others came from families in which intellectual and cultural interests were far more likely to be part of the customary events of their daily lives. In *The Story of a*

Novel Wolfe declares that for his kind of people, the idea of being an author was something strange and exotic, in no way part of their experience. This was hardly true for any of the others. Faulkner's great grandfather, for example, was a novelist, and Faulkner grew up in a university community in which his father was a college official. John Crowe Ransom's father was a distinguished linguist and theologian. Donald Davidson's father was a schoolteacher, his mother a musician. Robert Penn Warren's father was a banker, his mother a schoolteacher. Allen Tate's family was of distinguished, well-educated stock; his grandfather was a Latin teacher, and his great-grandfather a newspaper editor. Eudora Welty's father was president of an insurance company. And so on. The point is that in the upper-class South, from which all these authors came, there was always a literary and aesthetic tradition. Young men and women growing up in such circumstances would not ordinarily find that intellectual and aesthetic inclinations on their part automatically set them rigidly apart from their neighbors, isolated them from family and community.

With Wolfe it was very different; there was almost nothing in Wolfe's background and surroundings that would enable him to share whatever intellectual and artistic impulses he may have had as a small child. He could look for no real sympathy, no genuine understanding for any such inclinations. Whatever embryonic literary interests the young Wolfe must have possessed would have been kept solitary and secret. "My Shakespeare, rise!"

I do not want to make too much of this, but I think it no more than true to say that everything about Wolfe's childhood conspired to turn his deepest sensibilities inward, to cause him to erect a barrier between himself and the world around him, to give him a tremendous defensiveness about his literary and intellectual interests. Wolfe speaks of Eugene's "secret world, so fearfully guarded," and when he has Eugene write a composition in school describing a girl listening to a lark, it contains these words: "The girl has had a hard life. Her people do not understand her. If they saw her listening to the lark, they would poke fun at her." (My own guess is that this is probably an actual composition that Wolfe himself wrote.)

The picture Wolfe gives of Eugene Gant's boyhood is far from that of a happy, normal child in harmony with his environment. One continually encounters such sentences as these: "The agony and humiliation it caused him was horrible, but she was unable or unwilling to understand it . . ."; "The herd, merciless in its banded instinct, knew at once that a stranger had been thrust into it, and it was merciless at the hunt . . ."; "shame gathered in him in tangled clots, aching in his throat . . ."; "Once, deathly sick, but locked in silence and dumb nausea, he had vomited finally upon his cupped hands . . ."; "Eugene was startled and confused, feeling that his secret world, so fearfully guarded, had been revealed to ridicule . . ."; "He writhed with shame and humiliation . . ."; "his shame, his distaste for his employment was obvious, although he tried to conceal it . . ."; "He felt now the petty cruelty of village caste . . ."; "He rushed at the wall like an insane little goat, battered his head screaming again and again, wished desperately that his constricted and overloaded heart would burst, that something in him would break, that somehow, bloodily, he might escape the stifling prisonhouse of his life. . . ." It was not a pretty childhood.

Is it, then, entirely without explanation that this particular North Carolina youth, whose childhood was filled with wretchedness, pain, and bewilderment, whose innermost thoughts and feelings set him far apart from the attitudes of his family and community, whose deepest instincts and values were in continual conflict with those of his environment, should have developed into an adult who was preoccupied with himself, who considered himself "God's lonely man," who poured out an intense fictional assertion of his own uniqueness and of the justification for it? "He believed himself thus at the centre of life," Wolfe says of Eugene Gant as a youth. And at seventeen Wolfe wrote to his mother from Chapel Hill that "I am changing so rapidly that I find myself an evergrowing source of interest. Sounds egotistical, doesn't it?" I suggest that both remarks are literally true.

If in the instance of the other Southern writers of Wolfe's generation the breakdown of the patterns of the old community life produced a growing alienation from the values of the community, then it is hardly surprising that in Wolfe the sense of alienation should have been especially intense, manifesting itself in a violent, intensely lyrical assertion of separation and loneliness. The others at least grew up in a society that possessed a tradition of intellectual and cultural activity that, mannered and genteel though it was, permitted a measure of expression for the developing aesthetic sensibilities. With Wolfe there was no such outlet. I do not mean that his family did not recognize his talent; but it was something foreign and strange to them. There was no convention for him to follow, no accepted pattern, however inadequate, of formal, objective utterance; the Wolfe family's lower-middle-class situation had no place for aesthetic expression. Anyone who displayed intense artistic inclinations would have been considered a freak, a misfit. And when the qualities of mind that made Thomas Wolfe into a novelist instead of a stonemason or a real-estate salesman did come fully to light, there was not sur-

prisingly an explosive force to their emergence, a furious
emotional subjectivity that could be disciplined only with
great difficulty and always imperfectly.

As a child growing up in a North Carolina community, Wolfe knew the social milieu of the Southern
town for his own and experienced its breakdown in the
new century, but his view was greatly modified and distorted because of his personal circumstance and that of
his family. In H. M. McLuhan's words, "Wolfe has all
the passion without any of the formal means of con-
straint and communication which make it tolerable. He
was a Southerner by attitude but not by tradition." Small
wonder that before he turned to the novel, Wolfe failed
as a dramatist; the very nature of the theater, preclud-
ing as it does any save the most external modes of expression, was uncongenial to one whose aesthetic was
overwhelmingly autobiographical, subjective, lyrical. It
is said that *Look Homeward, Angel* was originally composed in the first person, and that Wolfe at one point
went through it substituting "he" for "I." *Of Time and
the River* actually was a first-person narrative at one
point, with David Hawke as the narrator, and the change
to Eugene Gant and the third person was done in the
publisher's office by John Hall Wheelock. If anything,
the change only intensifies the "romantic self-justification," because the apparent objectivity enabled Wolfe
to pretend all the more that he was writing about someone other than himself, and so he was not restrained
either by modesty or reserve. He told everything, omitted
nothing.

The circumstances of his childhood never lost their
hold on Wolfe's imagination. He spent his life trying to
understand and find an order for his experience. And the
longer he lived, the more experience there was to understand. The violence with which he was both drawn

toward and repelled by his past was such that he could
never step away from the immediate circumstance of his
personal experience and judge how it might best be employed for fiction. The personal experience *was* the fiction; he was unable to modify it or change it in any
essential respect. In *Look Homeward, Angel* Eugene
Gant quotes Catullus: "Odi et amo; quare id faciam." It
is an apt reckoning of Wolfe's attitude toward his origins; he castigates the South, his family, his childhood,
rages at his youthful circumstance; yet so strongly is he
drawn toward all of it, so obsessed is he with its memory,
that he cannot look at it with the objectivity needed to
master it in fiction.

In the later fiction the narrowness of Wolfe's viewpoint, the subjectivity with which he viewed his experience, was a crippling disability, for he could not describe
a man living among other men in a convincing fashion.
There are only fragments, moments of illumination. But
Look Homeward, Angel is bathed in color and light from
beginning to end. The child's world he saw whole, and
although Eugene Gant is in conflict with it almost from
the outset, this did not prevent Wolfe from describing
that world with great fervor and vividness. The fabric
of a small city's life is unrolled before us. We see its
workings, its hold on its inhabitants, especially on the
Gants who live there. We see a Southern community in
the toils of transition, growing from a small mountain
town into a busy tourist city; we see the inhabitants ad-
justing to accommodate themselves to the change. The
members of the Gant family embody the process. Eliza
Gant, the canny, conservative, slow-moving mountain
woman, becomes the real-estate speculator, the woman
of property, who participates zestfully in the commercial mania. Luke Gant takes to the business world

with great success. Ben Gant yearns for a home, love, certainty, and dies without them. W. O. Gant, a violent, tumultuous person, comes from the outside, settles down, but finds no peace for his mind. Eugene, born into the community as it is changing, is caught up in the process, cannot find a place for himself, and leaves to pursue his art in the shining city.

It is the process of the change that is foremost, and means most to Eugene and to Wolfe. From childhood Eugene is conscious of time and change. Finally these become the only reality, the only logic and order he can find for what he has known and been. Thus Wolfe wrote his novel of change and alienation. A boy grows up in a Southern town and goes off into modern America, leaving behind him death, taking with him only the memory of the past. So terribly and so indelibly had the process of alienation marked him that the art he went away to pursue became one of recapture, of searching the memories of the past for whatever reality there might be in life.

He was a thoroughgoing Romantic; his writing has the intensity of fiction written by an artist who is seeking furiously, through his literary craft, to impose on his recalcitrant experience his own highly personal valuations. This is the way it was! he insists, and in order to convince us of the justice of his contention, he marshals the force and excitement of a tremendous rhetorical talent. It is his chief concern in *Look Homeward, Angel*, his self-appointed mission: to recreate the circumstances of his childhood, to give to his chaotic experience the order and the importance of a work of art. He wrote a beautiful tale of growth and alienation, in which he, who had experienced it and known both, was the chief character. He recaptured the past, recreated his family, his community, himself, the love and the pain he had felt there, and the loss he knew as he saw it vanish in time.

So far as any American fiction endures, Altamont endures, in motionless vision, timeless chronology. In one great novel Thomas Wolfe fixed the transient world he knew so well into changeless art.

5

BURDEN'S LANDING:
All the King's Men
and the Modern South

Quentin Compson, in William Faulkner's *The Sound and the Fury*, is a young man from a once-distinguished Mississippi family who finds the modern world so meaningless that eventually he takes his own life. Jack Burden, in Robert Penn Warren's *All the King's Men*, is likewise the descendant of an old Southern family, but no one can say of him that he retreats from the modern world. Indeed, it might rather be maintained that he immerses himself in it. Still, his very immersion is a kind of flight. He throws himself into the main currents of politics and power in order to escape from Burden's Landing, where the first families of Louisiana still live in what seems to Jack a purposeless and ambitionless vacuum of diversion and unreality. He plunges into Louisiana political life as the aide of a highly untraditional, unaristocratic governor, and he tries to put Burden's Landing far behind him, to separate himself from its values and its memories. In the end he sells his home and leaves Burden's Landing for good, but not before undergoing the spiritual confrontation that is the story of *All the King's Men*. Only by coming to terms with Burden's Landing can he free himself from it.

105

All the King's Men is Robert Penn Warren's third novel, and I believe still his best one. All of his fiction, it seems to me, revolves about a similar theme: man's private responsibility for his public actions. I have entitled this essay "Burden's Landing" because it seems to me that in the particular relationship between Jack Burden, the protagonist, and the place in which he was born and grew up can be found a highly revealing commentary about modern Southern experience.

Since its publication in 1945, *All the King's Men* has had continuing success, both popular and critical. The reader of Warren returns to it again and again—and so for that matter has Warren, who has used the plot situation for three plays, the most recent of which received off-Broadway production. Warren describes the novel's widespread popular appeal to its "journalistic relevance" —its pertinence to public interest in the late Senator Huey P. Long of Louisiana, whose career bears strong resemblances to that of Willie Stark in *All the King's Men*. This is no doubt true in part, but I am not so sure that "journalistic" is the right word to use. It is not so much that Willie Stark's personality and career topically remind the reader of Long's, as that the careers of both Willie Stark and Huey Long exemplify a problem of continuing concern to all of us. Warren, by dealing in the way that he does with the fortunes of a political demagogue, touches on one of the most provocative and fateful questions of American experience—the sources, uses, and abuses of great political power in a democratic society, and the individual's responsibility to that society and to himself. The lures and limits of power seem to fascinate Warren, and since this novel is his most controversial and provocative treatment of the theme, I want to explore it in some detail. This involves, first, a consideration of Willie Stark.

When *All the King's Men* first came out, there was considerable debate among critics and readers about the relationship between Willie Stark and Huey Long. In general, the people who thought it was a fairly direct relationship tended to see Willie as the central figure of the novel. Others, however, disagreed, and insisted that Jack Burden, the narrator, and not Willie Stark, was the chief character in the book. Surely, now that the topical dispute over Willie's identity with Huey Long has died down, no reasonable reader can deny that it is Jack Burden, not Willie Stark, to whom the central experience of the novel occurs. On the other hand, the chief figure in that experience *is* Willie Stark. And because Willie does remind one forcibly of Huey Long, I should like to begin by considering that relationship.

Willie Stark is a poor boy from upstate Louisiana who becomes a demagogue and controls an entire state, until finally an assassin's bullet lays him low. In certain notable ways his life and career definitely resemble that of Huey Long, the Kingfish, who dominated Louisiana public life in the 1920's and early 1930's. Not long after *All the King's Men* appeared, the novelist Hamilton Basso, who had been an anti-Long newspaperman during the era of the Kingfish, castigated Warren for not portraying the Kingfish as the thoroughly dangerous dictator that he was. The complaint was also raised by the literary critic Robert Gorham Davis, who felt that the novel left much to be desired from the standpoint of proper democratic ideology.

Basso's objections were similar in essence to those made by citizens of Mississippi about the novels of William Faulkner, though from a different viewpoint. Good Mississippians complained that Faulkner maligned their state by portraying Mississippians as violent, lustful, degenerate, depraved folk. Basso, on the other hand, felt that Warren made Huey Long into a much more palatable phenomenon than he was, by portraying him as a man of good intentions who, though dictatorial and power-mad, nevertheless worked for the good of the poor folk of the state. In describing the existence of characters such as Joe Christmas, Faulkner was supposedly distorting the public perspective on "real life" as lived in Mississippi. And in making Willie Stark into a hero as well as a villain, Warren was, according to Basso, falsifying the "real-life" picture of Louisiana's most notorious public figure. But Warren as novelist was really doing only what Faulkner as novelist had done in *Light in August*. Just as Joe Christmas in that book was much more heroic, much more sympathetic to the reader than the drunken murderer from whose story the novel is alleged to have grown, so Willie Stark is given far greater moral dimensions and higher motivation than the Louisiana politician whom he resembles. In both instances there has been a transformation, until the "real-life" counterpart is no longer immediately recognizable. Basso, who fought Long and who wrote a novel, *Sun in Capricorn*, depicting him as a thoroughly evil man, was unable to read *All the King's Men* as a work of fiction; he saw Willie Stark as the counterpart, slightly disguised, of a flesh-and-blood politician, and he felt the disguise was flatteringly misleading and inaccurate. His assumption is that the novel's responsibility is to "real life"— not merely in the final estimate of the novel's worth, but at all points along the way. Warren is denied the use of "real life" unless he uses it journalistically.

Robert Gorham Davis also equated Long with Stark, and he objected, not to the misrepresentation as such, but to Warren's ideological failures. Warren made a man like Willie Stark into a hero, when such men were clearly Fascists, subversive of the democratic process,

and a menace to free society. "Warren does not ask—
the question apparently has no imaginative appeal for
him—whether American tradition does not demand that
we fight men like Long with all the democratic means at
our disposal in order to preserve in this country and in
the world free, open, pluralistic societies in which individual rights are protected by law and in which ultimate
control is vested below in the people and not above in
Willie Stark," ran Davis' criticism. Davis would have had
Warren approach his subject as John Dos Passos did in
another "Huey Long" novel, *Number One*. Warren's
responsibility, according to Davis, was to depict his
protagonist in proper political terms, since his protagonist was a politician; he should have stressed the in-
sidious nature of Willie Stark's political appeal to the
voters, shown him to be dangerous and dictatorial, and
not allowed Willie Stark's motives to have obscured in
any way the threat to democracy involved. If you deal
with Huey Long in fiction, Davis in effect said, you have
to do it the right way—which is to say, from the right
political perspective.

Again the process of converting "real life" into fiction
is misrepresented. For Warren did not write a political
novel "about" Huey Long. Whatever the Kingfish's
lineaments might have been in real life, Willie Stark in
All the King's Men is no simple Fascist demagogue. Dictatorial he may be, but he is a man with a mission even
to the last, with a strong social conscience and a burning
desire to bring to the rednecks of his state their full share
of the blessings of modern society. His grievous flaw—
we see it very early—is that mixed with this social mission is an avid taste for power, and a willingness to use
corruption in order to effect his ends. It is the taste for
power that eventually corrupts Willie Stark, and brings
about his downfall. Yet he retains some sense of his high

purpose to the end. Willie is a complex person, and his political nature is so thoroughly mixed with his moral and spiritual identity that *All the King's Men* transcends its political relevance to become a fable of men in the modern world of power. Nowadays, when the immediate memory of Huey Long and the Southern politics of his era has receded into history, the novel is as meaningful as ever, and as relevant to life in our day. Furthermore, as Robert B. Heilman and others pointed out in reply to Davis' strictures, Warren's view of Louisiana politics and of Dixie demagoguery was, so far as the novel was concerned, ultimately as scorching in its implications as anything Davis might have desired, and what Davis had mistaken for indulgence was in reality a searching exploration below the surface of political slogans into the very foundations of political magnetism and response. The apparent sympathy with which Willie Stark is portrayed is at the same time an indication of the weaknesses implicit in the democratic system.

Why, we may ask, has the career of Huey Long proved so fascinating as to prompt so many novelists to use it as a basis for fiction? For *All the King's Men* is only the best of a number of novels that deal with men like Huey Long. Basso's *Sun in Capricorn* and Adria Locke Langley's *A Lion Is in the Streets* draw almost directly on Long's career and personality. John Dos Passos' *Number One* and Sinclair Lewis' *It Can't Happen Here* are less closely adapted from life, but, especially in Dos Passos' novel, there are numerous similarities.

The answer is that Long's successes exemplify many of the central problems of our public life. The issues raised by his fiery career are of perennial interest, both in the South and elsewhere. For here was a man who exercised a tremendous imaginative appeal over the people of Louisiana, and indeed of neighboring states as well. In a state whose social progress in the twentieth century had been slow and inadequate, in which corruption and disregard for the basic welfare of large elements of the population were notorious, Long sprang into public notice as the spokesman for the downtrodden, the small farmers, the rednecks. For the first time in Louisiana politics the little man really had a voice in government.

And Long *produced*—this is what is important. He built good roads into the interior, provided better schools, built hospitals—and forced the business interests of the state to bear a fairer share of the taxes required to finance those needed services. He was no mere spellbinder, no ordinary, garden-variety Southern demagogue who stirred up class dissension without any objective purpose other than his own popularity. Alone among the folk politicians of the South, Long largely eschewed the race issue; he was too big a man to content himself with yelling "Nigger!" He had definite social objectives, and his electorate realized this, to the extent that for decades after his death the name of Long has continued to be a potent force in Louisiana politics.

For this reason Long's example is all the more relevant to our public life, and all the more sinister. The methods and techniques Long employed to achieve his ends, and many of the uses to which he put the power delivered to him by the voters, were among the darkest and most ominous in American political history. He bribed, threatened, bought and sold men, used violence, extortion, graft, employed various techniques of distortion, reputation-blackening, hate-mongering, and rabble-rousing, flouted representative government, made a mockery out of constitutional processes. Few weapons were too savage for him to use; no reputation was too upright for his sliming. He went from the governorship of Louisiana to the United States Senate, and at the time of his assassination in 1936 he was threatening to move from regional into national power and prominence. Of all the demagogues of the 1930's, he was the most fascinating, and potentially the most dangerous.

For Long gave a tongue to the rural masses, and he possessed the imaginative appeal needed to stir them into effective political consciousness. He vastly increased the interest of the average citizen of Louisiana in politics; he shook the state out of the profound political lethargy in which it had drowsed for many years. And his politics, for all the gesturing and fanfare, exuded *realism;* he dealt with the true issues, and he made people aware of their existence and importance. His career thus touches on the vital questions of effective political action in a democracy, and the consequences of popular participation in government, with all the attendant problems of responsibility in leadership and respect for due processes of law. He invigorated political democracy—and dangerously strained its checks and balances.

Thus the "journalistic relevance" of *All the King's Men* amounts to the fact that it touches on a very perplexing social problem in our time. That it is set in the South is appropriate, for it is in the twentieth-century South that the tension between the needs and claims of popular democracy and the role and use of law, tradition, and leadership have been often and dramatically spelled out.

"Willie Stark was not Huey Long...," Warren has declared categorically. "Certainly it was the career and the atmosphere of Louisiana that suggested the play that was to become the novel. But suggestion does not mean identity, and even if I had wanted to make Stark a projection of Long, I should not have known how to go about it. For one reason, simply because I did not, and do not, know what Long was like, and what were the secret forces that drove him along his violent path to meet the bullet in the Capitol."

The Willie Stark of the novel is a created character, with his own motivations, his own habits, his own identity as a fictional person. Whatever the suggestions of Long's career might be, no foreknowledge of Huey Long and Louisiana politics is required to make Willie a believable character; he stands by himself. He is preeminently the man of power, of popular appeal, engaged in political action. Warren has taken some of the elementary characteristics of Long's Louisiana and used them in creating a fictional world. The fact that some men who knew Long have objected to Warren's alleged misrepresentation and glorification of the Kingfish is actually a tribute to Warren's artistic objectivity; for as a novelist his aim in creating the character of Willie Stark was Willie's believability as a fictional being, the man about whose person the activities of the novel would center. Willie as pure villain, as hypocritical politician motivated by desire for gain alone, would be dramatically inadequate to give *All the King's Men* the meaning it contains.

By his very insistence upon making Willie Stark a strongly motivated, at least partly sympathetic figure, Warren was singularly able to comment dramatically on the needs and responsibilities of power, the relationship of private to public morality, the dangers of using evil means to secure good ends. Just as the disinterested observer cannot dismiss Huey P. Long as merely one more Southern demagogue, so Warren achieved realism by giving to Willie's life and death the believable human passion and motivation that enabled the author truly to examine and illustrate their real significance. Indeed, in terms of pure plausibility Willie Stark as Warren saw him is much more believable a phenomenon than Huey

Long as seen by a Hamilton Basso and others of Long's political foes; Willie's great appeal for the voters, and for the characters of the novel whose lives revolve about his, is much more credible and plausible than that exercised on the "real-life" Louisiana electorate by the entire villain and scoundrel depicted in most anti-Long accounts.

The point is that Warren, in choosing not to denounce Huey Long journalistically but to create a believable, coherent, motivated human being in Willie Stark, actually came closer to "real life" than did the mere journalistic accounts of the time. He did so because the artistic image of human life is not arbitrary and capricious, but subject to the logic of the artist's deepest experience as a human being, so that the artistic vision is *of* life. Huey Long, being a mortal, has turned out, now that the strength and passions of political controversy have subsided, to have been a human being, too. So that the most recent account I have read of Long, Professor T. Harry Williams' provocative little study, *Romance and Realism in Southern Politics*, shows us a "real-life" politician who strongly resembles Warren's Willie Stark!

The artistic independence, as it were, of *All the King's Men* from the literal demands of Louisiana politics is shown by the existence of Jack Burden and his key role in the novel. Though the action centers around Willie Stark, it is Jack Burden who is the chief instrument of the plot, the lens through which the actions of the various characters, including Willie, are focused and understood. What happens, and what it means, finally has importance because of its impact upon the characterization of Jack Burden. The novel is not about Willie Stark, but about what Willie means for Jack.

Jack Burden is Willie Stark's political aide. He is a newspaper reporter when he first meets Willie, and comes to know him well when Willie first runs for governor. A threadbare, idealistic young lawyer from the town of Mason City, Willie is pushed into the gubernatorial race by a political faction that wants to split the opposition vote between Willie and another candidate, in order to assure its own candidate's victory. Thoroughly duped, Willie campaigns earnestly and ineffectively until Jack and a political hack, Sadie Burke, inform him of his victimization. At this point the latent power and outrage in Willie explode, and he makes a fiery speech to the rural audience that has come to hear him, informing them of the trickery, urging them to support the opposition's candidate, and if he fails to serve them faithfully, to find someone who will. In this speech Willie's great oratorical ability and capacity for leadership first come forth; he holds his audience spellbound.

Later Willie runs again for governor on a reform ticket, Jack deserts his newspaper to work for him, and thereafter serves as Willie's right-hand man in politics, remaining with him until the last, when the assassin mortally wounds Willie in the foyer of the state capitol.

Willie's attraction for Jack is both ideological and personal. Jack believes in Willie's political goals, in his efforts to give the poor people of his state a fairer share of the benefits of government, in his vendetta against entrenched interests and the selfish political dealings of the opposition. To the end he is convinced that ultimately Willie Stark was on the side of the right.

But that is by no means Willie's sole attraction for Jack. Willie represents for him the example of power effectively used, of a driving force which can give purpose and meaning to life. Willie can *act*. He is not helpless before experience. His magnetic character, his surging energy, afford a focus and goal for Jack, something that Jack can believe in, work for, give himself to in full measure. Willie seems to provide the answers to experience, as Burden's Landing did not. Though Willie's methods are often arbitrary, arrogant, even cruel and vicious, Jack can tell himself, as Willie tells himself, that the ends are good. Jack not only subdues his patrician distaste for Willie's methods, but even serves as Willie's agent in putting them into practice—for Willie's personality and his objectives are enough, or seem at the time to be enough, to excuse cruelty, corruption, blackmail, disregard for law and life. Willie is The Boss; in his will is Jack's solace.

But not his peace or contentment. The Jack Burden who works for Willie Stark, carries out his often distasteful political assignments, is not a satisfied man. The manner in which Jack relates the story of *All the King's Men* is cynical, ironic, discontented; from the very first pages, when Jack describes a trip to Mason City with The Boss, his family, and entourage, we have a sense of tension, strain, desperation of spirit, that helps to show us the nature of Willie's hold on Jack. There is an atmosphere of expectation, of waiting for the neural stimulus of Willie's personality to explode into action before the crowd in Mason City. Willie provides a focus, an excitement, but it is not something wholesome or finally satisfying; instead it seems to serve as a kind of uneasy substitute for certain sounder bases of belief and value that are missing in Jack Burden's life. It is as if Jack, and the others as well, require something to give their lives emotional excitement and momentum, and they have turned to Willie because they can discover nothing else more substantial.

What has made Jack Burden feel such a need? When he tells us something of his past history we begin to get an idea. Jack is a member, by birth and rearing, of the old, genteel Southern society of Burden's Landing, a society socially and economically quite similar to that of the Compsons and Sartorises in the Faulkner novels. Jack's mother has been several-times married and divorced, and Jack thinks of her as incapable of love. He hardly remembers his father, the so-called Scholarly Attorney, who left Burden's Landing when Jack was a small child, and has become a religious fanatic, an otherworldly man who has never afforded to Jack the stability and love he might have expected from a father. It is Judge Irwin, a widower who lives nearby, who taught Jack to hunt ducks, make miniature soldiers and weapons, and otherwise gave him some of the adult guidance and companionship he missed from his father.

Jack's closest friends at Burden's Landing were Adam and Anne Stanton, whose father was once governor of the state. As a young man Jack fell deeply in love with Anne, who returned his affection but who refused to marry him until he decided on a career and showed evidence of being ready to make something of his life, and not settle back into the genteel inertia of Burden's Landing. This Jack could not do; he went to college and then to law school, but was not at all interested in a legal career. For awhile he did newspaper work, then he became interested in the study of history, and worked toward a doctorate, undertaking to edit the journal of Cass Mastern, a distant relative who died in the Civil War. The journal described how Jack's ancestor had done great wrong to a friend who had trusted him, which in turn caused an innocent Negro slave girl to be sold down the river, and how he had spent the remainder of his life attempting to rectify his misdeed. But Jack could not understand why his ancestor had behaved as he did, and so could not complete the editing of the journal. He left his studies and went back to newspaper work. Meanwhile he had married a voluptuous female named Lois, had eventually tired of her mental vacuity, and in disgust at the emptiness of their married life he left her. Finally the chance came to work for Willie Stark.

What was missing in Jack's life was any sense of purposiveness, any feeling of engagement. His existence at Burden's Landing did not provide him with principles on which any foundation could be constructed for action in the real world. Burden's Landing is cut off, remote; its patterns of life seem insulated from those of the everyday world beyond. There is an air of decadence and general ineffectiveness about the place. We get an indication of what is wrong with it in an episode in which Jack, by this time working for Willie, returns home and attends a party at Judge Irwin's home. The conversation turns to politics. Everyone present except Jack joins in denouncing Willie Stark and his influence on public life, and Jack realizes that they do so in his presence because they assume that, having been born and reared at Burden's Landing, at heart Jack *must* be with them: "I was just picking up a little, or maybe a lot, of change with Willie, but my heart was in Burden's Landing and they had no secrets from me and they knew they couldn't hurt my feelings."

But after awhile Jack interrupts with a question that astounds them all:

> "Doesn't it all boil down to this? If the government of this state for quite a long time back had been doing anything for the folks in it, would Stark have been able to go out there with his bare hands and bust the boys? And would he be having to make so many short cuts to get something done to make up for the time lost all these years in not getting something done? I'd just like to submit that question for the sake of argument."

The gentlefolk of Burden's Landing are incredulous, aghast. It has simply never occurred to them that a member of the families of Burden's Landing could entertain such sentiments. It is as if Jack were in another country; he feels alone, isolated in the group. Burden's Landing seems divorced from reality, from the flesh-and-blood world of politics and power and action that is his life with Willie Stark.

We understand then why Jack Burden left Burden's Landing.

The episode, which I think is a central one in the novel, throws into focus the relationship of Jack with Willie Stark. For Willie is *not* from Burden's Landing; he is not a member of the old Southern aristocracy that in bygone times controlled the state. He comes from upstate, poor-white stock; he is crude, uncultivated, not a gentleman. Willie represents everything that Burden's Landing scorns; he has no ancestors, no tradition, no code of manners and gentility. But he is squarely in touch with the realities of everyday life in Louisiana, with the sources of power and action in twentieth-century Louisiana society. In turning to Willie, Jack has sought the "real world," rejected the unreal, outdated attitudes of his class. Willie at least professes ideals that mean something for his time; Willie can act to rectify the evils in his society. Willie is living in the present, not in the past.

Yet though Jack Burden works for Willie Stark, takes his stand with Willie in the political and social arena, repudiates the standards of Burden's Landing for those of the state capitol, this is not to say that ultimately Willie Stark's version of reality is sufficient, either. For Willie *fails.* In substituting the values of unabashed expediency and pragmatic effectiveness for the virtues of honor and respect for law and for tradition, Willie finds only tragedy. To effect his ends, he dips too deeply in corruption, relies too heavily on force and cunning. In the end the power he acquires corrupts his soul, and the taste for power, as an end in itself, obscures the ideals for which ostensibly he has been striving. Willie's *modus vivendi* is that all men are incurably evil and selfish, and that the only way to create good is out of evil. His political machine, his whole procedure of operation is constructed thoroughly on pragmatic expediency, relying on the cupidity of men and the pure effectiveness of power.

Realizing the state to which he has fallen, Willie attempts to reassure himself that his original good intentions are still valid by resolving to build a great hospital, a symbol of pure good, untainted in its construction by expediency or compromise. Political needs force him to modify his resolve by allowing the building contract to be allocated for reasons of political advantage. But disaster strikes in his own family; his son is badly crippled in a football game in which because of his physical condition he should not have been allowed to play, and Willie realizes that it was his own arrogance and desire for boastful pride that was responsible for his son's playing in the game. He reverses himself, repudiates the building contract allocation, resolves anew to have the hospital built without any political considerations. But this he cannot do; his henchmen, whom he has used so effectively in the past, have depended too importantly on the graft from the building contract. They inform Adam Stanton, the doctor who is to direct the new hospital, that his sister Anne has become Willie's mistress. To Adam, this can mean only that Willie's action in persuading him to head the hospital was the result not of Willie's belief that Adam was the best qualified man for the job, but of a bribe given by Willie to Anne in exchange for her favors. Driven wild at the betrayal this seems to him, Adam guns Willie down in the capitol building.

Jack Burden too experiences tragedy. For at Willie's

behest he has conducted a private investigation into the past of his old friend Judge Irwin, who had come out for Willie's opponent in an election. Jack discovers that when a young man the Judge had accepted a bribe, which had resulted in the suicide of an innocent man. Jack tells himself that because what he discovered was "true," he has no responsibility in the matter, and he threatens the Judge with exposure if he will not withdraw his support from Willie's opponent. The Judge refuses, Jack leaves, and the Judge kills himself. Only then does Jack learn that he has in effect killed his own father, for it was Judge Irwin, not the religious fanatic who was once the Scholarly Attorney, who was his real father. It was Judge Irwin whom his mother had loved— she was, after all, capable of love.

And Jack knows, too, that in part he was responsible for Willie Stark's death. For he had shown Anne Stanton the evidence of Judge Irwin's early misdeed, in which her own father, then governor of the state, had been implicated, and it was this revelation of the weakness of the father she had so admired that had turned her away from Burden's Landing, and thrown her into Willie Stark's arms—like Jack, she too had been attracted to Willie's power and pragmatic effectiveness. In his effort to persuade Adam to take the directorship of Willie's hospital, Jack had also showed the evidence of his father's connivance in fraud to him. Thus when Willie's henchmen went to Adam with the evidence of his sister's liaison with Willie, they had been able to play on Adam's rage and shame, so that he went out and killed The Boss.

Jack himself had known of Anne's relationship with Willie for some time previously. When he first discovered what his childhood sweetheart was doing, he had climbed into his car and driven westward, all the way to to the Pacific. Devastated by the shock, he had decided then that the only real values in life were those of sensation, animal stimulation: "the dark heave of blood and the twitch of the nerve.... The words *Anne Stanton* were simply the name for a peculiarly complicated piece of mechanism which should mean nothing whatsoever to Jack Burden, who himself was simply another rather complicated piece of mechanism." He had come back then, resolved to work for Willie Stark. But then came the episode with Judge Irwin, and Jack realized that the conduct of the Judge when confronted with the evidence of his past disgrace had been no mere animal response. The Judge might have saved himself; he might have withdrawn his political support for Willie's rival, or he might simply have told Jack the facts of his parentage. But the Judge chose death to the betrayal of principle and of the woman he had loved. And there was Willie Stark's wife Lucy, whom Jack had always admired; in her conduct before and after Willie's death, she had shown far more than animal response.

So that in the agony of his real father's suicide, which he had caused, and Willie Stark's and Adam Stanton's deaths, which in a sense he had also caused, Jack learns that honor and love are not false qualities, that expediency and rationalization are not sufficient excuse for one's actions, that human beings must accept full moral responsibility for their own conduct, and that it is not enough to subordinate one's own sense of justice and honor to the demands of any external principle of long-range, expedient good. *He* is responsible; *he* must be the judge of his own morality and conduct. Only now can he understand what had baffled him before, the meaning for the conduct of Cass Mastern, his Civil War ancestor, who had faced up to his individual guilt.

Jack had rejected the sheltered, unreal world of Burden's Landing. The values it had prated—honor, truth, responsibility—had seemed unreal, detached from the actualities of life. But it was not the values themselves that were at fault; it was the failure of Burden's Landing to practice those values in terms of its own times, the limitations that the decadent society of Burden's Landing placed on those values. He had given himself over to Willie Stark, had sought to find in Willie's strength, Willie's goals, a substitute for the remorseless requirements of his own conscience, his own sense of responsibility in the world as a human being. He had done Willie's dirty work, telling himself that the goals that Willie professed justified the evil means. And the result of his flight, of his evasion of responsibility, had been tragedy.

Now, at the end, he is ready to marry Anne Stanton, leave Burden's Landing forever; he will go back into politics, this time with his friend Hugh Miller, a man of principle and high integrity. Only now is Jack really free of Burden's Landing. For all the time he had worked for Willie Stark, he had done so in an attempt to deny the sense of futility, of aimlessness, of unreality that he had felt there as a child. Burden's Landing, the weight of the past, is at last truly dead. He is prepared to cope with the modern world, but this time as an individual, exercising his own standards of honor and responsibility instead of seeking to avoid them by leaning on Willie Stark's strength. Now he will, in the closing words of the novel, "go out of the house and go into the convulsion of the world, out of history into history and the awful responsibility of Time."

Of William Faulkner, Robert Penn Warren has written that he has "taken our [Southern] world, with its powerful sense of history, its tangled loyalties, its pains and tensions of tradition, its pieties and violence, and elevated it to the level of a great moral drama on the tragic scale." The same might well be said of *All the King's Men*, which does all of those things. Nonetheless, there are several significant differences between Warren's novel and the great Yoknapatawpha County tragedies, and for the purposes of this essay, it is important to realize what they are.

In terms of Faulknerian mythology, Willie Stark is a Snopes, and Jack Burden is a Compson. But here we have a striking difference. For unlike the Yoknapatawpha Snopeses, Willie is no crass materialist, no rapacious, codeless, weasel-like creature who through his low cunning undermines the crumbling foundations of a collapsing aristocracy. Willie possesses stature, purpose, ideals. And Jack Burden is not very much like Quentin Compson; he is not driven away from the twentieth century, into suicide, by the burden of the past, the concept of an obsolete and unreal code of familial honor. Instead he seeks to come to grips with the demands of the modern world, its sources of power and authority, its values. In this respect he is unlike any of Faulkner's characters; if we compare his characterization with that of the only Faulknerian character who can cope with modern times and still retain his stature and dignity, the Gavin Stephens of the later novels, we will recognize that for all of Faulkner's tremendous artistic versatility, Warren has been able in *All the King's Men* to do what his older compatriot never successfully managed—the creation of an intelligent, believable protagonist living in and coping with the contemporary scene. The greatness of Faulkner lies elsewhere.

The theme of decline and fall, which Faulkner invested with tragic dignity and pathos, is thus importantly modified. Where Faulkner's Compsons and Sartorises are trapped within the historical process, unable to exist outside of it, Jack Burden battles valiantly to extricate himself and eventually succeeds. Perhaps the difference is that the aristocratic milieu of Yoknapatawpha County in which the Compsons and Sartorises exist is in the process of dying, while Burden's Landing is all but dead, and Jack Burden can find no illusion of vitality within it. He must therefore separate himself from it, or from important aspects of it in any event, and re-establish his values within a different social framework. There is no *life* to Burden's Landing; it is comatose, exhausted, existing in no relationship with the "real world." To live within it is to suffocate. This will not do for Jack—and it certainly will not do for Anne Stanton. Both of them insist on living. The problem is, how?

For in leaving the Landing for Willie's Stark's world of action and power, they do not leave all the standards of Burden's Landing behind them. That is to say, Jack definitely takes with him his consciousness of *role*. He is still very much the Southern gentleman of the First Families who believes he has the duty to bring to bear his intelligence, his authority and sense of responsibility, on the problems of the society into which he was born. The trouble with Burden's Landing is that it no longer permits him to do this; to remain in it and to frequent its society is to isolate oneself from the consciousness of responsibility and leadership that a place such as Burden's Landing once presumably embodied, but has ceased to embody. "Jack, what are you going to do?" Anne Stanton asks. And later, "You know I love you, Jack Burden, and I believe in you, Jack Burden, and you are not going to be like those people, Jack Burden." She will not marry Jack until she is convinced that he intends to make something of himself, which is to say, to leave the decadent idleness of Burden's Landing and engage himself in the "real world." But being involved with the sources of power and responsibility is not sufficient; it will not satisfy Anne, and it cannot satisfy Jack. He must live effectively in the modern world while retaining the sense of honor and justice, the belief in ideals and the necessity to act in accordance with those ideals, that Burden's Landing once possessed when it furnished leadership for the Louisiana community.

In Jack's mind—and in Warren's—these ideals have in no sense become outmoded. Man cannot live without purpose, without integrity, without social and ethical responsibility. The difficulty, which is Jack's problem in the novel, is to discover a method whereby one can be in contact with the sources of power and action while retaining the traditional ethical and social attitudes. How can a young man born to lead continue to exercise that historic role in modern society?

Jack remains the aristocrat, even in his dealings with Willie Stark. There is always a certain air of contempt for Willie, the untutored man of the people, a sense that Jack considers himself superior to The Boss, that he represents Willie's conscience, even while he greatly admires Willie's strength and his social purposiveness. Even though he recognizes that Willie is a born leader, that he possesses unique qualities of personal magnetism and social responsibility, Jack never quite loses the sense of condescension that the born aristocrat has for the plebian tribune. Jack, in effect, remains something of a snob, even while carrying out Willie's orders. And even Willie seems to respect Jack's aristocratic superiority; he allows him liberties, primarily that of conscience, that he will not grant to any of his other, less highborn hirelings. Willie apparently feels an obligation to justify his actions to Jack, to explain his purposes and motivations.

Willie is the man of action in the modern South, and Jack Burden retains a sense of patrician distaste for Willie's world and his method for dealing with it. Jack never *likes* Willie's world; he comes to grips with it out of a sense of necessity. Like Faulkner, Warren seems to have a horror of the slimy and slick conditions of the modern South, but unlike Faulkner he tends to view engagement in them as both possible and inevitable. That is, modernism seems to represent not so much catastrophe as necessity. And not only *All the King's Men* but all of Warren's fiction appears to be a kind of enforcement of that necessity. His protagonists cannot wither away and die; they must engage themselves in their society, and they must go about it as intelligently, and with as high a devotion to ideals, as possible. The trick is to rid themselves of those ways of viewing their responsibility to those ideals which have become outmoded and false, while still retaining the sense of mission and purpose. The ideals—truth, justice, loyalty, social responsibility, leadership—must be extended to fit the needs of a much larger segment of the society, to come to grips with the complex needs of modern industrial life. Inevitably this represents change, adjustment, compromise.

This requirement has led Warren in the direction of pragmatism. That is to say, the problem of how to get along in the modern world, and to equate a lofty but in part outmoded social ethic to its demands, inevitably has caused Warren as novelist to approach his chosen social milieu with an eye toward finding out what actually works. What portions of the old ethic are usable? How can the traditional values be renovated, as it were, to permit their accommodation to the needs of the present?

Willie Stark, as Warren points out, is an example of a too-great reliance upon expediency. The Boss, as Warren is anxious to indicate, is the social and political reformer who, because he is too willing to compromise with the immediate demands of a practical situation, is eventually corrupted by the power he thereby gains.

And Jack Burden, by contrast, is the thwarted moralist who is unable to work out a scheme of personal responsibility for his actions, and attempts to bury any notion of such responsibility in his total immersion in Willie Stark's cause. At this he fails; he cannot quiet his conscience. His very manner, wiseacring, cynical, is a defense against his own idealism. He must undercut his motives, must seek to cast doubt on the purity of his intentions. But he ends up by reaffirming his belief in ethical absolutes, tempered by the needs of the real world to be sure, but ethical absolutes just the same. His quest for such absolutes was the occasion of his espousal of Willie Stark and his cause. He is unable to accept Burden's Landing, because moral absolutes must have a direct relationship to life. He tries to accept another moral absolute—Willie's power, his ability to act, his social goals. But he proves equally unable to accept Willie, because Willie is a false absolute, a false source of moral strength.

This constant struggle on the part of Warren's characters to reconcile themselves to the practical, expedient demands of the moment and the unchanging tenets of an absolute morality has continued throughout Warren's fiction, and Warren's variations on the theme have left him open to criticism. In his testing of the validity of the uses of pure idealism, he has been accused of pursuing an "As If" philosophy—that is, of dealing with ethical and religious ideals as if they were only tactical devices for ordering reality, rather than being real in themselves. Not only is this sometimes charged to Jack Burden in *All the King's Men*, but the novel immediately following, *World Enough and Time*, has also been criticized in this respect. One critic, for example, has found a passage such as the following as representing something very much like the biological, chemical determinism of Theodore Dreiser: "But if Jeremiah Beaumont was a chip on the tide, he was a thinking and suffering chip, and his dearest thought was that he was not a chip at all but a mariner who had made calculations of tides and a decision for his course." What kind of a moral agent, asks this critic, can such a man as that be?

But this is to misunderstand Warren, I think, and to misunderstand novels. Warren doesn't come down on either side. He is completely concerned with the human position, which is to say, with the plight of men caught in the dilemma between absolute moral ideals and the demands of the immediate, "real" world. The truth is that Warren as a novelist assumes the reality of both, and presents his protagonists as attempting to equate the apparently contradictory realities through active moral agency. In *All the King's Men* each character must make his own accommodation. The Scholarly Attorney, Jack's ostensible father, withdraws from the world of action into an idealistic isolation from society. Adam Stanton seeks to do the same thing through devotion to pure science, and when he becomes aware of his failure, chooses unreasoning revenge and swift oblivion. His sister Anne lives in a world of values that no longer exists, and when the values are seen as having been compromised, she throws herself at Willie Stark. Judge Irwin, having compromised himself once, seeks to make repentance, and rather than compromise again, takes his own life. Willie Stark so compromises his own ideals that he loses himself in the values of the expedient world, and when he tries to hedge on his bargain, is shot to death. Jack Burden likewise discounts his personal integrity, and only through tragedy learns what can happen when ideals are disregarded. In fine, *All the King's Men* is "about" this dichotomy between moral absolutes and practical necessity, as dramatized in the lives of some human beings who must try to define themselves by conflicting standards. The reconciliation demanded thereby is no easy matter—and *All the King's Men* is, not surprisingly, a tragedy.

A tragedy, however, that ends in redemption. For at the close of the novel, having undergone the purging experience brought about by the downfall of Willie Stark and the attendant deaths of his friend Adam Stanton and his real father, Judge Irwin, Jack Burden is preparing once again to live in the real world of power and action. Married now to Anne Stanton, he will aid his friend Hugh Miller in a venture into politics. He will take with him a sense of duty, of personal moral responsibility, but tempered by the knowledge of the world. He has sold his house at Burden's Landing; neither he nor Anne wishes to live there any longer.

In the last analysis Jack Burden is still the aristocrat with the sense of duty, and he is back in his proper milieu, for unlike The Boss, his friend Hugh Miller is a man of culture, of highest moral principle. Jack has learned from history—the Judge's past, the story of his ancestor Cass Mastern—the ethical truth he needs to guide his actions in the present. He must leave Burden's Landing, because for him Burden's Landing and its ways constitute a limitation of his capacity to be fully alive and human. No longer does Burden's Landing embody the possibilities of honor, responsibility, leadership. In the world in which Jack Burden finds himself, he must redefine those values, so that they can function in a society that embraces Willie Stark and the hopes and aspirations that made him possible.

6

THE GOLDEN APPLES
OF THE SUN

*Time goes like a dream no matter how hard you run,
and all the time we heard things from out in the
world that we listened to but that still didn't mean
we believed them.*

MISS KATE RAINEY, in *The Golden Apples*

In American fiction there are two Mississippis. One is
William Faulkner's: a place of violent men and desperate
struggle, in which the forces of order and disorder contend in the epic battles that embody man's ceaseless
warfare with his human condition in time. The protagonists in this tragic combat are larger than life; they are
ruthless monsters of men such as Thomas Sutpen in
Absalom, Absalom! and Joe Christmas in *Light in August*, or they are whole dynasties of families such as the
Compsons and the Sartorises, or else they are arch-
villains and scoundrels such as Flem Snopes. All such
men do battle with their enemy, time; they rage at their
human limitations, seek to immortalize themselves, refuse
to concede their mortality. When they die, it is as tragic
heroes die, despairingly, knowing they are defeated.

The other Mississippi is a very different kind of place.
It is a tidy, protected little world, in which people go
about their affairs, living, marrying, getting children,
diverting themselves, dying, all in tranquil, pastoral fashion. Sometimes the "real world" peeps in on them, but
generally they lock it out, and agree to ignore it. They
do not contend with time; instead they pretend that it

131

does not exist. This is the Mississippi of the Delta: broad, alluvial country, bounded at the north by the city of Greenville and at the south by the confluence of the Yazoo and Mississippi rivers. It is rich farming land, known for its luxuriant cotton acreage, and it is dotted with large plantation homes emblematic of the old aristocracy that has presided there for decades. In miles it is less than two hundred from the northern Mississippi country about which William Faulkner writes, but spiritually it is much farther than that. To the citizenry of the Delta the Faulkner country is hilly, primitive territory, rough and barbarous. The Delta is not given to violence and to strident questing; it is a sprawling, accommodating countryside, and its ways are lavish, somnolent. Times goes like a dream in the Delta. It is Eudora Welty's country, her Mississippi.

William Faulkner's Mississippi is rightly known throughout the world. Few American novelists have been capable of writing genuine tragedy; between Melville and Faulkner there is perhaps not a single one. Faulkner is one of the twentieth century's greatest novelists in any language, and the Faulknerian universe that centers on the town of Jefferson in the mythical country of Yoknapatawpha is modern America's foremost fictional country. Miss Welty's Mississippi is less well known, but it is her own, just as Faulkner's is his property. Surely it requires considerable temerity for a novelist to write in the shadow of so massive an example as Faulkner. Miss Welty has not only done so; she has written with great originality, and her claim to her version of Mississippi experience has been convincingly staked out. Not so prolific an artist as her fellow Mississippian, she has nevertheless produced an impressive body of work: two full-length novels, two novellas, and several excellent volumes of short stories.

Her reputation, I think, is principally as a short-story writer. I propose, however, to consider her as novelist, because it seems to me that, for all her mastery of the short story, it is as a novelist that she is most interesting. In *Delta Wedding* and *The Golden Apples* (and the latter is a unit, not a collection of short stories, as I hope to show) she has done her most enduring work—work which is by no means mere "local color," but instead gives us a quite profound version of experience. Professor Willard Thorp, in his valuable *American Writing in the Twentieth Century*, errs when he dismisses her as a modern-day "local colorist," grouping her with Jesse Stuart, Marjorie Kinnan Rawlings, and Katherine Anne Porter, and saying only that "Miss Welty is at home in the Mississippi Delta region. . . ." She is certainly that; but she is much more than that. She is one of the most original writers of her time, and the apparent lightness— for want of a better word—of her style conceals a remarkably vigorous and penetrating sensibility. It is not the modern "local colorists" who are her peers; among her Southern contemporaries she ranks in stature and importance rather with the best—with Faulkner himself, with Warren, Wolfe. I am not proposing that her work is *as* important as Faulkner's, but I am maintaining that in scope and insight her two novels deserve to be compared *with* Faulkner's. She is no lightweight; she is not merely picturesque; she is a serious writer. She deals with some very important aspects of reality, and her art is one of great insight into such matters.

The most startling quality of Eudora Welty's art is her style: shimmering, hovering, elusive, fanciful, fastening on little things. Entirely feminine, it moves lightly, capriciously, mirroring the bemused, diverted quality of the people whom it describes. Like the hummingbirds that appear frequently in her stories, it darts here and

there, never quite coming to rest, tirelessly invoking light, color, the variety of experience. In *Delta Wedding* Laura McRaven watches from the coach window of the train as it approaches the town of Fairchilds:

> The land was perfectly flat and level but it shimmered like the wing of a lighted dragonfly. It seemed strummed, as though it were an instrument and someone had touched it. Sometimes in the cotton were trees with one, two, or three arms—she could draw better trees than these were. Sometimes like a fuzzy caterpillar looking in the cotton was a winding line of thick green willows and cypresses, and when the train crossed this green, running on a loud iron bridge, down its center like a golden mark on the caterpillar's back would be a bayou.

Like the land, the style is exotic, laden, rich in allusion and connotation.

But if it is feminine, it is also quite muscular, and its elusive, hovering quality is never vague or soft. Her art is highly complex, precise, and controlled, and the rich fabric of its texture contains a firmly patterned dramatization of people in a time and place, one that makes a considerable commentary on human experience. Her novels, it seems to me, present a unified, controlled picture of one sort of Southern life. It is the day-to-day existence of people in the small towns and rural areas, based strongly on the depiction of family and community, with a dissection of such groups that gives us an idea of just why they exist, and what they mean for the human beings who compose them. It is removed from high tragedy; there is little of the Faulknerian mode in Miss Welty's best work. But it does share one attribute of Faulkner's work: and that is that its ramifications extend beyond the borders of Mississippi and the South. Her writings may seem at first to be more "typical," but that is because the technique is more realistic than Faulkner's; no more

than Faulkner does Eudora Welty write local color. When you read her novels, you learn about *human beings*.

I emphasize the social quality of her fiction, because Miss Welty is highly conscious of that aspect of her people. They are great talkers, great visitors-about; they are at their most typical when present at weddings, card parties, music recitals, receptions, funerals, those occasions when people come together and share each other's company. They all live in communities, where everything is known, realized, accepted, talked about. At the same time they are individuals, with their private identities held secret from the world. Their very community existence, their constant coming and going in company with each other, is a way of protecting this privacy. In the family, in the community, certain things are known, and so those who belong can deal with each other in terms of the known, and thus avoid inquiry into private matters. "We never wanted to be smart, one by one," Shelley Fairchild records in her diary in *Delta Wedding*, "but all together we have a wall, we are self-sufficient against people that come up knocking, we are solid to the outside. Does the world suspect? that we are all very private people? I think one by one we're all more lonely than private and more lonely than self-sufficient." They go to their weddings, parties, funerals, recitals, and they converse and gossip, and each maintains his façade of group personality as a barrier to deeper probings, each of them in league with the others to keep the world at arm's length, protecting their private identity. They are the Fairchilds of *Delta Wedding;* they are the townfolk of Morgana of *The Golden Apples;* but each is a solitary, lonely individual, whose participation in the social group is a carefully if instinctively assumed arrangement whereby energy is expended along certain agreed-upon planes of activity, to the rigid exclusion of other private, solitary matters.

Miss Welty depicts these little social communities, these family and town groups, as protective devices that serve to ward off knowledge of certain vast, ungovernable facts of human existence in the world. Participation in the family and the community makes it possible to shut out the consciousness of time and mortality, to screen from one's vision what the unhappy Virgie Rainey, who cannot belong to the community, faces in *The Golden Apples:* "a horror in life...the separateness." Shellmound, the family seat of the Fairchilds, and the town of Morgana both exist so that those who belong can pretend an ignorance of the loneliness in life, the pathetic inadequacy of human communication and understanding.

At Shellmound the Fairchild ancestors look down from their portraits on the walls. The living members of the family think of them, converse with them even, as if they still were present. Death is denied, ignored; the family life goes on, organized, tranquil, ordered. Violence, agony, misery are kept removed from their lives. Occasionally one of the members of the group must deal with such things, but the family, as a family, shuts them from its consciousness. George Fairchild breaks up a knife fight between two Negro boys, oblivious almost of the peril involved. Later on, Shelley sees her sister's fiancé Troy Flavin shoot the ice pick out of the grasp of a Negro fieldhand, and is angered at the boldness, the decisiveness of the incident. "All at once Shelley was sickeningly afraid of life, life itself, afraid *for* life...." Troy should have been at the wedding rehearsal, and not away from it and dealing with life in so violent, so desperate a fashion.

For the Fairchilds everything is gentled, made human,

a part of their ordered world. Even the Yellow Dog (Yazoo Delta) train that comes by their plantation is diminutive, personalized. The locomotive engineer typically stops the train to get out and pick goldenrod. Once the Fairchilds are all crossing over the viaduct when the Yellow Dog comes along, moving slowly, its engineer asleep. The mentally retarded Fairchild cousin Maureen gets her foot caught in the tracks, and George Fairchild stays with her to extricate it, while the others scatter. Maureen holds out her arms to stop the train, which obediently halts.

On another occasion a cyclone had ripped through the Delta, and left cows bellowing everywhere in the ditches, but grandmother Laura Allen had insisted that her curtains must first be salvaged from the top of a tall tree before permitting her husband to take the Negro hands to rescue the livestock, "and then she had mended what could not help but be torn, so that no one could tell now which curtains they were." The violence is denied; one pretends that it never existed.

The "real world" *can* be quite violent, of course. Maureen's father, Uncle Denis, has gone off to the war and died there. When Uncle George broke up the knife fight among the hands, there was real blood on him. And the Yellow Dog, though seemingly well behaved so far as Fairchild kin are concerned, runs over and kills a girl, a strange girl whom Ellen Fairchild had seen in the woods and George had later slept with. But the Fairchilds prefer not to think about it. They are concentrating on the daily ritual, the bemusement of life.

Delta Wedding centers on the approaching marriage of Dabney Fairchild and Troy Flavin, the overseer at Shellmound. Troy, who comes from the Mississippi hill country, is about to enter the family, and the Fairchilds are uneasy about it, but they focus their attention on the wedding preparations. It will be a very fancy wedding, with little girls bearing shepherdess crooks and bridesmaids holding tiers of flowers in an ascending pattern of light culminating in the whiteness of the bride's gown. The gathering of the family for the affair is disturbed by the marital troubles of George Fairchild, who lives in Memphis. George, for whom the mannered, patterned world of the Fairchilds is not always sufficient, is married to Robbie Reid, a plain little "town girl" from the nearby community. But Robbie has run away; she has been angry ever since her husband had stayed on the railroad trestle with the half-witted Maureen, risking his life to save a Fairchild, for she feels that George had demonstrated that his family allegiance was stronger than his marriage ties. The Fairchilds themselves simply cannot comprehend why Robbie might be resentful; when she finally comes back to Shellmound for the wedding, they are furious with her.

But the wedding takes place, and everything goes serenely and as ordered. Life at Shellmound continues on in its tranquil way. Ellen Fairchild is going to have another baby. When her daughter Dabney and Troy Flavin come back from a three-day wedding trip to New Orleans—it is cotton-picking time, and they cannot stay away longer—the Fairchilds all go off to a picnic on the bank of the Yazoo River, where they lie in the cool of the evening, hear the insects singing, and watch the stars fall.

Yet there are undertones in their conversation that are faintly disturbing. George talks of coming back home from Memphis, ousting two aunts from a nearby family place, the Grove, and putting in livestock and fruit trees instead of cotton. Troy, the newcomer from north Mississippi, agrees with him. Aunt Primrose reveals that there are rats at the Grove; the remark is repeated several times. They are vaguely uneasy, as if beyond and below their peaceful, controlled world, other and more ominous things exist.

For the truth is that the closed little world of Shellmound is doomed; there is that feeling about the end of *Delta Wedding*. The wide world will come in; there will be disorder, change. George seems to symbolize it; his life seems to involve a greater urgency, more distress, more reality, than will fit comfortably into the Fairchild family pattern. And Troy is not a Fairchild; there is a directness, a sharpness to him that will make his life, and his bride Dabney's, something different from the Fairchild pattern. The old aunts are growing still older; and their primness, their sheltered kind of existence will die with them. Shelley, Dabney's older sister, who will soon leave for a trip to Europe and then to school in Virginia, has revealed through her secret diary that she too sees beyond the confines of Shellmound into a less-protected, less-mannered world. Even cousin Laura McRaven from Jackson knows things about the outside world that will not fit. " 'My papa has taken me on trips—I know about geography . . . ,' " she says. "But in the great confines of Shellmound, no one listened."

For Shellmound seems, in the very way that the story is told, to belong to a vanished past—1923, long ago. *Delta Wedding* is related as from a distance, as if remembered, a place of serenity and peace vanished in time—hovering, shimmering, a Land of Lost Content. Who "tells" the story of *Delta Wedding?* It is shown through the consciousness of various persons, but particularly of Laura McRaven, and we feel that somehow it is part of Laura's *memory* of the past. There is a precariousness, a fragility about it; we sense that it could swiftly collapse and vanish, that it is fated to do so. In its evanescence, its tenuousness, it already seems far away,

too wistful for comedy, too distant for tragedy. The
people of the little family community whose world is
Shellmound are destined, we feel, to be dispersed into
the larger, more "real" world, the rumors of which the
family identity can no longer serve to keep from the
consciousness of its inhabitants. They will die, or will
move on to other destinies, other strategies. Shellmound
cannot much longer protect them from the forces of
time and change.

With that sense, the novel closes. It has been the account of a wedding in a Mississippi family, but much
more than that has taken place. We have also been shown
something about time, and the way people respond to its
inexorable tread.

In one sense, it seems to me, Miss Welty has written a
sequel to *Delta Wedding*. It is the short story entitled
"Kin," in *The Bride of the Innisfallen*. "Kin" does not
involve the same family, but what happens in it is highly
appropriate to the way that *Delta Wedding* ends. The
short story is told by a young woman, Miss Dicey Has-
tings, who was born in Mississippi but now lives in the
North, where she is engaged to be married. On a visit
home, she and her cousin Kate ride out into the Delta
country to visit their ailing Great-uncle Felix at Mingo,
the family homestead. When Dicey enters she is at once
overwhelmed by the consciousness of time: "I looked
and saw the corner clock was wrong. I was deeply aware
that all clocks worked in this house, as if they had been
keeping time for me all this while. . . ." Great-uncle Felix
lies in his bed, murmuring about the past, and writes a
note to Dicey, whom he mistakes for a long-ago love.
While he writes, Dicey sees an old stereopticon near
his bed:

> It belonged to Sunday and to summertime. . . . My held
> hand pained me through the wish to use it and lift that

old, beloved, once mysterious contraption to my eyes, and dissolve my sight, all our sights, in that. In that delaying, blinding pain, I remembered Uncle Felix. That is, I remembered the real Uncle Felix, and could hear his voice, respectful again, asking the blessing at the table.

Preoccupied with her awareness of change and the passage of the years, Dicey says good-bye, and she and Kate leave. She remembers how beautiful and how tranquil life at Mingo had seemed once, and how it is so far away now. As they drive off, she seems to hear the very noise of time itself:

All around, something went on and on. It was hard without thinking to tell whether it was a throbbing, a dance, a rattle, or a ringing—all louder as we neared the bridge. It was everywhere in the grass and trees. . . . Then all was April night. I thought of my sweetheart, riding, and wondered if he were writing to me.

Mingo was just such a place as Shellmound once was, the seat of a numerous family, where everyone gathered, talked, grew up, became old. Now it is only an old house, with a dying man inside, and the ordered, tranquil life it used to contain has vanished with the people who once lived there. It is as if one of the young Fairchilds, or better still, as if cousin Laura McRaven had come back to Shellmound after a long time, and remembered it as it once used to be.

The events of *Delta Wedding* occur during a single week. Those of *The Golden Apples* span forty years of life in the little town of Morgana, Mississippi. In *Delta Wedding* a single family made up the characters, while in *The Golden Apples* a variety of townsfolk occupy the leading roles. Economically and socially the people of *The Golden Apples* are a cut below those of Shellmound; they are all of middle-class backgrounds. They have no plantation homes, and Morgana is considerably more democratic than the community centered on Shellmound. The leading families of Morgana are the Morrisons and the Starks, with the MacLains and the Raineys being of a somewhat lesser social rank. There is, however, no impassable gulf between them. Old Mrs. Lizzie Stark, the matriarch of the town, would but for her infirmities supervise events at the Rainey home when Mrs. Kate Rainey dies in the last chapter, and even so she sends her servant to help out.

The Golden Apples consists of seven episodes, most of them able to stand by themselves, but the cast of characters is the same throughout, and to read the book as a mere series of connecting sketches and stories describing a town's life is to miss the central structure of the book. *The Golden Apples* is more than a set of related tales; it has a coherent, unified narrative development, which builds up from story to story, and the meaning of any one of the episodes is not fully understood until the close.

As *The Golden Apples* commences, Mrs. Kate Rainey is telling a passerby about the exploits of Mr. King MacLain. Though married to Miss Snowdie MacLain and the father of twin boys, King seldom stays around home. For years on end, as Mrs. Rainey explains, King has largely kept away, appearing only at rare intervals. As Morgana's chief Far-Wanderer, he provides considerable excitement and material for gossip. He has been reported seen here and there—in Texas, at Governor Vardaman's inauguration in Jackson, everywhere. Mrs. Rainey is sure he has been in California; she doesn't know exactly why, but she pictures him there: "I see King in the West, out where it's gold and all that. Everybody to their own visioning."

Whatever King is, he is surely the favorite fertility

symbol for Morgana's womenfolk. As Mrs. Rainey concludes, "I'll bet my little Jersey calf King tarried long enough to get him a child somewhere. What makes me say a thing like that? I wouldn't say it to my husband, you mind you forget it." Throughout the course of *The Golden Apples*, King MacLain keeps reappearing. In "Sir Rabbit" he turns up in the woods near Morgana to seduce young Mattie Will Holifield almost before the very eyes of her unimaginative spouse.

King's role in *The Golden Apples* is an important one. Though this harmless, elfinlike little man spends most of his adult years away from Morgana, leaving his wife and family behind to shift for themselves, and coming home to await his death only in time for the last episode, he is nevertheless spiritually a part of the Morgana community all the time. His absence from the town is entirely geographical. In the eyes of all Morgana citizens he remains Miss Snowdie MacLain's husband and female Morgana's romantic dream.

By contrast, Virgie Rainey, Mrs. Kate's daughter, who is only four years old when the book opens, leaves Morgana only once and unimportantly. Yet she is never really a part of the community. Almost from the time we meet her, she is estranged from Morgana. This never changes, and the book is built around her estrangement.

The most important revelation of Virgie's role in the community occurs in the long story entitled "June Recital," as seen and remembered by young Loch Morrison and his older sister Cassie. Loch is ill of malaria as the story opens, but his sickness does not prevent him from gazing out of the bedroom window and even crawling out into a nearby tree and to the ground. As he watches from the window strange events happen in the deserted MacLain house next door. He has seen a girl and a sailor in a room upstairs, and in the downstairs parlor an old woman festooning pieces of old newspaper about the room. Then the old woman sets fire to the house, and in the excitement that follows, an odd ticking device, which we recognize as a metronome, is tossed out through the window. Loch climbs down and retrieves it. Later he asks his Negro nurse about the strange instrument he has rescued:

> "Louella, listen. Do you hear a thing ticking?"
> "Hear it plain."
> "Reckon it's going to blow up in the night. You can see it. Look on the washstand." All by itself, of its own accord, it might let fly its little door and start up. He thought he heard it now. Or was it his father's watch in the next room, already laid on the dresser for the night?
> "I 'spec' it will, Loch, if you wants it to," she said readily, and sat on in the dark. . . .

Metronomes mark time, and time is the key to "June Recital," and to the meaning of life in Morgana too. The metronome, and what it stands for, is bound up with Virgie Rainey's estrangement from the community. Once it had belonged to a German music teacher, Miss Eckhart, who some years before the day that Loch Morrison retrieved it had rented quarters in the Mac-Lain home, where she had given music lessons to the children of Morgana. In the story, Loch, who is quite young, and thus innocent of the knowledge of love, sex, and time, peers through his telescope as the strange things take place next door. He sees the sailor and the girl cavorting in odd fashion on a mattress in an upstairs room, while the old woman is strewing newspapers about downstairs. Loch calls to his sister Cassie to come and look at the peculiar goings on, but Cassie, who had been one of Miss Eckhart's pupils, is busy dyeing a scarf to be worn on an evening hayride. It is only when the old woman begins playing the opening bars of "Für Elise" on the piano that Cassie will come to the window. Because of the sunlight she can see little of what is going on in the abandoned house, but the music recalls past events. "Für Elise" was the favorite piece of Miss Eckhart's star pupil, Virgie Rainey, the only one of the music students whom the old German woman had considered really worthy of the music. Virgie had been Miss Eckhart's sole consolation in her lonely and frustrating work of teaching piano in the small Southern community. But now Virgie plays the piano in the movie house, while Miss Eckhart has long since been retired to the county home.

It was Miss Eckhart who was downstairs, and who set fire to the house, and when the smoke billows and shouts of fire are raised, the sailor and the girl upstairs, who is Virgie, hastily flee, and of course are seen by everybody. Cassie Morrison in particular watches as Virgie runs past Miss Eckhart, who is now being taken away by her keepers: "She clicked by Miss Eckhart and she clicked straight through the middle of the Rook party, without a word or the pause of a moment." The import of the climax has been admirably summed up by Robert Daniel in an essay, "Eudora Welty: The Sense of Place":

> Cassie, who fully recalls the past incidents that lead up to the present, cannot see into it; for one thing, she "was practicing on her ukelele again so she could sing to the boys." Loch, at the other window, sees the present fully, but is too inexperienced to understand it. . . .
>
> When Cassie comes back from the hayride, her thoughts return to Miss Eckhart and Virgie Rainey; and as she too falls asleep she grasps at least a part of the mystery. "Both Miss Eckhart and Virgie Rainey were human beings terribly at large, roaming on the face of the earth. And there were others of them—human beings, roaming, like lost beasts."

Virgie, alone of the music pupils, had felt the inexorable rhythm of the metronome, beating independently of the time of the community of Morgana. She had fought against what Miss Eckhart wanted to teach her, refusing to take her piano lessons seriously, to "be heard from in the world." Yet for Virgie, as for Miss Eckhart, the music had not been simply an avocation, a social accomplishment in the community—as it had been for Cassie Morrison. It was woven into Virgie's very consciousness. The beat of the music, with its metronomic awareness of an unchanging measure of time, was part of Virgie's very being.

At the close of the novel, when Virgie's mother has died and the funeral has taken place, Virgie drives seven miles away from Morgana to the nearby town of MacLain, and watches the rain fall. "October rain on Mississippi fields. The rain of fall, maybe on the whole South, for all she knew on the everywhere. She stared into its magnitude." She thinks of how King MacLain, who had winked at her the day before at the funeral, would soon die, and she remembers a painting of Perseus slaying the Minotaur that had once long before been on the wall of Miss Eckhart's studio.

> The vaunting was what she remembered, that lifted arm. Cutting off the Medusa's head was the heroic act, perhaps, that made visible a horror in life, that was at once the horror in love, Virgie thought—the separateness. . . . Because Virgie saw things in their time, like hearing them—and perhaps because she must believe in the Medusa equally with Perseus—she saw the stroke of the sword in three moments, not one. In the three was the damnation—no, only the secret, unhurting because not caring in itself—beyond the beauty and the sword's stroke and the terror lay their existence in time—far out and endless, a constellation which the heart could read over many a night.

Virgie knows then that, though she had denied Miss Eckhart to the last, she had never rejected her: "in the strange music of youth that is accepting of more than is given, she had accepted *the* Beethoven, as with the dragon's blood." Now it was part of her, that knowledge and that terror, and unlike Cassie Morrison and others of Morgana, she could not hide away from her knowledge of time and isolation in the everyday life of the community. The dragon's blood was on Virgie Rainey: "In Virgie's reach of memory a melody softly lifted, lifted of itself. Every time Perseus struck off the Medusa's head, there was the beat of time, and the melody. Endless the Medusa, and Perseus endless."

For the others in the community, Morgana acts to conceal such knowledge of the "real world." The everyday pursuits of business and pleasure in the small Mississippi community, the parties, the politics, the marriages and funerals, manage to keep the various inhabitants successfully diverted. Time flows by—forty years of it during the novel—but they manage to ignore it, and keep from themselves the fact of their individual loneliness and separation through immersion in community life.

What happens to a Morgana citizen who leaves the town is shown in the story "Music From Spain," in which Eugene MacLain, King's son now living in San Francisco, wanders aimlessly and vaguely about that city in company with a strange guitar-playing Spaniard, far away from the serenity and the sense of belonging enjoyed by the home folks of Morgana. Eventually Eugene returns home to live. His twin brother Randall has his troubles too, as recounted in the story "The Whole World Knows." His marriage almost fails, and he comes close to doing something desperate, but he recovers, rejoins the life of the community, and at the close is mayor of the town.

The communal guard must always be kept up. The role that Morgana plays for its inhabitants can only be effective if they act in concert to exclude from their lives any kind of stark, wholly passionate experience that would remind them of the world outside. This had doomed Miss Eckhart, for she had not been willing to subordinate her Beethoven to the everyday proportions of the town's social needs. In another story, "Moon Lake," Loch Morrison labors valiantly to resuscitate an orphan girl who had drowned in the water. The rhythm of the artificial respiration, like Miss Eckhart's metronome, is independent of Morgana time. In his intensity and heroism Loch presages his coming estrangement from Morgana. His companions feel awkward at his action: "I'll tell on him, in Morgana tomorrow," Jinny Love Stark remarks. "He's the most conceited Boy Scout in the whole troop; and's bow-legged." We are not surprised to learn at the close of the book that Loch has long since moved away. There is in Morgana no room for the individual act that transcends the need and desire for community approval. The heroic, the tragic, the artistic must be trimmed to fit into the complicated fabric of the town's doings. Without these proportions being insisted upon, the community cannot serve its proper function: it cannot screen out from its inhabitants' awareness the awful knowledge of individual separation and loneliness. Thus Loch Morrison must go away; and Virgie, though she refuses to leave, is not really a member of the community, because she cannot deny her inner knowledge to the extent that she is able to participate.

During the course of *The Golden Apples* we watch the citizens of Morgana come and depart. Like Shellmound in *Delta Wedding*, Morgana too has the sense of being part of a vanished time and place, described from a great distance. We see the townsfolk born and we watch them die, and time progresses steadily onward. They are prisoners in time; no condition, no relationship can remain meaningful. The deepest griefs, the most bitter enmities are eventually forgotten. Even King Mac-Lain, the spirit of the woods, ramble though he does, will one day be cut down. Before the unyielding progression of time, nothing may stand. But happily for them, most of the town's inhabitants are screened from this knowledge, and so find their lives endurable. To safeguard them against this awareness, the terrible contemplation of time's huge, impersonal intransigence, communities such as Morgana—and Shellmound—exist. So long as the inhabitants can keep themselves engrossed with the town's day-by-day pursuits, they can be spared the knowledge of loss in time.

This immersion in the affairs of the town Virgie Rainey could not manage, struggle valiantly though she did to do so. She dribbles away her life, never contented, taking a procession of lovers all of whom fail to answer her deepest needs. Once she did flee, but she came right back. At the end she is absolutely and thoroughly alone, past tragedy, past wanting. She stares into the rain falling on the South, and in company with an old beggar woman who has taken refuge under a tree from the shower as she has done, Virgie is left "listening to the magical percussion, the world beating in their ears. They heard through falling rain the running of the horse and bear, the stroke of the leopard, the dragon's crusty slither, and the glimmer and the trumpet of the swan."

This knowledge of time and the "real world," this awareness of separation, is closely tied to the achievement of beauty through art. Cassie Morrison, who senses this separateness about Virgie Rainey, had remembered some lines of a poem on the afternoon when she had heard "Für Elise" being played on the piano in the deserted house next door:

> Though I am old with wandering
> Through hollow lands and hilly lands
> I will find out where she has gone. . . .

As she sleeps, "she sat up in bed once and said aloud, 'Because a fire was in my head.' Then she fell back unresisting. She did not see except in dreams that a face looked in; that it was the grave, unappeased, and radiant face, once more and always, the face that was in the poem." So "June Recital" closes, and though Cassie remembered all the lines of the poem, Miss Welty did not let her recite them for us. But the poem is not so easily disposed of as that. It is Yeats's "The Song of Wandering Aengus," and not only do the last lines of that poem furnish the theme of *The Golden Apples*, but they provide its title as well:

> Though I am old with wandering
> Through hollow lands and hilly lands,
> I will find out where she has gone,
> And kiss her lips and take her hands;
> And walk among long dappled grass,
> And pluck till time and times are done
> The silver apples of the moon,
> The golden apples of the sun.

That was Virgie Rainey's quest, fight it though she tried; and its relentless requirements are what the townsfolk of Morgana would avoid. For time is wandering and death, and it is also music and art. Because a fire was in her head, Virgie Rainey could not rest, could not drive from her consciousness the beat of the metronome, could not fail to be aware of what Cassie knew only in dreams, that Morgana existed in order to shut out: "the grave, unappeased, and radiant face, once more and always, the face that was in the poem." For some, the little Mississippi community could afford surcease from the enormous and terrible problems of human identity and creation. But not for Virgie Rainey. She could not be diverted, could not trick herself into not knowing.

Surely this is far removed from the kind of pleasant quaintness that we customarily associate with local color. It is a very devastating view that Miss Welty has of society: it is a façade, a screen, she says, to disguise severe truths about human life. The truths remain valid; the society only hides them from sight.

No one would think to describe Miss Welty as a naturalistic writer; and really she is not that, because whatever her people are, they aren't mere combinations of "chemisms," to use Dreiser's term again. All the same, the universe they inhabit is not particularly beneficent and satisfying, and the lucky ones seem not to be, as Cassie Morrison says to Virgie Rainey, "you and Loch" —those who go away, who have "a life of your own, away." Rather, the fortunate inhabitants of the Welty universe are those who can stay at home and manage to divert themselves in society, thus keeping out of their consciousness the knowledge of their human plight.

If this seems to be saying that Miss Welty is making a positive virtue of stupidity and insensitivity, that is not quite the case. What she is intimating is that the world can be a very appalling place for those observant enough to look at it clearly, and that because of this, most people prefer not to do so. But it is not really a matter of choice; certainly Virgie Rainey tries not to know what she knows. And Cassie Morrison's mother tried to divert herself, and managed for a considerable length of time, but eventually she must have failed, for she took her own life. Perhaps I make too sharp a distinction between those who see and those who do not; for who knows what any of Miss Welty's people are really like, all the while that they go about their busy ways? Perhaps they all have the capacity to run wild at any moment; a certain air of exasperation exists about all of them, not excepting Mr. King MacLain himself.

There is a peculiar bemusement about Eudura Welty's characters. Even at their funniest, their most picturesque, they seem so very much in earnest. They work hard at playing games. It is even a little reminiscent of the manner in which the characters in Hemingway's *The Sun Also Rises* expend so much effort in concentrating on the routine, unimportant activities in life, such as walking down a street, crossing a bridge over the Seine, eating, drinking, in order not to think about their plight in time. Not that the desperation is anything nearly so close to the level of consciousness; Miss Welty's people are always a bit abstracted; their minds are apparently filled with all manner of thoughts that are not at all organized and catalogued. Even so, there is another respect in which they behave like Hemingway's expatriates: they cannot talk seriously with one another. A dialogue between any two persons in the Welty novels is an exchange only of the surfaces of their thoughts; they speak obliquely; what they say is only a remote approximation of what they are thinking. Like the characters of Henry James and Edith Wharton, we never know what they are actually thinking. They can trade gossip and trivia by the hour, but their innermost thoughts are never shared. Each of the main characters in both *Delta Wedding* and *The Golden Apples*, it seems to me, is an enigma. They are all private, secret, solitary creatures, very much like ourselves.

Here lies Miss Welty's finest accomplishment. By fixing on this contrast between the private consciousness and the social personality, she has created a version of "real life," without making it either too simple or too histrionic. She has convincingly dramatized a mode of existence. Her two novels ring with the authority of experience. She has looked into the lives of a Mississippi family and a town from the outside and inside both, and shown them for what they truly are, in a way that no one else has quite done, not even Faulkner. We *believe* in Shellmound, in Morgana. For we have seen those places as the participants see them, and we have also seen the participants, as they think of themselves and as they really are.

We can marvel at Miss Welty's objectivity, at the way she can look at her characters without being taken in by them, so that she can show us why they are acting in the way they do. At the same time she makes us share her compassion for all of them. There are no really unpleasant characters in either of the novels—not even Jinny Love Stark in *The Golden Apples*—for we understand them too well to judge any of them with entire harshness. Eudora Welty is both detached from and at the same time a part of what she writes about. She can understand the Fairchilds, and she can also know why little Laura McRaven could feel that "Jackson was a big town, with twenty-five thousand people, and Fairchilds was just a store and a gin and a bridge and one big house, yet she was the one who felt like a little country cousin when she arrived. . . ." She can understand Miss Lizzie Stark, but she can also understand Virgie Rainey. And she created them so that we can. She knows what belonging to a place means, for she also knows what it means to be estranged.

Is it too fanciful to see, in Virgie Rainey's relation to Morgana, the same kind of detachment from the community that made possible the art of writers such as Miss

Welty? Probably so, for Virgie after all never went on to play "*the* Beethoven." Perhaps it is Loch Morrison, who did go away, who is the better exemplar. Or better than that, perhaps, Cassie Morrison herself, who stayed on, who never married, lived in Morgana and was part of it by day and separate by night, knowing both the daily life of the town and the dream-borne vision of the goddess of the moon.

7

THE POETRY
OF AGRARIANISM

In the year 1930 there was published a volume of essays entitled *I'll Take My Stand: The South and the Agrarian Tradition*. Appearing just as the boom-or-bust economy of the 1920's was receding into the chaos of the Great Depression, it strongly criticized the business and commercial foundations of modern American life, and for contrast held up the agrarian society of the old, pre-industrial South. It urged Southerners to spurn the pleasures of modernism and to reaffirm their belief in an ordered, tranquil, religious life, close to nature and removed from the tumult of metropolitan ways.

There were twelve contributors to *I'll Take My Stand*, but the moving spirits were four poets: Donald Davidson, John Crowe Ransom, Allen Tate, and Robert Penn Warren. The subsequent achievements of these men in poetry, criticism, and fiction, as well as that of others of the contributors, such as the novelist Andrew Nelson Lytle, helped to earn for *I'll Take My Stand* some of the lasting attention it has enjoyed since its publication, but the book has made a considerable impact in its own right. The seriousness with which it has been received by economists, sociologists, and other social scientists, some of whom have gone to great pains to refute it, testifies to its effectiveness as social documentation. In seeking to rebut it, various commentators have demonstrated that the agrarian image of the Old South as depicted in the book omitted a number of quite unattractive aspects of Southern life, and that its prescription of an anti-industrial ethic for the South was highly unrealistic, so that in the three decades since the book was published the Agrarians' counsel was not followed by the South, which instead has raced ahead with its industrialism. Even so, the book continues to attract attention, and has now been republished in a paperback edition.

Yet perhaps the eventual importance of *I'll Take My Stand* does not lie in its commentary on the changing South; nor does it reside in the book's critique of modern society, which (rather than its specifically Southern aspects) has been the reason it has continued to be so provocative a document. Instead, the ultimate value of the book consists in what it has to tell us about Tate's, Ransom's, Warren's, and Davidson's positions as men of letters—and Lytle's, though in this essay I propose to confine my inquiry to the poets. It may be read, I think, in the same way we read the political pamphleteering of Pope or Swift, which is to say, not so much for specific commentary on contemporary political and social life (though it is highly interesting in that respect) but as a by-product of the mind of the poet, as clues to the attitudes that figure his literary productions. It is this that I want to try to show—how the agrarian image discussed in the symposium fits in with the poetry, provides it with an important thematic image, and helps to indicate the relationship of the literary work to the region from which Tate, Ransom, Warren, and Davidson came.

During the early and middle 1920's the Fugitive poets, as they were then called, were not particularly concerned with their identity as Southerners. Rebelling from the United Daughters of the Confederacy tradition in Southern letters, they had found self-conscious sectionalism a hindrance to their own literary development. In the later years of the decade, however, as they thought more and more about the role of poetry and the arts in American life, their attitude had changed. The United States of America of the 1920's seemed to them increasingly worshipful of material things, dedicated to a brazenly commercial society. Artistic taste was being debased to accommodate the needs of mass, commercialized culture. The domination of industrial and business interests was reducing the fine arts to the status of diversionary, nonessential activities. So overwhelmingly did American life seem given over to the pursuit of gain that aesthetic and religious impulses were all but ignored.

At this point the four leading Fugitive poets turned to the South. For as poets they were given to metaphor, and their instinctive recourse was to discover a poetic image for their critique of American society. In the history of the South they perceived the image of a region that had for many years resisted the domination of the machine, persisting in its agricultural ways even after military conquest, and well into the present century, and only then, in the 1920's, beginning to capitulate fully to the standards of American industrial society.

When measured by the dominant American ideal, the preindustrial South had been backward, but it had evolved a society, they felt, in which tradition, leisure, aesthetic and religious considerations had not been ignored in the pursuit of economic gain. Only in modern times, by bartering away its rural ways for the gaudy benefits of industrialism, was the South surrendering its spiritual heritage. What was wrong with the region, they felt, was not that it was backward and agricultural, but that it was failing to cherish its own highly civilized values. For it was the South, they believed, and not the industrial Northeast, that still retained the old American virtues, that still provided a style of living in which genuine religious and aesthetic experience were possible. As such, it might well provide an image of the good life, and thus furnish a needed corrective for America's headlong materialism. With that goal in mind, the Agrarian symposium was written.

I'll Take My Stand has been widely read as a primer for the Southern economy, and much effort has been devoted to refuting its apparent diagnosis of decreased industrialization and more yeoman farming as cure for the South's ills. Yet the book's value as social commentary did not and does not lie in that realm. Its true topical use is that of an extended metaphor, of which the image of the agrarian South is no more than the trope. What the book really concerned itself with was the nature of man in society. Far from being a perfectible person of unlimited possibilities, it said, man is a fallible, finite creature, whose welfare depended upon his living in a society devised to restrain his destructive impulses and further his more civilized virtues. But in his hunger for the material benefits of modern industrial civilization, modern man was ignoring his spiritual welfare and his moral obligations to society. He had erected a new god, Progress, and was attempting to make the contrivances of the new industrialism into the sole ends of life. Caught up in a race to exploit the natural world through applied science, man was losing touch with the real world, with aesthetic and religious values. His machines were brutalizing and coarsening him. The frail, tenuous spiritual insights of Western civilization, achieved so arduously over the course of many centuries, were being sacrificed,

and the result, if unchecked, could only be dehumaniza-
tion and chaos.

In the life of their own section they saw the dehumanizing process going on at a particularly attenuated
rate. Industrialism had been late in coming to the South,
and only in the 1920's was the full force of its impact being felt. In the contrast between what the Old South at
its best had been, and the New South that was coming
into being, they discovered a metaphor of what had happened to American life. And to dramatize the kind of
life that they felt Americans should seek, they held up
the image of the Old South.

It was the image of a society that very likely never existed, but one that should have existed, in which men could
live as individuals and not as automatons, aware of their
finiteness and their dependence on God and nature, imbued with a sense of the deep inscrutability of nature,
dedicated to the enhancement of the moral life in its
aesthetic and spiritual dimensions. In contrast to the
hurried, nervous pace of life in modern cities, the agrarian South was the image of a society in which human
beings could live serenely and harmoniously. Not dominated by lust for money and power, they could be free
of the tension and harassment of the modern industrial
community.

I'll Take My Stand was thus designed as a rebuke to
materialism, a corrective to the worship of Progress, a
reaffirmation of man's spiritual and aesthetic needs. Neither a treatise on economics, nor a guide to political action, nor yet a sociological blueprint, the Agrarian symposium was an image of what the good life could be.

As I have said before, this aspect of *I'll Take My Stand*
largely accounts, I think, for the continued life of the
book. Had its only importance been what it had specifi-

cally to say about the economics and politics of the
Southern states, it would soon have been forgotten. But
the fact that the Southern image was but the immediate
and topical statement of a much deeper and more general
aesthetic and religious attitude, and served primarily to
dramatize that attitude, caused the book to speak with
much greater authority and relevance than any merely
topical treatise on economics and politics could. Its imaginative appeal stirred many readers to whom the topical arguments by themselves would have seemed insubstantial and visionary. The book, in other words, spoke
to a very important and widespread human problem:
what is man's proper relationship to his environment?
Thus *I'll Take My Stand* gained a broad hearing, and
continues to be read and pondered.

Now this is well and good, but the question still remains: what does Nashville Agrarianism as promulgated
by Allen Tate, Donald Davidson, Robert Penn Warren,
and John Crowe Ransom have to do with their *poetry?*
For interesting though their Agrarian symposium is, and
cogent though its arguments may remain, the chief importance of these men is as poets and artists. "Captain
Carpenter" and the "Ode to the Confederate Dead" are
likely to be read when *I'll Take My Stand* becomes no
more than a footnote in American cultural history. The
question, therefore, is whether there is any important
relationship between the attitudes that occasioned the
Agrarian symposium and the poems these men have
written.

There is, I hope to show, a very definite relationship.
The basic attitudes toward human experience, and toward man's place in nature and in society, that are topically expressed in *I'll Take My Stand* are, it seems to
me, precisely those that give meaning to their poetry.

The poetry and the Agrarianism grow out of the same impulse, and the Agrarian writings constitute a topical, historical statement of certain attitudes and themes which in the poetry achieve a broader, more artistic relevance. In other words, the premises of Agrarianism are also the premises of the poetry. Arguments about society in *I'll Take My Stand* become themes and images in the poems.

Before taking up the poetry, it might be useful to summarize certain of these premises, so that we can then trace their presence in the poetry, and the ways in which they are modified by each of the poets. I would single out three such arguments:

1. Man is essentially a creature of nature, and the natural world best provides the norm whereby man can recognize his status, which is finite, and his condition of dependence, which is on God.
2. A society that is estranged from nature distorts human identity. The complexity of modern society forces man into a condition of spiritual fragmentation, in which he seeks to live by abstractions that fail to give order and wholeness to his experience.
3. Man is not a creature of the present moment alone, and he needs the ordering values of an historical tradition, with its classical heritage, its base in the cultured, leisured, harmonious life, its recognition of aesthetic and religious values, to define and regulate his conduct.

Such, I believe, were the basic assumptions of Agrarianism, and it now remains to demonstrate that they are likewise the assumptions of the poetry of four talented American writers.

It is convenient to begin with Donald Davidson, in whose work there is almost a literal, one-for-one correlation between the themes of Agrarianism and those of his poems. Nashville Agrarianism is part and parcel of

his poetic impulse; his verse specifically concerns itself
with agrarian topics, particularly in their specific Southern forms. A poem such as Davidson's "On a Replica of
the Parthenon in Nashville" is a direct appeal to the
values of the tradition-guided life, with its civility, its
reliance upon the classics, as contrasted with the restless
impatience of modernism:

> Why do they come? What do they seek
> Who build but never read their Greek?
> The classic stillness of a pool
> Beleaguered in its certitude
> By aimless motors that can make
> Only uncertainty more sure

Modern industrial existence, as symbolized by the direc-
tionless motorcars, is made to appear as a barbarous contrast to the pure, classical simplicity of the original
Parthenon, which with its friezes and Grecian columns
is entirely out of place in busy, modern urban life:

> But the sky drips its spectral dirt,
> And gods, like men, to soot revert.
> Gone is the mild, the serene air.
> The golden years are come too late.

He depicts the replica of the Greek temple in the contemporary Southern city as a helpless, futile gesture toward tradition by modern men who otherwise have ignored and forgotten that classical heritage and all the
wisdom it contained, and who have now "raised up this
bribe against their fate" while continuing to follow the
ignorant goals of debased modern industrial society.

Davidson's best poem, "Lee in the Mountains," is as
literally a Southern agrarian poem as has ever been composed. The image of General Lee, defeated but not dis-
honored, living out his final years in Lexington and occupied with the editing of his father's memoirs, is of a

man who still believes firmly in the cause for which he
fought so well:

> God too late
> Unseals to certain eyes the drift
> Of time and the hopes of men and a sacred cause.

He is resolved, unlike his father, never to write of the
battles he has fought:

> The rest must pass to men who never knew
> (But on a written page) the strike of armies,
> And never heard the long Confederate cry
> Charge through the muzzling smoke or saw the bright
> Eyes of the beardless boys go up to death.

He asks himself whether the crass present times justify
the valor and sacrifice of the War:

> Was it for this
> That on an April day we stacked our arms
> Obedient to a soldier's trust? To lie
> Ground by heels of little men,
> Forever maimed, defeated, lost, impugned?
> And was I then betrayed? Did I betray?

He feels that the spirit of the cause is still alive, that if
called upon to do so the Southern people would again
rally to his standard and give battle to the invaders from
the North:

> The sunken flag would kindle on wild hills,
> The brooding hearts would waken, and the dream
> Stir like a crippled phantom under the pines,
> And this torn earth would quicken to shouting
> Beneath the feet of ragged bands—

But it is all over, just as he had foreseen long before the
War, and it is not his duty to summon the regiments
again. Rather, it is his task to remind the young men of
their duty to the land and to tell them that despite defeat
the hope of man rests in submission to God's wisdom:

a just
And merciful God Who in this blood once shed
On your green altars measures out all days,
And measures out the grace
Whereby alone we live;
And in His might He waits,
Brooding within the certitude of time,
To bring this lost forsaken valor
And the fierce faith undying
And the love quenchless
To flower among the hills to which we cleave,
To fruit among the mountains whither we flee,
Never forsaking, never denying
His children and His children's children forever
Unto all generations of the faithful heart.

The truth and solace of God are thus embodied in an agrarian image of the flowering hills and fruited mountains, where earthly hope and certainty reside in a life close to nature. There is where he belongs: "The fortune of the Lees goes with the land / Whose sons will keep it still." The elegiac tone of the poem is sustained by the image of the great Confederate military chieftain who, having fought for the land he loved, lives in the mountains in fealty to God's will. The passionate devotion of Lee to the Southland, his faith in a just God, his belief that, though beaten in battle, the South remains strong in its resolve and devotion, all serve to create an image of a people bound by historical loyalties and blood ties, imbued with a religious attachment to the land and to the past.

Davidson's use of the Southern historical tradition and the agrarian heritage of the region is direct and uncomplicated. The historical birthright is available to him as a poet without irony or qualification, and the image of the agrarian South can be thrown into immediate and direct contrast with modern urban existence, to serve as a rebuke to the aimlessness, the tawdry materialism of contemporary life. His most ambitious poem, "The Tall Men," is built directly on the contrast between the uncomplicated, vigorous life of the Tennessee frontiersmen and the compromised plight of the modern, city-dwelling Southerner. In what might be described as the quintessential Nashville Agrarian judgment, he speaks of

> this gray city, blinded, soiled, and kicked
> By fat, blind fools. The city's burning up?
> Why, good! Then let her burn!

And his final admonition to his fellow citizens is to

> remember the rifles
> Talking men's talk into the Tennessee darkness
> And the long-haired hunters watching the Tennessee
> hills
> In the land of the big rivers for something.

John Crowe Ransom's version of agrarianism in poetry is less literally Southern and topical, and more contemplative. Agrarianism was the good life, the most civilized kind of existence possible to man. His objection to contemporary industrial society was that it denied the individual the attainment of the good life, by providing a chaotic, fragmented existence, dividing human experience into little isolated compartments, setting apart emotion from intelligence, and promoting a dehumanized, abstract version of human life. Ransom's poem "Painted Head" announces his verdict on modern society. The head painted on the canvas—the intelligence, the brain —has been set apart from the body and made to seek reality on its own intellectual terms, without consideration of the body. He remarks the

> instinct of heads to be
> Absolute and to try decapitation
> And to play truant from the body bush.

But the artist, in "unhousing by abstraction this once head," has painted it as something ugly and undesirable, and thus

> Makes repentance in an unlovely head
> For having vinegarly traduced the flesh
> Till, the hurt flesh recusing, the hard egg
> Is shrunken to its own deathlike surface.

Intellect for its own sake, abstract theorizing without taking into account the senses, without allowing for the emotions, is a distortion of experience. The aesthetic life is one that envisages intellect and emotion as equally essential aspects of reality, and does not seek to ignore the full body of experience:

> Beauty is of body.
> The flesh contouring shallowly on a head
> Is a rock-garden needing body's love
> And best bodiness to colorify
>
> The big blue birds sitting and sea-shell flats
> And caves, and on the iron acropolis
> To spread the hyacinthine hair and rear
> The olive garden for the nightingales.

Modern industrial life for the Agrarians is just such a life of abstraction, of social formula without proper accounting for the particularity of human experience. For Ransom the agrarian image is of the kind of life in which leisure, grace, civility can exist in harmony with thought and action, making the individual's life a wholesome, harmonious experience. When Ransom writes of nature, it is almost never as wilderness, but as farmland. His agrarianism is of the old Southern plantation, the gentle, mannered life of leisure and refinement without the need or inclination to pioneer. The necessity for order and stability is uppermost in Ransom's world. His poems reflect his abhorrence of (and, paradoxically, his fascination with) disorder; they are full of violence, bloodshed, gore. In "Necrological," for example, a friar observes bodies on a battlefield:

> Not all were white; some gory and fabulous
> Whom the sword had pierced and then the grey wolf
> eaten;
> But the brother reasoned that heroes' flesh was thus,
> Flesh falls, and the postured bones lie weather-beaten.

A slaughter is likewise in prospect in "Armageddon," as the faithful of the Lord, having been recalled to right opinions after their momentary fraternization with Satan, prepare for battle:

> With scourge they mortify their carnal selves,
> With stone they whet the ax-heads on the helves
> And seek the Prince Beelzebub and minions.

Judith of Bethulia, in another poem, waylays the invader in his tent, after which the Lord's hosts

> smote them hiding in our vineyards, barns, annexes,
> And now their white bones clutter the holes of foxes,
> And the chieftain's head, with grinning sockets, and
> varnished—
> Is it hung in the sky, with a hideous epitaphy?
> No, the woman keeps the trophy.

The violence is always presented with mannered gentility, a sense of chivalric decorum in language, that serves only to underscore and emphasize the terror of the action. The famous "Captain Carpenter," for example, is an agrarian gentleman of the old school, courteous, traditional, chivalric and true, who rides out to confront the modern world, with lamentable results. First he meets "a pretty lady and all her train" who "played with him so sweetly" but then seized a sword "and twined him of his nose for evermore." Next he encounters a stranger rogue, and at once

> drew upon him out of his great heart
> The other swung against him with a club
> And cracked his two legs at the shinny part
> And let him roll and stick like any tub.

The Captain loses one encounter after another. His trouble is that he goes about his questing in the traditional, chivalric style, while his opponents will not fight fair. The wife of Satan "bit off his arms at the elbows." He "parted with his ears" to a black devil, and he yields up "his sweet blue eyes" to another. Finally "the neatest knave that ever was seen" steps out and falls upon the Captain:

> I would not knock old fellows in the dust
> But there lay Captain Carpenter on his back
> His weapons were the old heart in his bust
> And a blade shook between rotten teeth alack.

The knave, "with gentle apology and touch refined," thereupon "pierced him and produced the Captain's heart." So much for the Captain. Yet for all his ineffectiveness there is something admirable about him:

> God's mercy rest on Captain Carpenter now
> I thought him Sirs an honest gentleman
> Citizen husband soldier and scholar enow
> Let jangling kites eat of him if they can.

And as for the Captain's murderer,

> The curse of hell upon the sleek upstart
> That got the Captain finally on his back
> And took the red red vitals of his heart
> And made the kites to whet their beaks clack clack.

Is not Captain Carpenter, in all his forlorn bravery, very much a Southern gentleman to the manner born, who tries to go about his life in a traditional way, only to be hewn to pieces by vicious rogues with no compunctions about honor and dignity? Indeed, does not this renowned "citizen husband soldier and scholar" fall before the onslaught of modernity? If so, there is no doubt about where Ransom's sympathies lie; ironic he may be concerning the Captain's limitations for the kind of combat he faces, but Ransom is not on the side of the barbarians. And there is the intimation, too, that though life has dealt unkindly with the Captain, he has nonetheless done what he should, and his defeat is not entirely without compensations. The medieval ballad form, the quaint, bloodless diction, the mannered formality of the language, all contrast with the violence of the deeds described, so as to give the poem an ironic, mordant tone.

Throughout Ransom's poetry there is the same kind of irony, brought about by the conjunction of a stylized, formal attitude of discourse and some of the most vicious, sanguinary subject matter in all of modern American poetry. Little children die; old maids see their gardens deflowered; spinsters are buried; country mountebanks boast of the ferocity of their pets; ladies of high degree die "after six little spaces of chill, and six of burning"; Christ smites Antichrist; Judith of Bethulia waylays the heathen; blue girls are reminded of "a lady with a terrible tongue, / Blear eyes fallen from blue, / All her perfections tarnished"; little girls observe their pet chickens die of poison; lovers "with individual tigers in their blood" thereupon "rend and murder trying to get undone"; old campaigners bleed to death; dogs pip a farmer's "bull of gentle pedigree"; and so on. Here are typical lovers as depicted by Ransom:

> In Heaven you have heard no marriage is,
> No white flesh tinder to your lecheries,
> Your male and female tissue sweetly shaped
> Sublimed away, and furious blood escaped.
>
> Great lovers lie in Hell, the stubborn ones
> Infatuate of the flesh upon the bones;

Stuprate, they rend each other when they kiss,
The pieces kiss again, no end to this.

In "Prelude to an Evening" he depicts a happy family
circle, with father come home from the office:

Do not enforce the tired wolf
Dragging his infected wound homeward
To sit tonight with the warm children
Naming the pretty kings of France.

Ransom's poetry is that of a gentleman of culture and
refinement confronting the savagery and horror that
lie beneath the veneer of everyday modern life. The
elegance of the diction, the quaintness of the metaphor
serve to intensify the desperate nature of the predicament. Everywhere about him he sees violence and terror,
and he is appalled at what he sees. Ransom's agrarianism
is an assertion of the value of ritual, manners, tradition,
as a way of disciplining the passionate violence of the
world, while helping to realize its frail loveliness. His
most overtly agrarian poem is "Antique Harvesters," in
which Southern life is depicted as a fox hunt, a typical
Ransom strategy:

Here come the hunters, keepers of a rite;
The horn, the hounds, the lank mares coursing by
Straddled with archetypes of chivalry;
And the fox, lovely ritualist, in flight
Offering his unearthly ghost to quarry;
And the fields, themselves to harry.

Violence and bloodshed are subsumed in the figure of the
fox hunt, which becomes so ritualistic that there is no
intimation of slaughter whatever; the fox seems in no
danger, for the whole performance is formal, deliberate,
figurative. As for the farmers who till the fields in which
the gentry have come riding, they perform their agrarian duties in the best pastoral fashion, with no intimation

of calloused hands, hookworm, pellagra, or the evils of the sharecropper system:

> Resume, harvesters. The treasure is full bronze
> Which you will garner for the lady, and the moon
> Could tinge it no yellower than does this noon;
> But grey will quench it shortly—the fields, men, stones.
> Pluck fast, dreamers; prove as you amble slowly
> Not less than men, not wholly.

The motif is religious; the South is identified with the Virgin, and the farmers' loyalty to the South with fealty to Her. It is all ritualistic and mannered, and the poem closes with an injunction to the young men to honor and keep the vigil and the devotion to the land that the old men have kept. For Ransom, the good life is one in which soul and body, passion and intellect, tradition and the full savoring of experience, all can exist harmoniously. His notion of civilization is of something precious and fragile, to be cherished at all costs as the single leaven to the darkness and violence of the world, the sole way to gentle the brute passions of men. He saw Agrarianism as the occasion for that kind of life.

For Ransom, as for Davidson, the historical image of the Old South is of a society that was real, that formerly existed, one that could be identified, despite certain flaws, with the good life. Though Ransom has since veered from that position to a far greater extent than Davidson, the conviction is inescapable, if one reads their Agrarian writings of the period, that both men held a full and literal belief in the historical Old South as the true exemplar of an agrarian society as realized in the New World. Perhaps with Ransom there was an element of conscious strategy in his espousal of the cause, a sense perhaps of desperate bravado, but with both of them the Agrarianism was strongly literal. It was not simply a

kind of metaphor, a symbol; it was something to be trans-
lated into social, political, economic behavior, something
that could be willed into performance. Turn back, they
seemed to be saying; it is not too late even yet.

By contrast, the historical heritage and the agrarian
life are separated from the protagonist of Allen Tate's
"Ode to the Confederate Dead" by more than an act of
will. Tate's modern man, like Davidson's, is lacking in
belief and purpose, but it is not simply a matter of his
obstinacy in ignoring the agrarian wisdom of his fathers.
Rather, his plight is rendered the more desperate through
his separation from his history by an impassable gap in
time, so that not only does he lack access to his tradition,
but even the ability to define reality through it. The
Confederate dead are anonymous, removed, beyond historical identification:

> Row after row with strict impunity
> The headstones yield their names to the element,
> The wind whirrs without recollection;
> In the riven troughs the splayed leaves
> Pile up, of nature the casual sacrament
> To the seasonal eternity of death

Thus Tate's vantage point, instead of involving the passing of a judgment from above on the failure of the
modern man at the cemetery gate to abide by the heritage of his past, is much more directly that of the moderns themselves. In this way their plight in time is depicted with much more both of sympathy and of an-
guish. The watcher at the gate feels cut off, isolated, alien
to the precept of the dead soldiers whose monument
he sees:

> The brute curiosity of an angel's stare
> Turns you, like them, to stone,
> Transforms the heaving air

Till plunged to a heavier world below
You shift your sea-space blindly
Heaving, turning like the blind crab.

Submerged in the depths of his emptiness, lacking mobility and direction, he is able to focus his attention only on the physical scene before him:

Dazed by the wind, only the wind
The leaves flying, plunge

These dead Confederate soldiers, he thinks, possessed courage, certainty, belief in their cause, and so were able to act in the world, to sacrifice their lives in battle with the conviction that their death could have meaning:

You know the unimportant shrift of death
And praise the vision
And praise the arrogant circumstance
Of those who fall

He tries to imagine the fury and excitement of their day of battle, the heroism and the passionate commitment they could possess. But such belief, such behavior, are beyond his own conjecture; a prisoner in time, locked within his own sensibilities, the modern man cannot evoke for himself a coherent explanation for such behavior:

You hear the shout, the crazy hemlocks point
With troubled fingers to the silence which
Smothers you, a mummy, in time.

The attitude of modern man is seen as a kind of desperate civility, a mannered helplessness. Living in a time when action seems divorced from reason, passion from belief, knowledge from conviction, he is at a loss as to how to confront the example of the dead soldiers, whose own lives were based on the wholeness, the coherence, the firm commitment to experience that their modern descendant at the gate lacks:

What shall we who count our days and bow
Our heads with a commemorial woe
In the ribboned coats of grim felicity,
What shall we say of the bones, unclean,
Whose verdurous anonymity will grow?

There is no meaningful response that can be made; to the modern man, life and death have no explanation beyond the physical cessation of consciousness, for human experience does not appear as a believable, intelligible activity, possessing any truth outside of one's private consciousness. Lacking conviction, estranged from history, modern man exists only from day to day:

Night is the beginning and the end
And in between the ends of distraction
Waits mute speculation, the patient curse
That stones the eyes, or like the jaguar leaps
For his own image in a jungle pool, his victim.

As for the watcher at the gate, who sees the Confederate gravestones as the emblems of a day when the confusion of belief present during his own time was not yet such as to cripple the soldiers' ability to act with conviction, what meaning can he discover in the scene at the cemetery? No answer is forthcoming; the sole conviction that remains for the modern man is that time *is*. Beyond that, he can be sure of nothing except his own subjective existence in time and his estrangement from the past—and that all men are mortal. With that thought he turns away from the cemetery.

In Tate's poem the South's past, the life of the Old South and its great day of battle, are so far away from the modern Southerner that he cannot even comprehend them. The Southern Agrarian image for Tate symbolized a wholeness, a meaningfulness to human experience, that modern society lacked. It is held up as the kind of existence that the fragmented industrial society of our own day cannot offer its members. But how can that agrarian state be regained? Seemingly only by a violent reassertion of belief in the desirability of wholeness, of order reinforced by tradition and spiritual commitment; before one can regain the image, one must first regain one's belief in the *need* for the image. For even that is absent, so prevalent is the disorder. Much of Tate's poetry is concerned with the search for a tradition. In "The Mediterranean," modern man's quest is likened to that of the Trojan wanderers in the *Aeneid*, and it is only through the realization of their own desperation that they can attain their goal, by turning back to the values of their own tradition:

> And we made feast and in our secret need
> Devoured the very plates Aeneas bore

It is not until then, through his regained historical experience, that the modern man can confront reality, deal with the real world:

> Now, from the Gates of Hercules we flood
>
> Westward, westward till the barbarous brine
> Whelms us to the tired land where tasseling corn,
> Fat beans, grapes sweeter than muscadine
> Rot on the vine: in that land were we born.

Typically the good life, the life of order, purpose, achievement, assumes an agrarian image, since for Tate it is that kind of existence that affords man the serenity and contentment that he seeks.

Tate's agrarianism is that of an image of the life man should desire, a life imbued with tradition, conviction, belief. Modern man, habituated to the materialism of his own chaotic experience, is denied any such purposefulness. Tate's allegiance to Agrarianism was a commitment to the search for order and meaning, an assertion of the primacy of religious and aesthetic values over those of the modern marketplace. In his later writings his interests turned from Southern history and Agrarianism to more specifically religious themes, culminating in his own conversion to the Roman Catholic Church. Throughout his literary career, both in prose and poetry he has dealt with the plight of dehumanized modern man, and the consequences of his spiritual fragmentation, with the contrasting image of the good life being first agrarian and historical, and later Catholic and religious. Almost always the perspective from which the observer has looked has been squarely that of modern man, whether Southerner or not, suffering from the consequences of unbelief. The intensity of Tate's commitment to that perspective has produced poetry of great strength and pathos.

Robert Penn Warren's lyric poetry, like Allen Tate's, depicts the condition of modern man suffering from unbelief, but his poems are if anything more private than Tate's, less social in their conception. Tate's modern man is emblematic of modern society, which suffers from its failure to discover religious foundations for its action. It is "*we* who count *our* days and bow / *Our* heads with a commemorial woe." One is always conscious of the social function. Warren's modern man, however, is entirely isolated within the society, and suffers only his own private agonies. There are no watchers at cemetery gates in his poems, for even that is an action with public as well as private implications. There are only solitary individuals discovering their own predicament, for the most part devoid of the responsibility for any historical or social representation. His people are locked in with their loneliness; it is not a mode of thought with them, as it perhaps is with Tate's watcher at the cemetery gate, but a literal fact, a condition of being.

The function of the agrarian image for Warren is as an environment in which man can most clearly discern his plight in time. This plight is not importantly social, though one might make some social observations about the way in which the poet sees the plight. But Warren does not make them. It is the condition of being mortal that interests him. Growing fields, harvest time, season prodigality serve to remind him of mortal transience. Of "Croesus in Autumn" he writes:

> Should then gruff Croesus on the village bench
> Lament the absolute gold of summer gone?
>
> Though this grey guy be no Aurelius
> Surveying the ilex and the latin vine,
> He might consider a little piteous
> The green and fatal tribe's decline.

In the poem entitled "Calendar" the winter season likewise gives notice of mortality:

> The days draw in:
> Southward, the red suns trim
> Daily, and dim, and spin
> Their bleakening paradigm.
> Summer has been.

The onset of autumn causes the poet to think of the dead, and he asks whether any meaning still remains for their former existence, and whether those now alive will in their turn come to signify anything.

In the seven-part poem "Kentucky Mountain Farm," Warren utilizes the image of hills and mountain rocks to remind men of the paltriness of mortal effort. The rocks of the opening section rebuke men for their act of will and possessiveness involved in springtime ploughing and planting:

> quit yourself as stone and cease
> To break the weary stubble-field for seed;
> Let not the naked cattle bear increase,
> Let barley wither and the bright milkweed.
> Instruct the heart, lean men, of a rocky place
> That even the little flesh and fevered bone
> May keep the sweet sterility of stone.

The fact is that Warren's poetry contains little or no imaging of an agrarian existence, whether Southern or otherwise, as constituting a method of achieving the good life. Its function in Warren's poetry is rather that it enables the human being to visualize his plight more clearly than a social mirror might do. Warren sees man as essentially a phenomenon of nature, belonging in nature. The condition of being human, however, has brought about his alienation from nature, which leads him to question his existence, to become aware of his compromised fate. Nature is the norm; and man, by virtue of his intelligence, has been estranged from it. In "Pondy Woods" a Negro fleeing from a lynch mob is instructed by buzzards that

> we maintain our ancient rite,
> Eat the gods by day and prophesy by night.
> We swing against the sky and wait;
> You seize the hour, more passionate
> Than strong, and strive with time to die—
> With time, the beaked tribe's astute ally.

Man's human position renders him more complex and introspective, and sets him to covet what the other phenomena of the natural world do not think to desire: meaning for his existence, a secure place in time, lasting accomplishment. To this presumption nature serves as a rebuke. Nature in its passivity is seen as far more enduring, far more complete than man, as in the poem "The Last Metaphor," in which a man goes out to look at the winter landscape:

> Assuredly the planet's tilt will bring
> The accurate convulsion of the year—
> The budding leaf, the green, and then the sere,
> After winter burst the fetid spring.
>
> After April and the troubled sod
> Fell summer on us with its deathly sheaf,
> Autumnal ashes then and the brittle leaf
> Whereunder fructified the crackling pod.
>
> Now flat and black the trees stand on the sky
> Unreminiscent of the year's frail verdure.
> Purged of the green that kept so fatal tenure
> They are made strong; no leaf clings mortally.

All warmth and quickness must pass, slipping away with mortality, and the only wisdom is that of birth, growth, death; further search than that for purposiveness is certain to be disappointed.

For Warren, then, the agrarian image is an assertion of the supremacy of dumb nature, the massive reality of the natural world as contrasted with the doubt, the ignorance of thinking men with their pathetic searching for values beyond those of nature. In this respect Warren seems almost Emersonian, but without the earlier poet's easy optimism about cosmic unity and Transcendental purpose. It is in nature that man confronts the ultimates. He is essentially *of* nature, one of its phenomena, but cut off from it now. The homeward trek of the protagonist of "The Ballad of Billie Potts" is depicted as one of the most elementary of actions in life, true of all living creatures. Each living thing struggles without success to escape the limitations of time, to find some meaning for its life by going back to its beginnings, hoping somehow to discover its true identity, the self that existed when young and seemingly independent of time's law of decline and fall:

> The bee knows, and the eel's cold ganglia burn,
> And the sad head lifting to the long return,
> Through brumal deeps, in the great unsolsticed coil,
> Carries its knowledge, navigator without star,
> And under the stars, pure in its clamorous toil,
> The goose hoots north where the starlit marshes are,
> The salmon heaves at the falls, and wanderer, you
> Heave at the great fall of Time, and, gorgeous, gleam
> In the powerful arc, and anger and outrage like dew,
> In your plunge, fling, and plunge to the thunderous
> stream:
> Back to the silence, back to the pool, back
> To the high pool, motionless, and the unmurmuring
> dream.

History for Warren is a record of man's individual efforts to assert his identity in time. At no point in his lyric poetry does Warren set up the history of the Old South as a corrective to modern experience. His agrarianism consists, so far as his poetry (and even, I think, his fiction) is concerned, primarily of his belief in the superior version of reality afforded by natural and rural life. Modern man is out of place, and his estrangement from nature is a sign of it. That is all; no more than that.

Elsewhere Warren has spoken of the past as "a rebuke to the present; ... it's a better rebuke than any dream of the future. It's a better rebuke because you can see what some of the costs were, what frail virtues were achieved in the past by frail men." Nashville Agrarianism was for him "a protest ... against a kind of dehumanizing and disintegrating effect on your notion of what an individual person could be." But it will be noted that these are relative values; the ultimate questions remain unresolved. Typically Warren's historical personages are not heroes, except by virtue of the boldness of their efforts to assert themselves and the resulting catastrophe of their failure to do so. This is true both of Warren's poetry and his fiction. In "The Ballad of Billie Potts" pioneers come into the wilderness of Kentucky and proceed to recapitulate their human culpability. In the long narrative poem "Brother to Dragons" the dream of Thomas Jefferson is analyzed and shown to be flawed, just as that of modern man is flawed. In *World Enough and Time* the life of nineteenth-century Kentucky is marked by the same kind of greed and evasion of responsibility as that of turn-of-the-century Kentucky in *Night Rider,* and modern-day Kentucky in *The Cave.* The achievements of Willie Stark in *All the King's Men* are doomed from the beginning by the very conditions of their achievement; and so on, in each of Warren's works. Man is human, and therefore mortal and sinful. In the wilderness, in nature, man can come to his closest awareness of his ultimate limitations.

Warren's version of frontier life is greatly different from that of Donald Davidson in "The Tall Men" and others of the older Fugitive's poems. Davidson's Tennessee backwoodsmen are, by virtue of their primitive simplicity, free of the pettiness and compromised fate of modern man. Warren's pioneers are revealed as men who face the same problems and limitations as modern men. Their pioneering status, away from urban society, merely makes their difficulties come into sharper focus. In Warren's poetry, environment finally matters very little; wherever he lives, man must confront his own identity.

His agrarians are not virtuous husbandmen; there is little of the pastoral corrective in them. Where John Crowe Ransom writes lovingly of gentle, mannered farmers, and sees the agrarian existence as the most civilized of lives, Warren's men in nature are anguished mortals caught in time, for whom the stony fields of winter are withering reminders of human transience, and the forest a place where the crimes of culpable humanity may be re-enacted.

Warren was the youngest of the four poets. Born in 1905, he was seven years the junior of Tate, who was born in 1899. Both poets were undergraduate students at Vanderbilt University in the years just after the First World War. Ransom and Davidson, on the other hand, were veterans of that war, and were members of the Vanderbilt faculty in the Fugitive days. Ransom was born in 1888, Davidson in 1893. This difference, it seems to me, is of some significance. For we have seen that, especially during the years when Nashville Agrarianism was in full vogue, the two older poets were able to make a full historical equation between the good life and the Old South, one that was largely free of the bleakly ironic qualifications in Warren's poetic image of agrarianism. And though Tate, who would seem to stand midway between the two positions, could image the life of the Old South in terms of its superior efficacy for human beings, he nevertheless seemed to view it as a modern, from a pathetically impossible distance. One has the feeling that for Ransom and Davidson, Southern agrarianism was still something they could imagine as actually *attainable,* in the strategic sense at least. For Tate, in his poetry at any rate, it was far more remote, while for Warren it was little more than an attitude toward experience. Both Tate and Warren cast their lot, so far as poetic strategy is concerned, fully with the compromised moderns; the modern predicament is *their* predicament. Not so Ransom; he remains a gentleman of the old school, though skeptically aware, as in "Captain Carpenter," of the quixotic aspects of his position. And as for Davidson, there is no doubt as to where his allegiances lie. The vantage point of his poems is not that of a modern suffering from the loss of a tradition; he assumes the tradition, and he urges the moderns back to it. "Rush out into the night," he advises his fellow citizens:

> take nothing with you,
> Only your naked selves, your naked hearts.
> Fly from the wrath of fire to the hills
> Where water is and the slow peace of time.

For all four poets, Agrarianism performed the function of a usable poetic myth. I do not mean by this that it was something divorced from all reality. Myths are by no means counterfeits for reality, but indeed may often contribute to and serve as an ordering pattern for much of the experience of real life. Nor in so saying am I attempting a judgment, one way or the other, of the political, social, or economic efficacy of Nashville Agrarianism. Rather, I would emphasize the imaginative function of Agrarianism in the poetry of these four distinguished Southern writers. It enabled them, as poets, to regulate their experience, to bring together in a controlling image some of the diverse insight and sense-data of their lives. For Donald Davidson, Agrarianism has been a method for undertaking a poetic critique of the estate of man in the modern South. For John Crowe Ransom, it constituted an image of the good, harmonious life of gentleness and dignity, in which men might best cope with their mortal condition. For Allen Tate, it provided an image of the kind of life in which action was possible and conviction attainable. For Robert Penn Warren, it furnished a superior index to reality, a condition whereby man could confront his true self. For all of them it permitted a signal criticism of the life they saw around them, an assertion of design and harmony, a rebuke to some of the disarray of twentieth-century industrial society. Intimately associated with the society into which they had been born and grew to manhood, it took for its image the rural experience of that community and occasioned a far-ranging commentary on the Southern past and present. Thus the Agrarian image lies inseparably within their work, not merely as codified or programmed in their topical manifesto for the South, but as given the artistic dignity and the imaginative order of poetry.

8

WILLIAM STYRON:
Notes on a
Southern Writer
in Our Time

In 1951 a young Virginian, William Styron, published his first novel. Entitled *Lie Down in Darkness*, it was the story of a young woman whose existence grew increasingly desperate until finally she took her own life. The novel was received with considerable acclaim, and reviewers prophesied a distinguished future for its author.

In an interview with David Dempsey, Styron readily admitted that he had first begun *Lie Down in Darkness* immediately following an intense reading of the novels of William Faulkner. And indeed, there were more than a few obvious similarities to Faulkner's fiction, notably with *The Sound and the Fury*. Both novels were set in the South. In both there were a family with an alcoholic father, a selfish mother, and several children, one of them mentally retarded. Both had protagonists who wandered about a city far away from home, clutching a timepiece, before jumping to their deaths. Both had faithful Negro servants who went to church to mourn the disintegration of their white folks. Another Faulkner novel, *As I Lay Dying*, was built about a family's journey to inter a coffin. In *Lie Down in Darkness* a family's

185

trip to the cemetery to inter a coffin provides the frame for the novel. And so on.

All the same, Styron's novel was not simply warmed-over Faulkner. For one thing, it had a contemporaneity to it, a sense of dealing with moderns in the modern world, that is not present in Faulkner. For Faulkner's attempts to use the contemporary urban milieu to create fiction, notably in the last two volumes of the Snopes trilogy, have been melodramatic and unsatisfactory. By contrast, Styron's novel was set convincingly in a contemporary setting, and was fully of the present moment in its concerns and attitudes. Where so much fiction by younger Southern writers seemed like inferior Faulkner, Styron's talent was recognizably his own; and as with the better Faulkner novels, it had the sense of *mattering*, of dealing with characters who definitely stood for something as human beings. Nor was it composed with the terse understatement typical of so much present-day American fiction. It had the high rhetoric, the sounding language, of the best fiction of Faulkner, Wolfe, and Warren.

Here, then, was a novelist who seemed to write squarely within the Southern tradition, and yet was definitely his own man. He was, furthermore, quite young—only twenty-five when his first novel appeared —and he obviously possessed the kind of stylistic mastery emblematic of the truly gifted writer. There was no apprehension of his first novel's having been a fluke, depending for its impact on a lucky combination of topical subject matter and the author's momentary psychological attitude, as was true of a novel such as James Jones's *From Here to Eternity*. The novelist who could write *Lie Down in Darkness*, one felt, could and probably would follow it with other novels of similar or higher caliber. This opinion was confirmed a year later when

Styron published a novella, *The Long March,* a vigorous tale of Marine reservists called back to duty. It too bore the mark of the writer thoroughly in control of his craft.

What happened then was very strange. For almost a full decade, William Styron did not publish another novel. Though rumors of a new work in progress recurred, year after year went by with no new fiction by Styron. Yet paradoxically, instead of gradually dropping from sight in public reputation as novels by other good writers were published and achieved recognition, as one might expect to happen to the author of a good first novel who did not produce additional work, William Styron's stock kept right on rising. On the strength of that one novel and the novella, he came to enjoy the kind of literary prestige that few other writers commanded. Critics habitually referred to him as one of the handful of really distinguished novelists of his generation. He was interviewed, quoted, repeatedly cited and discussed. For the better part of ten years he possessed a reputation that the author of a half-dozen good novels might well envy.

Lie Down in Darkness was a good book, and everything that was said about it in the way of the augury it held was justified. But good as it was, one is hard put to explain the extraordinary growth of Styron's reputation in terms of it. It was no *Look Homeward, Angel* or *The Sound and the Fury.* It was surely not, for its time and place, the kind of novel that *Sister Carrie* had been during the 1900's. To an extent it was derivative. It had flaws aplenty. Though it thoroughly warranted its author's being marked as a man to watch, a potentially important novelist, it was after all only a single, well-written, medium-length novel, and not a sustained body of literary work. So that one might ask why its author, during the 1950's, gained the astonishing reputation he enjoyed. Was it something else besides the book itself? One of Styron's contemporaries, Norman Mailer, jealously hinted as much in *Advertisements for Myself*, suggesting that it was Styron's own doing. "Styron has spent years oiling every literary lever and power which could help him on his way, and there are medals waiting for him in the mass-media," Mailer wrote. Exactly how Styron managed this feat Mailer did not bother to explain.

In any event, the reputation was there, and it outran the novel, with the result that when in 1960 Styron did bring out a second novel, what happened might have been expected. *Set This House on Fire* was treated to a torrent of critical abuse the like of which has seldom been seen in our time. On all sides it was roundly condemned. If one believed most of the review media, it was almost inconceivable that any novelist could have produced as bad a work as William Styron had done on his second try. The Most Promising Young Novelist Of His Generation was thoroughly denounced. The popular critics and the academic reviewers seemed to compete in the rage and intensity of their abuse, and not content with demolishing *Set This House on Fire*, some went back and decided that *Lie Down in Darkness* was not really so good, either.

Was *Set This House on Fire* really so bad as everybody said it was? Not at all, I think. In fact, it was quite a good book. Like its predecessor it had flaws, perhaps more vulnerable ones, but in almost every way it was a more ambitious, more deeply perceptive work. It was a novel such as no other writer of Styron's generation could have produced; it contained some of the best writing of its day. But if this is so, then what explains its devastatingly hostile reception? Why was it singled out for such a barrage?

The answer, I think, is to be found in the *kind* of book

that *Lie Down in Darkness* was, and the reasons why that novel, in contrast to the second book, enjoyed such a stunning success. It has to do with the difference between the kind of book that *Lie Down in Darkness seemed* to be, and the kind of book it really was. For when it first appeared it seemed to be something very different, and much more familiar, than what it actually was; and the reasons for this have to do in large part with Southern literature from Faulkner onward. The history of Styron's two novels is closely tied in with what Southern writing has been during the past several decades, and what it can and might be in the future. I want now to discuss Styron's work in this light. For what is involved, I believe, is not only the history of one young novelist's career and reputation, but the whole question of the continuation of a literary mode into a new generation. I am not talking about "influences," nor am I concerned importantly with cultural history as such. Rather I shall seek to deal, by inference at least, with the deepest and most elementary relationships between a book and its times, between art and culture, between one writer who comes from a particular region and the writers of that region who preceded him. And without claiming for a moment that the concerns I shall be examining are the *conscious* concerns either of writer, or region, or reader, I shall seek to show what, in William Styron's own time, which is ours as well, it means to be a "Southern" writer.

The central character in *Lie Down in Darkness* is a young woman, Peyton Loftis. Born of a well-to-do Tidewater Virginia family, she grows up in the seaport city of Port Warwick. Her father, Milton Loftis, is a lawyer. Once he had political ambitions, but over the years he has become much more interested in his golf game and in social drinking. Helen Loftis, Peyton's mother, is the child of a sadistic, puritanical army officer, who has left her a substantial fortune. Peyton is the older of two daughters; the second child, Maudie, is mentally defective. Milton Loftis is inordinately fond of Peyton, and far too indulgent. He cannot bear to jeopardize her affection for him, even momentarily, by denying her anything she demands. By contrast, Helen Loftis is highly resentful of her daughter's hold over Milton, and at crucial moments her jealousy is revealed in words and acts of great cruelty. The older Helen grows, the harder her personality becomes. Milton, meanwhile, becomes infatuated with another woman, Dollie Bonner, who gives him the idolatry and the softness that his wife will not provide.

After a violent scene with her mother, Peyton goes off to school at a fashionable Virginia women's college, and never really returns home to live, though several times she tries and fails. Her life becomes increasingly unhappy. At crucial junctures Milton fails to provide her with the guidance and firmness she needs in a parent, while Helen denies her the motherly affection she craves. When Maudie sickens and dies, Helen accuses Peyton of causing her death. Several times a reconciliation between mother and daughter is attempted, but Helen's insane jealousy always wrecks it, despite the advice and encouragement that an Episcopal minister, Carey Carr, attempts to give to Helen.

Finally Peyton goes to live in New York, where she falls in love with a Jewish painter, Harry Miller. In a final effort to gain her mother's love, she comes home to Port Warwick for the wedding ceremony, but just when all seems to be going well, the mother's obsession and hatred are viciously reasserted, and the day ends in bitterness and misery. Peyton and her husband return to New York, and Peyton thereupon steadily destroys her own marriage by continually "testing" Harry's love through acts of selfishness and cruelty. At length she begins to sleep with other men, whereupon the tormented Harry forces himself to leave her; and, when a final, pathetic attempt at reconciling him fails, Peyton commits suicide by leaping from a building. Her body is brought home to Port Warwick and buried. Thus the plot of *Lie Down in Darkness*.

First let it be reiterated that it is a *good* novel; there is no doubt of that. Styron's sense of psychological complication is such that the descent of Peyton Loftis into darkness is convincingly motivated. Just as in Faulkner's *The Sound and the Fury*, the novel is an account of the failure of love. Had Milton Loftis' love for his daughter been less selfish, so that the father had been willing to incur his daughter's momentary displeasure by insisting that she do what was right rather than what she wished to do; had Helen Loftis' firmness been the product of genuine love and understanding for Peyton and not a hypocritical mask for jealousy and hostility; then Peyton might have grown up into someone who is able to love in her turn. But Milton sought in Peyton the affection that Helen did not provide him, and Helen struck out at Peyton in order to punish Milton. Thus Peyton has known for love only indulgence on the one hand and poorly masked jealousy on the other; and when she marries, she seeks a relationship on just those terms. She demands and must have continual forgiveness, and the acts she commits in her quest for proof of such forgiveness are too reprehensible for her husband to condone. Along with this goes an insane jealousy, in which she magnifies small failures on her husband's part into evidence of monstrous unfaithfulness; no sooner does she feel that Harry has forgiven her for her own misdeeds than she begins at once to berate him unreasonably and psychotically for imaginary infidelities. Thus Harry must play the part of forgiving father on the one hand, and erring husband on the other, neither of which roles he merits. In psychiatric terms, Peyton must first re-enact her relationship with her father, and then her mother's relationship with her father. It is too much, finally, for Harry to accept, if he is to retain his own sanity. Whereupon, denied the only kind of love that she can recognize, Peyton takes her own life. A father's weakness, a mother's cruelty have brought about a daughter's destruction.

Set against a background of upper-middle-class, urban Southern society, the story is one of real dramatic tension. Peyton's struggle to save herself, more rending because of her own recognition of her plight, deeply engages the reader's sympathies. Intelligent, compassionate, with a great capacity for loving and being loved, she is doomed to frustration and pain, and when finally she succumbs to the forces that are dragging her downward, there is a genuine tragedy in her fall. Similarly, the characterization of Milton Loftis is a moving picture of weakness and ineffectual love. Milton too is aware of his plight, and his efforts to save himself and his family are pathetically moving. Helen Loftis, I think, is somewhat less effectively drawn; the psychological motivations for her conduct are never fully apparent, and must only be conjectured. The role of the family's Negro servants is too obviously contrived. Unlike Dilsey and her family in Faulkner's *The Sound and the Fury*, Ella and La Ruth in *Lie Down in Darkness* do not fill the dramatic position in the fortunes of the Loftis family that would justify Styron's use of them as tragic chorus.

Despite such flaws, however, *Lie Down in Darkness* is a successful, well-written work of art. As a first novel it surely justified those who saw in its author a writer of much promise, who might be expected to produce other works of distinguished fiction. To begin with, it was decidedly moving, and had genuinely tragic overtones; and it was the first novel to appear in the postwar period by a young writer of whom that could be said. Not one of the other postwar writers had been able to produce such a book. The best of their novels were ponderous, naturalistic works such as Mailer's *The Naked and the Dead*, and Jones's *From Here to Eternity*, both the products of writers of obvious passion, but written, I think, somewhat crudely. Both were war novels. Of the two Mailer's was the better written, but much of its power came out of its author's, and its readers', detestation of war and military life. In Jones's case that was about *all* that could be said for his book. In each instance a sense of civilized outrage, on the part of novelist and reader, contributed much to the success of the work.

By contrast, Styron's book was not a war novel. Its intensity was attained by the author's fictional craftsmanship, his talent at characterization, his insight into the tension and desperation of a modern, Godforsaken urban existence. Such a novel had not appeared in some time, and the public was hungry for a writer who could produce more. It was thus quick to hail *Lie Down in Darkness*, and to hope and expect that Styron would be able to follow with other and even better books. Furthermore, in the decade that followed its publication, no other competitor appeared in sight. Good as Saul Bellow's *The Adventures of Augie March*, J. D. Salinger's *The Catcher in the Rye*, and other novels by writers such as Nelson Algren, Bernard Malamud, and Herbert Gold were, their works seemed infinitely more private, less public in their dimensions than Styron's one novel did. There was not the sense of any of these authors speaking so directly to the experience of his times as Styron did in *Lie Down in Darkness*. Peyton Loftis' downfall seemed to say something about the day and age that the more limited predicaments of the heroes of other novels did not. Styron alone seemed capable some day of producing really important literary work, novels that could stand up to the best books of the prewar novelists.

More specifically, *Lie Down in Darkness* seemed very much in the Faulknerian mode. Not that it was derivative; quite the contrary. There had been and would continue to be numerous Southern novels that *were* derivative, that seemed to be imitation Faulkner. William Humphrey's *Home from the Hill*, for example, was almost a parody of the Yoknapatawpha novels, until halfway through when it left the primitive milieu of such stories as "The Bear" and descended into modern melodrama. The thing about Styron's novel was that, while it seemed to come out of the same literary and cultural tradition that had made Faulkner's fiction so profoundly moving, it created its own kind of tragedy, and did not rely on the secondhand insights of Faulkner and his contemporaries. Styron, in other words, seemed to be doing what good writers have always done: he used his tradition, rather than let himself be used by it.

That literary mode, it must be emphasized, had produced much of the finest American fiction of the twentieth century. It had avoided the sodden determinism of the naturalistic school of Dreiser, Dos Passos, Steinbeck, and Farrell, and had been able to achieve fiction in which human beings could be made to behave as free agents, able to pit their wills against their society and the limitations of their mortality in meaningful dispute. It had been able, too, to depict men in a necessary and inescapable relationship to society, so that the conflict between the private conscience and public circumstance could seem real. The characters of Faulkner, Wolfe, Warren, Lytle, and the others were not in arbitrary, casual contact with the world around them; they were inescapably a part of society, and any lasting isolation from society constituted a tragic condition. If society was hostile, it was never indifferent. Furthermore, these men's characters were not creatures of the moment; they existed in time, and the past affected them in crucial ways. Finally, the basis of their morality and the sources of their behavior were not only social and biological but religious as well; their transgressions were not ultimately against men, but through men against God.

When *Lie Down in Darkness* appeared, the Southern literary mode had been the productive force of distinguished fiction for almost three decades. It had set up certain expectations on the part of the reading public. The reader had become, as it were, habituated to conceiving of tragedy along certain lines. When Styron's novel came along, therefore, it fell heir to a by-then familiar literary tradition, and was read in terms of that tradition. Here was another fine Southern novel, with the implied promise that the author would be able to sustain and develop his talent within the accepted mode. The Southern literary tradition was thus manifestly continuing into the postwar generation.

This seemed all the more important since, up until then, and in the years immediately following the publication of *Lie Down in Darkness* as well, no other Southern novel by a younger writer seemed to hold out such promise. Truman Capote's *Other Voices, Other Rooms* had been too exotic, too private to allow one to feel that its author would be able to produce major work. Carson McCullers' fiction, interesting though it was, seemed limited in its scope; it stopped short of the tragic, contenting itself with a poignant exploration of surfaces. Flannery O'Connor's decidedly promising talent was limited in range and breadth; it seemed to fulfill itself adequately only in the short-story form. Certainly James Agee's *A Death in the Family* was an excellent and quite original work, containing passages of great beauty and force; but its mode was not that of high tragedy, and besides, Agee had been dead for two years when his novel appeared. To be sure, Robert Penn Warren was obviously of major stature, even though he never seemed to repeat the achievement of *All the King's Men;* while Andrew Lytle's *The Velvet Horn* was both its author's best work to date and as good a novel as almost any written by a Southern writer. But these two, like Faulkner, were members of the previous generation of Southern writers, the generation of the high renascence. So for that matter were Eudora Welty and Caroline Gordon; both had been publishing fiction since before the Second World War.

In the post-World-War-II generation of Southern writers, then, Styron stood alone in his achievement, and in the nature of that achievement. If the Southern literary mode was to retain its importance in contemporary American literature, William Styron seemed to be the writer who would lead the way.

Assuredly, I do not mean that the average reader was aware of all this when he encountered *Lie Down in Darkness,* though I suspect that many reviewers were, and to a greater extent than they perhaps realized. But I do think that when Styron's novel was published, it appeared to fit into a literary mode that a generation of excellent novelists had educated the reading public to understand, so that the reader was able to bring to *Lie Down in Darkness* an expectation and a frame of reference that the novel seemed to fill. This made possible a kind of cumulative public response that, at the time of publication and during the decade that followed, helped to give the novel its vogue, and contributed greatly to the nature and extent of Styron's reputation. Here, one felt, was another first-rate writer in the familiar Southern style, one seemingly able to create genuine literary tragedy. And that it *was* tragedy he had managed, there could be no doubt; had not Faulkner, Warren and the others already done just that, and in the same way?

Let me quote from one of Styron's more perceptive critics, John W. Aldridge. Writing in 1956, Aldridge spoke of the "Southern elements of the novel—particularly the elements of fundamentalist religion, regional guilt, and the contrast of races," as being "so powerful that if anything they seem excessive to the motives of the characters and perpetually to overcome them." He noted Helen Loftis' "Southern gentlewoman madness" and "the whole Southern blood-guilt." He remarked that "it is significant that it is after she marries and goes North that Peyton becomes overtly psychotic." Or lest I appear to single out Mr. Aldridge, who I believe has somewhat different thoughts on the matter now, let me quote from a review that I wrote of *Lie Down in Darkness* shortly after it appeared in 1951. I find, rather to my astonishment, that I did not have much to say about Styron's Southernness as such, but even so the criteria I used for the evaluation were clearly taken out of the familiar experience of the Southern novel. I remarked that "the Loftises want something, and none of them knows what it is. What they want is a purpose, a reason for being. In the final chapter Mr. Styron contrasts their aimlessness with the happy faith of their Negro servant, who is untroubled by acedia. The servant believes, and on the foundations of that belief is able to conduct a satisfying life." Note that this is an accurate description of the role of Dilsey in *The Sound and the Fury*—but not at all, as I shall try to show, of the servants in Styron's novel.

The question I should like to propose now, a decade after *Lie Down in Darkness* was first published, and with the hindsight that comes of having observed the progress of Styron's literary fortunes over ten years, is whether such inferences as Mr. Aldridge and I made, and those of many another critic as well, were accurate. Was *Lie Down in Darkness* a novel of originality, but one written essentially within the accustomed Southern mode, achieving its tragic force in approximately the same manner as the novels of Faulkner, Warren, and others in the Southern tradition? Or did the "Southernness" only *appear* to be important, and was *Lie Down in Darkness* in important and vital respects quite another *kind* of novel than those of Faulkner and the others, significantly different in its version of human experience, its conception of society and of people, so that the familiar Southern motifs were considerably less important than had seemed true at first reading? In other words, had Mr. Aldridge and I and various other critics reviewed William Styron's novel, or had we in effect reviewed a new novel by William Faulkner?

Earlier I noted some obvious resemblances between *Lie Down in Darkness* and Faulkner's *The Sound and the Fury*. Since the latter novel is one of its author's two or three greatest works, and since the dimensions of the tragedy of the Compson family are so central to the Southern mode—were instrumental, indeed, in fashioning that very mode—I want to compare the manner in which that novel realizes its tragic potentialities with the way in which Styron's novel does.

The Sound and the Fury is concerned with the collapse of the Compson dynasty in the modern world.

Once great, the family has fallen upon evil days, and the novel describes its death throes and final spiritual extinction. The failures of the fathers have been visited upon the children. Jason Compson III drowns his days in alcoholic futility; his wife is a self-pitying hypochondriac who prattles about her past while failing to give her children the love they need. Quentin Compson holds forlornly to an outmoded concept of Compson honor, and when its inadequacy becomes apparent, commits suicide by drowning. Candace Compson seeks to find in promiscuity the affection denied her by her mother. Jason IV survives by abandoning all pretense of Compson honor and becoming a Snopes in everything but name, a vicious, embittered, smalltime speculator and defrauder. The degradation of the family is symbolized by Benjy, whose helpless imbecility represents the dead end of a century of family tradition.

At first glance *Lie Down in Darkness* would seem to involve a greatly similar situation. Milton Loftis is a father who numbs his futility in alcoholism; indeed, his own father had a way of talking that was much like Jason Compson III's manner of addressing Quentin. Like Mrs. Compson, Helen Loftis is self-pitying and selfish, and takes out her frustration on her daughter. Peyton Loftis, like Candace Compson, turns to promiscuity in her need for affection, and like Quentin Compson she walks about a Northern city carrying a timepiece before seeking the oblivion of suicide. And the mentally defective Maudie is surely the Loftis counterpart of Benjy Compson. In both families, too, there are faithful Negro retainers who mourn the downfall of their white families.

Yet are the situations really similar? Like the Compsons, the Loftises are the modern descendants of a once-distinguished Southern family. But the implications of this in *Lie Down in Darkness* are very different. The Loftises exist entirely *in the present*. Milton Loftis' alcoholic stupor is not importantly the result of changed times. There is no outdated concept of Loftis honor, no heritage of former leadership to be lived down. Milton is not the sot he is because of the impossible burden of the past; his failure is entirely the result of personal weakness. His spinelessness must be blamed on his own character, not on the decadence of a fallen dynasty. Likewise, Helen Loftis is no Mrs. Compson; she is no morose worshiper of her family's past, but a twisted psychotic, whose sin is not hypochondria but insane jealousy. And her daughter Peyton's tragedy is not the result of a massively decadent family past, but of the personal failure of her parents. Though both Peyton Loftis and the young Compsons seek hopelessly for love and strength, the causes of the absence of those commodities are very different; with Peyton they lie in her parents' personal shortcomings, while with Quentin and Candace they are the result of the degradation of a dynasty in their time. They are *dynastic*, not personal. They are caused by *history*.

The difference is all important. For where the downfall of the Compson family symbolizes the crash of formerly great dynasties in time, and the central tragedy consists of the downfall of a once-great family, the death of Peyton Loftis in *Lie Down in Darkness* involves no such sense of the collapse of generations, no important implication that the sins of the dynastic past have caused the debacle of the present. In other words, in Styron's novel the historical dimension is almost entirely absent. Peyton is not the product of a family's and a region's history; she is a young woman whose own parents' failures rob her of the hope of happiness. What she is and is not can be blamed on Milton and Helen, and, in any important respect, no further back than that. Where Faulkner created a Greek-like tragedy, reminiscent of the fall of the House of Atreus, Styron produced a domestic tragedy that had no element of fated dynastic downfall about it.

We can see this clearly if we compare Maudie Loftis and Benjy Compson. The idiot Compson child is the proof of a family's downfall and disgrace, the barren fruit of exhausted loins; Maudie Loftis is only an unfortunately marred child. We do not see in her plight the judgment of fate on a dynastic collapse; she is not symbolic of the guilt of generations. She is a poor, pathetic little girl, bereft of her faculties, and nothing more. Missing entirely is any kind of implied commentary on family ambition and ancestral failures; Maudie's idiocy is the chance result of a biological freak. Not history, but biology, is to blame.

If we think upon the meaning of all this, we will recognize, I think, something essential about *Lie Down in Darkness*. And that is, that it is not a community tragedy but a private one. The relationship of the Loftises to the city in which they reside is vastly different from that of the Compsons to the county of Yoknapatawpha. Upperclass Port Warwick society, as seen in the occasions upon which it gathers in *Lie Down in Darkness*, is pleasure-seeking, decadent, even dissolute. But it is not anachronistic. It is not a holdover from a better day. There is little sense that what has happened to Milton, Helen, and Peyton Loftis is symbolic of the historic decline and fall of the Tidewater Virginia gentry. Port Warwick society is urban, cosmopolitan; it clings to no historical image of itself and its role. We can, if we wish, *infer* the death of the aristocratic tradition from its present condition, but any such inference will be based on our extraliterary historical knowledge, not on the manner in which Styron actually builds his tragedy. There is no concept of Loftis role within the community, no presumption of leadership that is no longer respected. Milton Loftis had political ambitions at one time, but not because he felt a sense of an expected family role, of habitual function of command. It is entirely a matter of personal ambition with him. And when he fails to act on those ambitions, there is no feeling of his having betrayed a public trust, but only of his personal inability to make something of himself.

In short, the Loftises live in Port Warwick, but they are not and were not Port Warwick, in the way that the Compsons once *were* Yoknapatawpha County. If their decadence mirrors that of the community's upper social stratum, it is not the decadence of an historical tradition gone to seed, but that of a very modern, hedonistic segment of urban rich society living without faith and purpose. In *The Sound and the Fury* the emphasis is on an aristocratic family's abandonment of historical role; in *Lie Down in Darkness* it is on the general immorality of modern society. How the society got that way is, whether explicitly or by implication, not part of the story.

Contrast, for example, the description of Quentin Compson's last day at Harvard with Peyton Loftis' last day in New York City. Both are far from the country of their origins. Both are doomed souls. But how different are the implications! Quentin's estrangement from his home *constitutes* his tragedy. His alienation from Yoknapatawpha County is emblematic of his failure to cope with the modern world; he is the ineffective oldest son and heir of the once mighty Compson dynasty, and his isolation is not only one of place, but of time. What Quentin is estranged from is the role of the Compsons as leaders of the community, a role that is vanished in time. Cut off from his tradition, he wanders aimlessly about Cambridge, meditating on his plight, until finally he weights his clothes with lead window sashes and dives from a bridge into nothingness.

With Peyton Loftis, by contrast, we have no sense that her tragedy consists in her isolation from Port Warwick, no feeling that she belongs not in New York but in the community into which she was born, and that she is walking forlornly about the city because of her family's failure to fill its accustomed historical role back home. John W. Aldridge, as we have seen, noted that "it is significant that it is after she marries and goes North that Peyton becomes overtly psychotic." But is this really significant, in any important dramatic sense? It is not because Peyton is unable to go home to Port Warwick that we are distressed; on the contrary, we were rather relieved when we learned that she had departed, and our distress is at her isolation *in* the metropolis, from the husband she loves and who loves her. Is it a matter of New York's having *caused* the appearance of the psychosis in overt form, or was the psychosis already all but present, and was the move to New York only a futile attempt to postpone its imminent onset? Peyton's flight is her one last chance to retrieve her life; and her destruction is fated because of what her parents have been and have failed to be to her, not because of her estrangement from the society into which she was born.

In both novels the cause of the isolation is ultimately spiritual. Both tragedies symbolize the plight of human beings in the modern world. But where Faulkner saw it in historical terms, involving the blood-guilt of generations, Styron saw it in social terms, an indictment of modern society as symbolized by the selfishness and weakness of the Loftis family. In *The Sound and the Fury* a dynasty collapses; in *Lie Down in Darkness* a family breaks up.

Much has been made of the religious implications of Styron's novel. In my review of the novel, as already mentioned, I contrasted the aimlessness of the Loftises with the sturdy faith of their Negro servants, and remarked, rather clumsily, that "the servant believes, and on the foundations of that belief is able to conduct a satisfying life." To be sure, the religious implications are there, but is it as simple a matter as I proposed, that of a mere "contrast of races," to use Mr. Aldridge's phrase? I think not. For Styron does *not* neatly juxtapose the futility of the Episcopal minister Carey Carr's attempt to lead Helen Loftis to true repentance on the one hand, with the magnetic efficacy of Daddy Faith's healing spiritual balm for the Negroes at the riverside in the final chapter. Instead the contrast is much more complicated, and considerably more ironic. For while it is true that Carey Carr's gentle, benevolent brand of modern theology is so lacking in moral force, so watered down in precept, that it cannot persuade Helen Loftis to overcome her jealousy, is Styron actually proposing in its stead the kind of primitive fundamentalism displayed by Daddy Faith and his constituency? Hardly. For Daddy Faith, effectiveness is clearly attributable entirely to the ignorance, the lack of sophistication, the love of flashy showmanship and weakness for dubious hocus-pocus of his audience; Daddy Faith is a faker, a false prophet. "Who loves you, my people?" he asks. "You, Daddy! Daddy Faith! You loves us! You, Daddy!" they shout back. "You, Daddy! Yes, Jesus, you loves us!"

But Daddy Faith certainly is not Jesus Christ; he is in no sense divine; indeed, his establishment is a gaudy parody of all known religions. He is effective in his charlatanry because of the gullibility of his audience. The idea, then, that Styron was criticizing the diluted intellectualism of Carey Carr's religion and its inability to provide ethical guidance for Carey's white parishioners by tellingly contrasting it with the primitive soundness of Daddy Faith's fundamentalism, is a misrepresentation of Styron's attitude. If anything, he seems to be making a much bleaker pessimistic observation, which is that the moral usefulness of religious truth decreases in direct proportion to the increase in the intelligence and sophistication of the believer. The implication is that religion can function effectively as a morality *only* when its communicants are ignorant and superstitious.

Here again the difference between *Lie Down in Darkness* and the comparable occurrence in *The Sound and the Fury* is revealing. The scene in Faulkner's novel in which Dilsey momentarily leaves the Compson household in the throes of its disintegration and takes Benjy to the Negro church to hear the preacher from St. Louis is one of the most dramatic in the novel. But contrast the two preachers. Daddy Faith is a flashy, gaudy showman. The preacher in *The Sound and the Fury*, though no mean performer in the pulpit, has nothing of the humbug about him. Though primitive and untutored, his sermon rings with sincerity, and his congregation is deeply moved. The minister's words speak directly to Dilsey, and she is moved to utter her simple but rending summation of all that has happened to the Compsons:

> "I've seed de first en de last," Dilsey said. "Never you mind me."
> "First en last whut?" Frony said.
> "Never you mind," Dilsey said. "I seed de beginnin, en now I sees de endin."

The point is that Faulkner's presentation of the Negroes at church, though written in dialect and presented in a kind of pastoral simplification, is deadly serious. There is no sense of ironic qualification, no element of condescension involved. The variety of religion is simple, but not ignorant. Unlike Styron, it seems to me, Faulkner *is* contrasting, directly and dramatically, the formless chaos of the white folks with the unlettered but deeply felt faith of Dilsey, and this quality of belief in Dilsey enables her to give to the Compsons some of the love and strength that they themselves cannot attain. In her loyalty, her compassion and faith, Dilsey is clearly superior to her white employers. Dilsey believes, and can act on her belief; believing, she endures, while the Compsons, who have no such firm theological conviction, are doomed to perish.

To recapitulate, then, the apparent resemblance of Styron to Faulkner in respect to certain important aspects of experience is only a surface similarity. Upon closer examination Styron turns out to have a significantly different attitude toward many things. Where Faulkner envisions the disintegration of a leading Southern family as something dynastic, the result of the spiritual and moral exhaustion of generations of aristocratic Southern life, Styron portrays it as being psychological, the result of the personal weaknesses and sins of a father and mother. Faulkner's tragedy is historical; Styron's has no important basis in the past. The failure of the Compsons is the failure of the Southern aristocracy; that of the Loftises is the failure of the effete rich. Faulkner's tragedy is deeply rooted in a region and its history; Styron's takes place in a recognizable place, but its dramatic causes lie almost entirely in the present. For Faulkner the fatal consequence of the breakdown of traditional Southern leadership is to isolate its heirs from their heritage; in Quentin's and Candace Compson's separation from Yoknapatawpha lies the tragedy. In Styron the isolation is not from an accustomed heritage and role, but from society in general, whether in Port Warwick or New York. Thus, while both writers see isolation from human society as tragic, the older writer's conception of society is of something involving a particular locale and region, with a known history, while the younger writer conceives of society in much more general terms. Quentin as a character could properly exist only in Yoknapatawpha County; Peyton might have done as well, if not better, in the metropolis.

In other words, both writers' attitude toward society is the same—they see a man's isolation from it as a violation of his human position; but with Styron this is only an attitude, while for Faulkner the attitude is inextricably connected with a particular society and a particular history, and the very nature of the man is inseparable from the man's historical role within his society. And while, as with Faulkner, Styron's attitude likely is the product of a particular kind of society and a particular history, the specific circumstances and the specific occasion that brought about the attitude are largely missing in Styron's work, while in Faulkner the attitude goes hand in hand with the circumstances that produced it.

That this is an important difference is clear: for the difference, it seems to me, is precisely that between the South in which William Faulkner grew up and that in which William Styron grew up. It is the difference between two separate generations of Southern writers and of Southern life. For the South of the 1900's and 1910's was painfully caught up in the process of breaking away from the old concept of community, the old, fixed patterns of life in a society in which inherited beliefs and accustomed roles played a central part in the conduct of life, in which the individual's identity was supposedly

208 THE FARAWAY COUNTRY

still defined within the community. Faulkner's novels, and in differing ways those of the other writers of his generation, record the breakdown of this older South before the onset of modern urban life. The attitudes toward society, toward history, toward theological and ethical values had been clearly embodied in specific institutions: a particular society with established roles and customs, a specific history, an accepted theology with a revealed ethic. In the growing failure of these specific and concrete institutions to provide order and authority for the human beings who sought to live within and through them, there lay either tragedy or comedy, depending upon the literary imagination concerned with them.

In Styron's South, however, that of the 1920's and 1930's, the process of social dissolution had proceeded much further, and the institutions had ceased importantly to embody the attitudes any more: no longer were there accepted and established roles. The history was no longer a living and concrete reality. And the particular theology could no longer be accepted as gospel truth. To an important degree the attitudes that grew out of these institutions still remained valid, and still do so: a belief that the individual belongs in society, that he is not a creature of the moment, that he needs the authority of religious conviction to guide his conduct. These are indeed present in Styron's novel. They are, however, no more than attitudes; they are not embodied in tangible institutions. And if Styron, as I think, is the leading Southern writer of his generation, and if he is in any important sense representative of his generation, then there would seem to be a significant change in the Southern literary imagination in the present generation, those writers who were born during or shortly after the First World War, growing up in the changing South during the 1920's and 1930's and writing their novels in the years after the Second World War. They would appear to constitute a generation that is much further removed than its predecessors from the concepts of a particular kind of community, of man as a creature of a particular history, and as a creature whose life is ordered by a particular scheme of theological belief.

For Styron's generation of Southern writers, who grew up in a greatly changed South, only the general attitudes, the general ways of looking at human experience, remain real. And what we might expect from these writers, then, is a literature that involves the examination of these attitudes as they survive, or fail to survive, in a very different kind of experience. That, I believe, is what we have in *Lie Down in Darkness:* not a Faulknerian tragedy at all, but a literary exploration of the potentialities of certain surviving attitudes for imparting meaning and order to modern human experience, an experience that by no means is identical with traditional Southern life as described and assumed in the work of the earlier writers.

If all this seems far removed from the accustomed concerns of fiction, think of it in specific terms. What, once again, is the difference between Dilsey at church on the one hand, and the contrast between Carey Carr and Daddy Faith on the other? Is the difference not that Faulkner assumes the reality of the theology, and measures the decadent Compsons against it, while Styron does not assume the theological reality, but instead explores its validity, showing both its failure to possess any meaning for the Loftises, and in the case of their servants, the charlatanry that must accompany the religion for it to succeed? Faulkner is not examining the validity of the theology; Styron is doing precisely that, and his implication that theological conviction would be desirable for the Loftises is the product of an attitude toward religion and society, not because of the theological validity of the particular religion itself.

What Faulkner *is* questioning is the validity of the historical tradition of aristocratic Compson leadership in the twentieth-century South. But here, by contrast, Styron conducts no such examination. He cannot even take such a tradition seriously; what little he presents of it is mouthed by Milton Loftis' aged father, long before the events that constitute the central tragedy of the novel. And Milton's memories of his father bear little dramatic relevance to the condition in which Milton finds himself as an adult. The theme of decline and fall, so far as it relates to a particular historical tradition, does not importantly exist in Styron's novel. By implication he may be said to show the results of the failure of such a tradition, but if we reach such a conclusion it is because of what we know about Southern literature and Southern history, and because of Styron's attitude, but not because Styron gave any dramatic embodiment to the theme of historical decline and fall in his novel, and thus attested to its concrete reality.

And finally, consider again the inescapability of Quentin's relationship to Yoknapatawpha County in *The Sound and the Fury*, as compared with Peyton's to Port Warwick in *Lie Down in Darkness*. Faulkner, it seems to me, *assumes* that Quentin should have a role in the community of his birth, and in Quentin's inability to discover such a role Faulkner sees a commentary on Quentin and on the times. But Styron does not make that assumption at all. He examines Port Warwick, finds it wanting; whereupon he sends Peyton northward. There is no sense of a killing estrangement, no sense that Peyton's failure to find a meaning for her life in the metropolis is due to the fact that she does not belong there, but in Port Warwick. Either kind of community would do for her, New York perhaps better than Port Warwick— and neither kind will do. The trouble is in Peyton, and in her parents' failure, and in crass modern times in general. We do not feel that because Peyton cannot live in Port Warwick there has been an historical betrayal of what the community should have been and what Peyton should have been. What we do feel is that Peyton belongs somewhere, a part of some society. And once again, this is because of the author's attitude toward the individual in society, not because of any inference that there ought to be a community such as Port Warwick presumably used to be and that Peyton ought to have been able to find a role and a meaning for her life within that particular kind of community. Styron's imagination is not wedded to that kind of community, and that kind of person. He does not see the disappearance of either as fated, and therefore tragic.

So far as Southern writing in our time is concerned, then, the question that William Styron's fiction occasions is the whole problem of continuity. If there has been developed over the course of several decades a kind of Southern literary mode, a tradition as it were; then, on the evidence of Styron's books, how is it surviving today? Just what is the relationship between Southern literature as we have hitherto known it, and a Southern writer of a new generation who does not assume the inevitability of a relationship between his characters and the kind of historical community that we think of as Southern, who cannot take seriously the importance of the continuation of a tradition of leadership in the modern South, and who does not measure his characters' ethical and spiritual conviction by their obedience to the authority of a particular kind of Protestant theology? We should have to conclude, I think, that such a writer's relationship to that tradition is significantly different from that of any of the older writers within that mode. We should have to conclude that he is joined to them, insofar as those things are important, principally by his attitude—an assumption on his part that a community role is desirable, that a traditional basis for experience is a good thing, that men without theological conviction live fragmented, chaotic lives—but an assumption not embodied in concrete institutions and shared experiences.

And if, then, it is only a matter of the survival of an attitude, not of the embodiment of the attitude in particular institutions, is not the next order of business the examination of the *assumptions themselves?* Not the institutions, but the assumptions. And insofar as a specific Southern literary tradition is concerned, where does that leave us?

It leaves us, I think, with William Styron's second novel, *Set This House on Fire.* For almost a decade preceding its publication, and on the strength of one good, medium-length novel, Styron was widely held to be America's Most Promising Younger Novelist. I have conjectured as to why this came about—the particular state of the American novel at the time of the appearance of *Lie Down in Darkness;* the emergence of a novelist who could *write,* and not merely relate; the inherited prestige of a particular literary mode into which it seemed to fit so well, a mode that had been notably proficient in producing distinguished fiction, so that the reading public had been educated to respond to the dimensions of that mode. And I suggested that because *Lie Down in Darkness* seemed to fit into that mode, and yet to possess an originality of its own, reviewers and readers were quick to recognize Styron as potentially a very important writer.

In short, it was as if the appearance of *Lie Down in*

Darkness constituted an assurance that the kind of contribution Faulkner, Wolfe, Warren, Welty, and the others had been making to American fiction for two decades and more was not going to dwindle and die, but could flourish for another entire literary generation.

Nine years elapsed, during which time a new novel by Styron was often rumored and once even announced, but without its appearing. Then, in the late spring of 1960, finally came *Set This House on Fire*. Unlike its predecessor, there was nothing tidy and portable about it; it was a big, hulking affair, two hundred thousand words long, the size of *Look Homeward, Angel* almost. It did not take place in Port Warwick, though the narrator came from there. In fact, though it was remembered and related by two men while fishing and reminiscing in Charleston, South Carolina, it did not importantly take place in the South at all, but in New York, Paris, and a small Italian coastal town. None of the customary trappings of the Southern novel was present: there were no Negroes, no First Families, no church services, no blood-guilt of generations, no oversexed Southern matrons. It was thoroughly, completely modern, even cosmopolitan. There were expatriate artists, Italian peasants, Greenwich Village cocktail parties, pornographic orgies, American tourists in European cities and towns, movie-making, Army PX's, philosophical Fascist policemen, and so forth. People quoted Ortega y Gasset and Wilhelm Reich, listened to Buxtehude and *Don Giovanni*, preferred Frankie Laine to Johnny Ray, worried about the decline of American capitalism. And—quite unlike most Southern novels—the protagonists engaged in long, probing psychological analyses of their inner souls, after the manner of Proust and Dostoyevsky. The story told was not at all Faulknerian; it was about a young artist who after a frightening stay in the lower depths won his way back to sanity. It was as if Eugene Gant had gone through the kind of furnace experience that Jack Burden underwent in *All the King's Men*, perhaps—but in Europe, not in Louisiana, and politics and the South were not involved. But to say that is to say very little, for Jack Burden never really ceased to take seriously all manner of verities that Styron's Cass Kinsolving not only flouted but even ignored. Styron's new novel was simply not a "Southern" novel at all, in the way that Southern novels had been written by his predecessors.

The new novel, as I have noted, was straightaway treated to a hostile critical barrage such as few other important works of fiction in our time have received. It was called romantic, melodramatic, pompous, sentimental, inflated, chaotic; it was self-pitying; it was even un-American. To repeat, the Most Promising Younger Novelist of his generation had fallen flat on his face.

The question I asked before was why, if *Set This House on Fire* was as I think a quite respectable novel, it came in for so hostile a reception. And the answer I proposed had to do with the nature of Styron's first novel, *Lie Down in Darkness*. That book had earned its author an impressive reputation, partly on the strength of the kind of novel it had seemed to be. To repeat, it seemed to be "Southern," Faulknerian; it seemed an extension, into our own day, of the Southern tragic mode, to fit into the mode even while giving it an original twist. But in reality Styron's first novel was significantly different; the specific experience that it related was not handled in the traditional way; only the attitudes remained close to the tradition, without their accompanying embodiment in concrete experience.

Set This House on Fire confirmed that break. And this time, there could be no mistaking the difference. By all rights, Styron should have produced in his second book another "typical" Southern tragedy. But he did not. He did not write the kind of book he was supposed to write at all. The novel that he brought forth after nine years of silence was far removed from the familiar mode of Southern fiction. And this, I think, caused a tremendous disappointment.

The nature of that disappointment was all too obvious: this young, talented novelist, so heralded, so praised, had failed to do what was expected of him. He had not continued the literary mode of Faulkner, Wolfe, and the others into the new generation. Seemingly he had veered off in another direction. And the new direction did not permit the familiar kind of tidy, smoothly formed tragedy that *Lie Down in Darkness* had seemed to be. By its very nature it demanded the groping, restless, searching type of novel that Styron produced.

What I am suggesting is that, just as readers and reviewers read *Lie Down in Darkness* as if it were automatically a novel in the Faulknerian mode, and praised it highly for that, they read *Set This House on Fire* with precisely the same expectation, and since this time the novel did not remotely fit the mode at all, they denounced it. Styron, the apparent heir to the best of the Southern literary tradition, had seemingly betrayed that tradition.

Yet had he? I am not so sure of it. It seems to me, rather, that Styron's second novel *was* an extension of the Southern literary imagination into a new generation, was in fact perhaps *the only possible way that the mode could be made to stay alive.* And I believe that, when we look back in retrospect at the first novel, we can see that *Set This House on Fire* was exactly the kind of novel we might have expected Styron to write, if what we took to be his major stature was true; it grows squarely out of the implications of the first novel, and represents a coming-to-grips with the true concerns of the author's experience—an experience, I believe, that is still very much Southern, but in significant respects not that of the previous generation of Southern writers. To illustrate what I mean, I must first review the plot of *Set This House on Fire*.

There are three main characters in the novel: Mason Flagg, a would-be playwright, Cass Kinsolving, a painter, and Peter Leverett, a lawyer. Flagg is a wealthy, clever, bedeviled young man, who is always "going to write" a play but never does. Handsome, conversant in the arts, a brilliant talker, he spends his days and nights in quest of some ultimate sensation, usually sexual. Sex, he keeps insisting, is the only frontier left to modern man. Essentially Flagg is a fraud, a poseur, in some ways reminiscent of the character Starwick in Thomas Wolfe's *Of Time and the River*.

Cass Kinsolving is a painter who cannot paint. A Southern boy, he is wedded to a sweet and not very intelligent woman named Poppy, and they have several children. A considerable portion of his time is spent in getting and remaining drunk.

Peter Leverett, through whom much of the story is related, is a boyhood friend of Mason Flagg's, who goes to visit Flagg in the Italian coastal town of Sambucco, where the major events of the novel take place. Peter is from Port Warwick, Virginia, the scene of *Lie Down in Darkness*. The new novel begins when Peter travels to Charleston, South Carolina, where a now-regenerate Cass Kinsolving is living and painting, and together they piece out the details of what happened in Sambucco, where a young peasant girl had been raped and Mason Flagg killed.

We see Mason Flagg, in other words, through the eyes of two persons—Peter Leverett, who knew him as a youth and as a young man, and Cass Kinsolving, who knew him in Sambucco just before his death. It is here that the chief structural flaw of the novel lies. For if this novel were primarily a study of Mason Flagg, what made him into the harried and driven creature he was, what drove him to his death, then the structural scheme that Styron chose to give his story might have sufficed.

But important though the character of Mason Flagg is in this novel, it is not in him that the chief meaning of the story is to be found. Rather, the central figure is the painter Cass Kinsolving.

For most of the novel, Cass is a man in bondage. In Paris, before he goes to Sambucco, he lives in an alcoholic daze, tortured by his inability to paint, spending his time drinking, wandering about, pitying himself, doing everything but confronting his talent. At length he moves his family down to Italy, where he comes under the sway of Mason Flagg. At one point Flagg even forces him, in exchange for his largesse, to paint a pornographic picture for his collection. Cass also becomes enamoured of an Italian peasant girl, and steals medicines in a hopeless attempt to save the life of her father, an old man in the last stages of tuberculosis.

Peter Leverett, about to leave Rome for the United States, drives over to Sambucco to visit Mason Flagg, arriving in time to witness the cataclysmic events that end the novel. The peasant girl is raped by Mason Flagg, then brutally murdered. Flagg is found dead at the foot of a cliff. The solution to these crimes is discovered by a philosophical young Italian policeman, who allows the culprits to go unpunished by the law.

The meaning of these events exists, as I have said, not in Mason Flagg's life but in Cass Kinsolving's. When Peter Leverett and Cass meet several years later to analyze what happened at Sambucco, Cass is well again, doing the painting he could not do in Europe, earning a living, caring for his wife and family. And though this novel is a murder mystery, the principal question it proposes is why Cass was for so long in bondage, unable to paint the pictures he wanted to paint and unable to receive and return the love of his wife and children.

In the events that come to a climax at Sambucco, I think, we do find out why. Cass was unwilling to accept the responsibility of his own talent, unwilling to face up to the fact that it alone could accomplish its own perfection. He wanted to find a form for his art outside of himself, when he alone it was who could give his art, and therefore his life, reason for being. He could not put up with his creative limitations and work his way out of them. He looked outside of himself, to the society, the people, the institutions surrounding him, for what could be found only within himself.

This was the hold that Mason Flagg had on him. For Mason could provide wealth, afford the glamor and excitement of "life," "experience"—or so Cass tried to pretend. Throughout the novel Cass attempted to deny the personal responsibility of his talent, attempted to substitute external experience for the dedication to artistic creativity that for him could be the only true account. He sought escape into "life," in alcohol, in false visions of Wordsworthian "ecstasy" that gave him the illusion of beauty, in Mason Flagg's largesse and phony dilettantism, in an insubstantial, idyllic romance with the peasant girl, in a quixotic and forlorn attempt to doctor an old man back to health. All these activities were ways of avoiding his own true mission and refuge—the remorseless requirements of discovering how to paint the pictures he wanted to paint. And because he was an artist, all these false externalizations of his need failed.

The attainment of this realization, through grief and

pain, constitutes the development of the novel, and though it requires five hundred pages and two hundred thousand words, as a story it is dramatically and artistically convincing. When at last we put down this novel, we have witnessed the resolution of a rending conflict within a man.

Why, however, is Cass so constituted that it takes him so long to find out what at last he learns? We accept the reality of his bondage to "life"—but how, we may ask, did it come to be? The answer is there, but—and this, I think, is the major structural defect of *Set This House on Fire*—it does not lie in the experience of Cass Kinsolving. Instead, it is found in the characterization of Peter Leverett.

For it was Peter, not Cass, who grew up with Mason Flagg, who through him was exposed to the delusion of self-fulfillment through external "experience," instead of through personal creativity, who was progressively tempted by Mason Flagg's advocacy of false gods. The spiritual duel between Mason Flagg and Cass Kinsolving that constitutes the dramatic struggle of *Set This House on Fire* was begun long before Cass went to Sambucco and encountered Mason Flagg. It commenced in Virginia, when Mason and Peter were students in preparatory school together. As Peter wrote of his attitude toward Mason then, "his wealth, his glamorous connections, his premature ease with the things of the flesh— they worked on me a profound fascination." It is this attitude that is transferred, as it were, by the author to Cass Kinsolving, a Cass who has been miserably wasting his time in Paris trying to be an artist without painting, and who wanders down to Sambucco when even the opportunities for self-delusion possible to him in a city such as Paris begin to fail.

Mason's last, despairing attempt to "own" Cass Kinsolving by raping Cass's girl friend was the culmination of a long battle. Why did Mason try to dominate first Peter Leverett and then Cass Kinsolving? Because he knew that they alone, of all those who comprised his acquaintanceship, could judge him as an artist. Tempted though they both were, they alone did not confuse what Mason did with the true artistic responsibility. At one point, early in the novel, one of Mason's admirers praised him to Cass in these words: "That Mason. Now there's a boy for you. A genius. Figure everything he's got. The eyes. The nose. The *expression*. Everything. It's uncanny, I tell you. Just like his dad." "You've read his play?" Peter asks him. No, the man replies, "but he's told me about it. It can't miss, I tell you. It's a natural. The boy has genius." But genius is a matter of plays written, not plays talked about, and Peter and Cass know it. Mason could bribe others, but he could not bribe them. They would not be owned.

But what is Cass Kinsolving's relationship to Peter Leverett? In the novel ostensibly both are friends of Mason Flagg, and that is all. Dramatically, psychologically, however, they are more than that. *They are one and the same person.* We meet Cass Kinsolving in mid-passage, a painter who cannot paint, a created, believable character. It is Peter Leverett's past history, not Cass's, that explains why Cass cannot paint. Peter Leverett, in other words, *becomes Cass Kinsolving.*

Now from a strictly logical point of view, that ought certainly to compromise Styron's novel. How can the experience of one character serve to create the characterization of another and entirely different man? But I want to emphasize that nevertheless we *do* believe in Cass Kinsolving. As a character he is convincing, and the events that give the novel its conflict and its resolution happen to him, not to Peter Leverett. So perceptive and

imaginative is the characterization of Cass that the explanation of how he got that way, though interesting, is
not finally at primary importance. Though logically we
know that the early experience happened not to Cass but
to Peter Leverett, dramatically and psychologically the
development of the characterization is so secure that as
readers we do what in terms of plot logic we should not
be able to do: we give Peter Leverett's experience to
Cass. We accept him, when he turns up in Paris, for
what he is on the basis of what we know about Peter
Leverett.

Building upon it, Styron succeeds in making Cass
emerge as a formidable characterization, a figure that
almost anyone who has ever attempted to paint or write
or otherwise create artistic work can recognize. Cass
Kinsolving is a familiar and crucial figure of our time,
the artist seeking reality, confusing it with "life," strug-
gling to locate it in his work. And coming as Cass Kinsolving does to us, the heir, so to speak, to a generation of
fictional protagonists by Southern novelists, it seems to
me that his plight thoroughly mirrors the situation that
confronts the Southern writer of Styron's generation—
a generation for whom the traditional institutions and
embodiments of values have been so seriously modified
that a new relationship between attitudes and values on
the one hand, and "real life" on the other, must be created. To do that, the values and attitudes themselves must
be examined. And what Styron makes his fictional artist
learn is what Allen Tate once said about the poet Hart
Crane. Crane, he declared, "is betrayed, not by a defect
in his own nature, but by the external world; he asks of
nature, perfection—requiring only of himself, intensity."
The poet, says Tate, did not face up to the obligation "to
define the limits of his personality and to objectify its
moral implications in an appropriate symbolism." The

Cass Kinsolving whom Peter Leverett visits in Charleston several years after the events of Sambucco has accepted that obligation, though he never speaks of such things at all. Wrongly constructed or not, the characterization is there.

Why, one asks, did Styron separate his characterization in this way? My own notion is that Styron himself did not fully recognize the essential connection between Peter Leverett's experience and Cass Kinsolving's. The actual origins he gives for Cass are not important to the novel. Cass was a boy from a small coastal town in North Carolina, the son of an Episcopal minister, who was left an orphan at the age of ten and brought up by a Methodist uncle and aunt. During the Second World War he landed in an army psychiatric ward, took up painting as therapy, was later married, and went to Europe to live and paint. It is interesting, though, that when Cass wins his way to sanity and takes his family back home to America to live, he goes not to North Carolina, but to Charleston, South Carolina, a seaport city—precisely what Port Warwick, Peter Leverett's home, was.

As for Peter Leverett, he too goes home in the novel, but early in the story, before he visits Cass in Charleston and they recall the events of Sambucco. When Peter stops by at Port Warwick there is a moving scene in which his father takes him driving about the city, and he is greatly struck by the changes that have taken place. Port Warwick now

> had grown vaster and more streamlined and clownish-looking than I thought a decent southern town could ever become. To be sure, it had always been a ship-building city and a seaport (visualize Tampa, Pensacola, or the rusty waterfront of Galveston; if you've never

seen these, Perth Amboy will do), and in official propaganda it had never been listed as one of the ornaments of the commonwealth, but as a boy I had known its gentle seaside charm, and had smelled the ocean wind, and had lolled underneath giant magnolias and had watched streaked and dingy freighters putting out to sea and, in short, had shaken loose for myself the town's own peculiar romance. Now the magnolias had been hacked down to make room for a highway along the shore; there were noisy shopping plazas everywhere, blue with exhaust and rimmed with supermarkets; television roosted upon acre after acre of split-level rooftops and, almost worst of all, the ferryboats to Norfolk, those low-slung smoke-belching tubs which had always possessed their own incomparable dumpy glamour, were gone, replaced by a Yankee-built vehicular tunnel which poked its foul white snout two miles beneath the mud of Hampton Roads.

Port Warwick, that is, is the *New South*—the South of modern times, in which the comfortable, sleepy old landscape is hardly recognizable. Peter and his father stop at a service station, and while there, Peter suddenly divines that almost on the very spot of reclaimed land where the gasoline pump now stands, there had once been a marsh creek where he had almost drowned and had been rescued by a Negro crab fisherman. Awed at the thought of the change that had taken place, in himself above all, he thinks that

perhaps one of the reasons that we Americans are so exceptionally nervous and driven is that our past is effaced almost before it is made present; in our search for old avatars to contemplate we find only ghosts, whispers, shadows; almost nothing remains for us to feel or see, or to absorb our longing. That evening I was touched to the heart; by my father's old sweetness and decency and rage, but also by whatever it was within me—within life itself, it seemed so intense—that I knew to be irretrievably lost. Estranged from myself and from my time, dwelling neither in the destroyed past nor in the fantastic and incomprehensible present, I knew that I must find the answer to at least several things before taking hold of myself and getting on with the job.

But what does Peter find out, in the ensuing story? He finds out what happened to Cass, not to himself. So if, as I have suggested, the young Peter Leverett is the young Cass Kinsolving, then several things are obvious. Peter's (and therefore Cass's) past is, figuratively and literally, buried in time. The creek where he almost died is covered by acres of fill dirt, upon which the properties of the new industrial South have been constructed. He cannot, as he says, dwell in the "destroyed past." When Cass Kinsolving, in effect the adult Peter Leverett, goes home, it is to a city which in many ways is like Port Warwick, but which is not Port Warwick. Charleston resembles Port Warwick in that both are seaports, both are on tidewater, both are surrounded by salt marsh; but except for the fact that both are seaports, their particular histories are quite different. There is thus, so far as Cass is concerned, no continuity of community, of history, of family role. But in Charleston, to a much greater extent than in Port Warwick (which is Newport News, Virginia), the evidence of the past does survive into the present. It is very much more an historical town, much more leisurely and quaint, in its waterfront areas at least, than Port Warwick. In other words, the general climate of everyday life in the older, less-industrialized South remains for Cass, but *without any personal, institutional ties to it on his part.* He lives there, but he is not of it.

Before Cass comes to Charleston, he is adrift, homeless, cut off from his past. He wants to paint; he cannot. He is married, with children; he wants to love them and care for them, but he cannot. He cannot discern any order and meaning to his experience. What he finally learns, in the frenzied chaos that produces the catastrophe at Sambucco, is that only through respect for his own personal integrity, as a human being and as an artist, can he give his life the order he seeks. He cannot look for his order and purpose in "life," in the institutions of the exterior world, in his environment, but only within himself. He must face his responsibilities, paint his own pictures. Then, and not until then, can he go home, to America, to the South.

What Cass had to know, before he could go home, was what Peter Leverett knew, about his childhood, about the place where he grew up—that it was, in Peter's words, "irretrievably lost." But also, as Cass finds out, that for a man to live and create, it must be replaced by order and purpose within oneself. For a world without order and purpose, without the values of love, self-respect, compassion and responsibility for one's fellow human beings, is a world of chaos and fragmentation, ending in the blind destructiveness of Cass at Sambucco. The results of what Peter Leverett has known produce the condition in which Cass finds himself in Paris and Sambucco. From this condition Cass manages finally to extricate himself.

In effect, Cass Kinsolving completes the symbolic journey begun by Peyton Loftis in *Lie Down in Darkness*. In the first novel Styron's protagonist left Port Warwick. In the second novel Cass Kinsolving comes home to Charleston. Earlier I sought to demonstrate how Peyton's background, society, and tradition had failed, not in terms of directly producing her own dramatic plight, but through their absence, their failure to be importantly present at all. Peyton dies in New York, estranged not only from Port Warwick but from human society as well. Now Cass Kinsolving comes back to the South, but not until he can furnish within himself the order, stability, and continuity he needs to exist, to live with other human beings.

What I am getting at is that *Set This House on Fire* is, among other things, an examination of the validity of certain precepts by which people live: an examination conducted on *Southern* terms. Cass Kinsolving's particular past is dead, forgotten, inoperative—but Cass as Styron describes him is nevertheless a man who requires the stability of belonging to a place that is anchored in time and that possesses order and stability. As Cass tells Peter Leverett in Charleston,

> "Funny thing, you know, in Europe there sometimes, when everything got as low as it can get for me, and I was hating America so much that I couldn't even contain my hatred—why even then I'd get to thinking about Charleston. About how I'd like to go back there and live. It almost never was in North Carolina, or the pinewoods up there in Columbus County where I was brought up. I didn't want to go back there and I sure as hell didn't want to go back to New York. It was Charleston I remembered, straight out of these memories I had when I was a boy. And here I am." He pointed across the wide harbor, radiant and gray-green and still as glass, then in an arc around the lower edge of the town where the old homes, deep in shade, in hollyhock and trumpet vine and bumblebees, had been defiled by no modish alteration, no capricious change. "You'll search a long way for that kind of purity," he said. "Look at that brickwork. Why, one of those houses is worth every cantilevered, picture-windowed doghouse in the state of New Jersey."

What Styron has done has been to describe the terms on which a man such as Cass Kinsolving can find such order and tranquillity for his life. It is emphatically made clear that Cass is unable to do without these commodities, but equally there is no intimation that he can find them in the life and institutions lying outside of himself. He must do it on his own. Cass can finally live in Charleston, when Peyton was unable to live in Port Warwick or New York and he himself in Paris and Sambucco, because he is creating—which is to say he is drawing his spiritual sustenance from within himself. Until he can do this, the environment makes no difference and the past is of no help. Cass himself is an orphan; Peter Leverett's Port Warwick is buried beneath the fill dirt; the traditional Southern circumstance, with its historical notion of role, its institutions, its community order, means nothing anymore.

We remember Faulkner's Quentin Compson in Cambridge; for him too the Southern past no longer enabled him to define himself as a man. The difference is that Quentin's failure to discover his role was inextricably connected with his failure to embody the values of a Yoknapatawpha County that no longer existed; while, contrariwise, Cass's eventual success in finding his place comes *before* he joins the community. Quentin left the stability behind him, geographically and in time; Cass brings to the community his own stability. Cass is in effect a new man, prepared to sink down roots in the community—but a different kind of a community for him, one in which there are no historical and social links with his past. Quentin's hope for stability and sanity rested in institutions, traditions, concepts of role, theological authority that no longer existed. Cass Kinsolving knows nothing about such things; he creates his own salvation.

The stability and order he finds cannot be dissociated from religious values—the ability to love, to care for one's loved ones, to act justly and responsibly, to be kind and generous. And these things Cass has learned to do, through realizing his own private integrity as a human being. "A man cannot live without a focus," Cass remarks at one point. "Without some kind of faith, if you want to call it that. I didn't have any more faith than a tomcat. Nothing. Nothing! . . . I was blind from booze two thirds of the time. Stone-blind in this condition I created for myself, in this sweaty hot and hopeless attempt to get out of life, be shut of it, find some kind of woolly and comforting darkness I could lie in without thought for myself or my children or anyone else." But let it be noted that if Cass has acquired such faith, it is personal, and apart from any revealed theology. We recall that his father was an Episcopal minister, and that he was brought up by Methodists. At one point, too, Cass describes his first sexual experience, with a female member of the Jehovah's Witnesses sect, who comically remarks to him that "That's one thing you'll find out about us Witnesses. We're right liberal as concerns social contacts." If we wish finally to describe Cass's attitude as being essentially religious, there is certainly no hint that its basis lies in any of the theological systems of his childhood. In describing Cass at Sambucco, Styron examined what Cass needed to do in order to achieve order, integrity, and tranquillity, and showed Cass living in hell on earth when he tried to do without spiritual conviction and moral responsibility. The redemption was from within.

I have spoken of Styron's fiction as embodying the the traditional Southern attitudes toward man's place in society, his need for order and stability, his desire for the love and responsibility that come from the authority of religious conviction, but without the institutions, the experience of life that embody those attitudes. I have said that *Lie Down in Darkness* possessed those attitudes, but without their fictional grounding in the traditional Southern institutions. In *Set This House on Fire* Styron may be said to have proceeded with an examination, inherent in the fictional process, of the terms by which such attitudes can survive and flourish in modern life—how Cass Kinsolving, a Southerner of our time and place, can live and cherish and create. It is as if, where the hell of *Lie Down in Darkness* lamented their absence, the purgatory of *Set This House on Fire* described their reacquisition. But the conditions whereby they could be regained necessarily involved a complete alienation from the time and place in which they had once existed, and from which they had disappeared. Cass Kinsolving's entire separation from the South was, in effect, a severance from all lingering institutions and traditions that once might have, however inadequately, embodied those attitudes. He was indeed a man without a country. So that for Styron, *Set This House on Fire* represented a clearing away of the debris, as it were, of the Southern fictional texture—all the accustomed embodiments of setting, history, community that for so long have provided the experience from which Southern literature has been created, now swept away, like Peter Leverett's memories of the past, in the fill dirt upon which a new and modern experience was erected. Not in Port Warwick, but in Paris and Sambucco, was Cass Kinsolving's full initiation in the cauldron of modern experience conducted. All his surviving attitudes, his ideals, his emotions were there examined and tested, and finally made to depend for their reality on his own inward and personal acceptance of them.

Whereupon he returned home. What, though, of Cass's alter ego, Peter Leverett? It may be noted that Peter Leverett no longer lives in the South. At the end of the novel, Cass writes to him that he "wanted to tell you how glad I am that N.Y. goes O.K. for you now." And there is no reason to suppose that Peter Leverett will be any more or any less happy living in New York than Cass seems to be in the South. To each one, "home" means something different. It is involved more importantly with what is going on inside them than with the place in which they have settled down to live and to work. For both these fictional characters live in a faraway country now, and that country, bound though it is to the "real world" by the pinions of time and memory, is finally a country of the mind.

Even so, it still bears a notable resemblance to a particular American region. Thus Cass Kinsolving, seated with Peter Leverett in a boat, fishing:

> He rebaited his hook and cast out the line again, squinting against the light. The river shores were immensities of shade—water oak and cypress and cedar; the heat and the stillness were like a narcotic. "September's a good month for this kind of fishing," he said after a long spell of silence. "Look over there, over those trees there. Look at that sky. Did you ever see anything so *clean* and beautiful?"

For Cass, who has come back, there is still the marshland, the water, the fishing, the sun. Changed and altered almost beyond recognition in many respects, it is even so the South.

POSTSCRIPT:
A Look Backward
and Ahead

In May of 1956 there was held at Vanderbilt University a reunion of the Nashville Fugitives, the group of young poets who in the early 1920's had edited and published *The Fugitive*, a little magazine which in the several years of its life earned an international reputation for the quality of some of its verse. Two of those who returned to Nashville that May had been teachers during the early 1920's: John Crowe Ransom and Donald Davidson. Others had been undergraduate students: Allen Tate, Robert Penn Warren, Merrill Moore. Among the other Fugitives present were William Yandell Elliott, now a noted political theorist; Alec Brock Stephenson, Jesse Wills, and Alfred Starr, now business and professional men of Nashville; and Sydney Mttron Hirsch, who had been important in the group's formation. Also at the reunion were two men who had been Vanderbilt undergraduates just after the Fugitive period: Andrew Nelson Lytle and Cleanth Brooks. For three days the Nashville Fugitives argued about poetry and reminisced about *The Fugitive* times. What they said was taken down on tape, and a transcript has since been edited and published by Vanderbilt University Press.

The Fugitive had been a typical little magazine of the period, in format and editorial dynamics similar to dozens of others published during the 1920's and afterward, both in the South and elsewhere. Most of the other magazines have been long-since forgotten, and the editors who conceived them and the poets who contributed to them likewise forgotten. But *The Fugitive* will hardly be forgotten any time soon. Had any little literary magazine before or since contained so much talent on its editorial board? Had the pages of any other little magazine contained as many poems still read and admired decades afterward? Had it not played a leading role in what had turned out to be a literary revolution?

Hearing the Fugitives talk and reminisce, one could not doubt, if indeed one had ever doubted, that their coming-together at Vanderbilt University in Nashville, Tennessee, during the 1920's had not been a merely fortuitous coincidence, that one could not attribute merely to chance their presence in that room almost forty years later. Too much feeling of a time and place was involved, too strong an awareness of their existence as a group, of their origin and identity as Southerners of a particular epoch in the life of a particular region.

Of the several Fugitives who had gone on to become professional men of letters, all had come to Vanderbilt originally from small country towns. Of good families, they had been sent to the university in Nashville to be educated; presumably they would go back home afterward and become leading citizens of their communities. But they had not gone back home. The intensity of their commitment to literature had led them far away from the community of their origins, into the cosmopolitan world of letters, of which they were now distinguished citizens.

The Southern Literary Renascence may be said to have begun with the formation of the Fugitives just after the First World War. Of the Southern writers who today enjoy the greatest critical reputations, not one had appeared importantly in print before John Crowe Ransom and Allen Tate began publishing regularly in *The Fugitive*. Ellen Glasgow and James Branch Cabell were really of the previous generation, and though in the 1920's, when the Fugitives were first meeting, their popularity was very high indeed, it has since receded, and when one thinks of modern Southern literature, one is likely to have in mind the generation of Faulkner, Wolfe, and the Fugitives.

No one can predict how much of the literature written by members of the Fugitive group and by the other Southern writers of their generation will survive. Contemporary reputations are the most treacherous of things. "Sir, we are a nest of singing birds," said Dr. Johnson of the poets of Pembroke College, Oxford. Who now remembers any of them except Johnson himself? Yet there was also Johnson's famed Literary Club, which gathered at the Turk's Head Tavern. The members of that group also possessed widespread contemporary reputations, and in this instance their contemporaries seem to have been correct, since today many of them are not at all forgotten. One simply does not know about such things.

On July 6, 1962, at the age of sixty-four, William Faulkner died. Of all the modern Southern writers, he was the greatest. No matter what may be the eventual fate of his contemporaries' books, his own appear destined to survive for many years to come. So far as his contemporary audience can tell, he seems to be one of the truly great figures in twentieth-century literature, to be ranked with Proust, Joyce, Yeats, Eliot, and Mann. The news of his sudden death did not come with the shock that Ernest Hemingway's death had occasioned the summer before. In part, no doubt, this was because of the difference between the personalities of the two men. Hemingway was a public figure, a celebrity. His photograph was familiar to millions. He projected the force of his personality upon his time. By contrast, Faulkner was quiet, unobtrusive; he shunned publicity, preferring to let his books speak for themselves.

But in part, too, the difference had to do with their art. There was a curious quality of incompleteness about Hemingway's lifework; though he had written five full-length novels, a number of excellent short stories, and several other books, everyone had been hoping that he would produce one more major work to crown his career, something better than anything he had yet done. His death meant that such a work would never be written, unless by chance it waited unpublished among his manuscripts. Barring this unlikely happenstance, we would have to be content with what we had.

The passing of Faulkner, on the other hand, brought no such regret for work left undone. By and large, he had said what he had to say. His lifework was complete. The books of his later years, however they may have varied in quality, did not substantially modify a reputation that rested primarily on a group of novels written in the late 1920's and during the 1930's and early 1940's. I doubt that even his fondest admirers would insist that he had it in him to surpass that earlier work. He had used his talents to the fullest extent, made the most of what he had been given. He cannot be fitted into a blighted generation; we cannot point to the time, the place, the condition of the culture as explanation of his failure to write better books. He did his best, not once but on a number of occasions. The shelf of books he leaves behind is all the achievement that any man might desire.

He created a mode of tragedy, explored it to its utmost, used it to write his finest novels. His death came after that mode had been made to bear its richest possible yield. That mode was the Southern mode; it involved a special way of looking at experience and evaluating it. Thomas Sutpen, Quentin Compson, Joe Christmas, Flem Snopes, the Bundrens—one reads of them in the fullness of their rhetoric and the matchless reality of their human persistence in time. By comparison, Hemingway's characters seem oddly vulnerable and uncertain, Dos Passos' flat and colorless. Wolfe's are closest, perhaps, to Faulkner's vitality and magnitude—Old Gant at least could inhabit a world as rich and evocative as Faulkner's. This is not the only legitimate kind of fictional world; but is there another in American literature since Melville's that is as soundingly heroic and vivid?

If the coming of the Fugitives to Vanderbilt in the early 1920's was the beginning, then Faulkner's death marks the closing at least of one phase of the Southern Renascence in literature. I do not mean, of course, that good books will not continue to be written by Southerners of Faulkner's generation. He was but one, the most gifted perhaps, of a number of talented writers, most of whom are still very much alive and active. Several months before Faulkner's death Katherine Anne Porter brought out one of the most impressive novels of her generation—*Ship of Fools*. Robert Penn Warren is still producing regularly. We have surely not heard the last from Eudora Welty or Andrew Lytle. Before the writers of Faulkner's generation have completed their work, it is likely that the body of novels, stories, and poems that constitutes the Southern Literary Renascence will be appreciably larger than it now is.

All the same, he was the foremost writer of his time in the South. Without him the Southern Renascence would have been a greatly impressive cultural phenomenon, but I doubt that it would have seemed to dominate American literature as completely as it has. And if Faulkner's achievement is to be equalled or surpassed, it will have to be by one of the writers of the generation subsequent to his own. Of those who have appeared thus far, none seems likely to do so.

So far as we can tell, then, the Southern Renascence, in the form that we have known it, is coming to an end. A time and a place have produced a body of distinguished writing. No one would think to explain the nature of that distinction merely by examining the time and the place; as well attempt to explain *Hamlet* by a study of Elizabethan England. Even so, when one looks at William Faulkner and his contemporaries, observes their sudden arrival on the literary scene when before them there was very little, notices the many similarities in the way they use language, the way they write about people, the kind of life that interests them, one is convinced that literature grows out of a culture, and that theirs has grown out of the twentieth-century South, and has its roots in Southern history and life.

That culture is changing, rapidly. The South that Faulkner, Wolfe, Tate, Ransom, and their contemporaries knew when they were growing up in the years before the First World War was vastly different from the South between the wars. Thus the present generation of Southern writers, most of whom were born in the 1920's and grew to manhood in the 1930's and 1940's, many of them serving in the armed forces during the Second World War, writes out of a different experience, and the fiction and poetry show it. I have used the novels of William Styron, whom I think is the best Southern novelist of his generation, to indicate something of what is involved. That experience, as I have tried to show, is no less markedly Southern than its predecessor's, but it is one in which many hitherto typical Southern attitudes and institutions have been called into question. And if this was true during the 1920's and 1930's, then what may we not expect from the generation still in school, that which gew up in the 1940's and 1950's, when the South underwent changes in its social fabric perhaps more sweeping in character than ever before?

The point is that if Southern literature is to continue to play so important a role in national letters as it has done since the 1920's, it will have to be constructed on new foundations, based on markedly different conditions of experience, and will thus constitute a recognizably new and different phase of the Southern Literary Renascence. Its writers, forced to find new responses to new situations, cannot write in the forms developed by Faulkner and his contemporaries, without first subjecting those forms to an extensive remodeling and alteration. The new Southern writing will have to be, as I have sought to show in my discussion of Styron, substantially different in its values, its attitudes, its techniques, from that of the previous generation. The age, in Ezra Pound's phrase, demands the image of its own special grimace, and what has sufficed before, no matter how splendidly, will no longer suffice.

The best writers of the newest generation already reflect this difference in attitude and approach. In poetry it is especially noticeable: who would think to link the work of Randall Jarrell and James Dickey with that of John Crowe Ransom and Allen Tate? In fiction the difference is likewise evident. Not only Styron, but Peter Taylor, Elizabeth Spencer, Shirley Ann Grau, Peter Feibleman, George Garrett, and Reynolds Price seem to me to be writing out of an experience that is in many respects greatly at variance with that of their predecessors. Even Madison Jones, Shelby Foote, Walter Sullivan, and Flannery O'Connor, the last of whom is surely one of the best short-story writers of our time, do not seem to write their fiction in the way that the previous generation of Southern writers has done.

A single example may help to illustrate something of what is involved here. Consider, briefly the role of the outsider, the man from a different kind of life and culture, in the work of a writer such as Faulkner. I think of Joanna Burden in *Light in August*, or of Sutpen in *Absalom, Absalom!* In each case the stranger, however grotesquely, becomes a part of the Southern landscape and is, albeit with difficulty, subsumed into the patterns of Southern life. Compare either with the eastern European immigrant in Flannery O'Connor's "The Displaced Person." Mr. Guizac in that story is eventually killed, but not until he has irretrievably disrupted the customary patterns of Southern rural society. What in Faulkner is self-sufficient, more powerful than outside forces, is in Miss O'Connor's story far more vulnerable. The outside world breaks into Miss O'Connor's Southern scene as it does not do into Faulkner's. I suggest that the difference has to do in large part with the different experience of two generations of Southern writers.

It is not the experience, however, but what the writer does with it, that matters. And at this point no one can say whether the next phase of the Southern Renascence will equal the attainment of the generation preceding it. That Southerners will continue to write, and the rest of the nation continue to read their books, seems beyond question. All the evidence is to continuing vitality; each year produces a new crop of Southern writers. Consider that within the past several literary seasons we have seen the advent of Walker Percy's excellent novel, *The Moviegoer*, Joan Williams' *The Morning and the Evening*, Harper Lee's *To Kill a Mockingbird*. If none of these works is a major novel, the appearance of all three would seem to indicate that any pronouncement concerning the termination of the Southern Literary Renascence would be quite premature.

Yet, it may be asked, is any of the younger generation of Southern writers really in the same category as Faulkner, Wolfe, Warren, Welty, as Tate or Ransom? Whatever the attainments of the newer writers, so far as we can judge of such matters, are they not of a distinctly lower order of merit?

One would have to admit that none of the newer writers seems to be of quite such major stature, though several of them appear to have the potentialities for that kind of development. Of these, as I have said, Styron seems to me to come closest, but that is a matter of opinion. Whether his future work will justify the high value that many readers place on him remains to be seen. Likewise it remains to be seen whether additional young Southern writers, of greater stature than any of those now writing and publishing, will not arise. Each year new candidates continue to come forth.

Let us, however, turn from such dubious speculation. What is important is not what might happen, but what has happened: a literary renascence, a rich outpouring of artistic genius such as few times and places have ever before enjoyed. William Faulkner, Robert Penn Warren, Thomas Wolfe, Katherine Anne Porter, Andrew Lytle, Eudora Welty, Carson McCullers, Caroline Gordon; Allen Tate, John Crowe Ransom, Donald Davidson; William Styron, Flannery O'Connor, Peter Taylor, Randall Jarrell. All from one American region, during a few brief years. So incredible a galaxy of talent! Could any time and place, hopeful that its memory will survive, look for a more lasting monument?

NOTES

Page 3: The complex matter of Mark Twain's attitude toward Hannibal and his use of it in fiction has recently been brilliantly analyzed by Henry Nash Smith in *Mark Twain: The Development of a Writer* (Cambridge, Mass.: Harvard University Press, 1962).

Page 5: Miss Glasgow's comments on the South, both in her book of prefaces, *A Certain Measure* (New York: Harcourt, Brace and Co., 1943), and in her posthumous autobiography, *The Woman Within* (New York: Harcourt, Brace and Co., 1954), from which the quotation here is taken (p. 105), are not among the least informative parts of that Social History of Virginia she claimed to have worked on all her life.

Page 6: Or, if the *Library of Southern Literature* is too formidable, the biographical sketches of Mildred H. Rutherford's highly amusing *The South in History and Literature: A Hand-Book of Southern Authors from the Settlement of Jamestown, 1607, to Living Writers* (Atlanta, Ga.: Franklin-Turner Co., 1907) will do as well. My favorite is the essay on Judge Logan E. Bleckley, of whom Miss Rutherford says that "many of his decisions have become classics in literature as well as laws" (pp. 744–47).

Page 11: Warren's *Paris Review* interview appears in *Writers at Work: The Paris Review Interviews*, edited by

Malcolm Cowley (New York: Viking Press, 1959, pp. 183–207).

Page 19: Allen Tate discusses this matter of literature as the product of change in society in his essays on "Emily Dickinson" (pp. 197–213) and "The Profession of Letters in the South" (pp. 265–81), in *On the Limits of Poetry* (New York: Swallow Press and William Morrow and Co., 1948).

Page 22: Hubbell's comments on Cable are contained in his excellent *The South in American Literature, 1607–1900* (Durham, N.C.: Duke University Press, 1954, pp. 804–22). The quotations from Richard Watson Gilder's correspondence with Cable are from Arlin Turner's *George W. Cable* (Durham, N.C.: Duke University Press, 1956). Edmund Wilson's revaluation of Cable, in the form of a review of Turner's biography, appeared first in the *New Yorker* for November 9, 1957, and was subsequently incorporated into *Patriotic Gore: Studies in the Literature of the American Civil War* (New York: Oxford University Press, 1962, pp. 548–86, 593–604). Wilson was writing about Cable as early as February 13, 1929, when he reviewed a biography of Cable by his daughter in the *New Republic*, subsequently reprinted in *The Shores of Light* (New York: Farrar, Straus and Young, 1952, pp. 415–20).

Page 27: The emergence of the Jim Crow laws during the 1890's and early 1900's is chronicled in detail in C. Vann Woodward, *The Strange Career of Jim Crow* (New York: Oxford University Press, 1955). The current fracas in the South is concerned mostly with their continued presence, and it is interesting to realize that where Negro demonstrations against them have been greeted with violence, it is usually by the descendants of those same up-country rednecks who forced their passage.

Page 44: Cullen's book on *Old Times in the Faulkner Country* (Chapel Hill: University of North Carolina Press, 1961), written in collaboration with Floyd B. Watkins, is chiefly valuable as a reminder that without the genius of a Faulkner, the social history of Mississippi would be a very dull affair. Interestingly enough, Ellen Glasgow,

in *A Certain Measure,* displayed a similar attitude toward the Faulknerian approach to Southern life (see
p. 69).

Page 61: In my discussion of religion in Faulkner, especially
in *Light in August,* I have borrowed liberally from
Robert D. Jacobs' "William Faulkner: the Passion and
the Penance," contained in *South: Modern Southern
Literature in Its Cultural Setting* (New York: Double-
day–Dolphin, 1961, pp. 142–76), edited by Mr. Jacobs
and myself.

Page 73: Jonathan Daniels analyzes Wolfe as a North
Carolinian in *Tar Heels* (New York: Dodd, Mead and
Co., 1941). The essay, "Poet of the Boom," is reprinted
in *The Enigma of Thomas Wolfe* (Cambridge, Mass.:
Harvard University Press, 1953, pp. 77–90), edited by
Richard Walser.

Page 83: C. Hugh Holman's edition of *The Short Novels
of Thomas Wolfe* (New York: Charles Scribner's Sons,
1961) presents five such works, as Wolfe wrote them
and published them serially; their far greater effectiveness in this form than when broken up and incorporated
in the later "novels" is quite evident.

Page 86: Edward Aswell describes the process of editing
Wolfe's posthumous manuscripts in "A Note on Thomas
Wolfe," contained in Wolfe's *The Hills Beyond* (New
York: Harper and Bros., 1941, pp. 349–86). See also
Wolfe's letter to Aswell, dated May 6, 1938, in *The
Letters of Thomas Wolfe,* edited by Elizabeth Nowell
(New York: Charles Scribner's Sons, pp. 757–59).

Page 87: I am glad to report that since this essay was written, Mr. Richard S. Kennedy has published *The Window of Memory: The Literary Career of Thomas
Wolfe* (Chapel Hill: University of North Carolina
Press, 1962), in which he gives in detail the astounding
history of the editing of Wolfe's manuscripts. This
monumental work of research makes it clear that until
Wolfe's manuscripts are edited and published as they
were written, and not as Edward Aswell reworked
them, we will have only a very imperfect idea of Wolfe
as a writer after *Of Time and the River.*

Page 90: Wolfe's letter to Aswell about his "Gant-i-ness" is dated February 14, 1938, and is contained in *The Letters of Thomas Wolfe*, pp. 710–19.

Page 92: Anyone familiar with my own book on Wolfe, *Thomas Wolfe: The Weather of His Youth* (Baton Rouge: Louisiana State University Press, 1955), will recognize that I have changed my mind considerably about the chapters of *The Hills Beyond*.

Page 101: McLuhan's essay, "The Southern Quality," appears in *A Southern Vanguard*, edited by Allen Tate (New York: Prentice-Hall, 1947, pp. 100–21).

Page 101: One wonders why Wolfe's editor thought that *Of Time and the River* would profit from being changed from first to third person discourse. It seems to me that quite the reverse is true; placing the book in the first person would have the psychological effect of making it seem to be confessional literature, while in the third person it seems to be special pleading. It would be interesting to read *Of Time and the River* as a first person narrative.

Page 102: The point about Wolfe's relationship to his family, and the aptness of the Catullan quotation, is made by John Peale Bishop in his excellent essay, "The Sorrows of Thomas Wolfe," which appears in Bishop's *Collected Essays*, edited by Edmund Wilson (New York: Charles Scribner's Sons, 1948, pp. 129–38).

Page 106: Warren wrote a preface to the Modern Library edition of *All the King's Men*, which was also published in the *Sewanee Review*, LXI, No. 3, 476–80. The dramatic version of *All the King's Men*, published by Random House in 1960, also appeared in the *Sewanee Review*, LXVIII, No. 2, 177–239.

Page 107: Basso commented on "The Huey Long Legend" in *Life* for December 9, 1946, pp. 106 *ff.* Davis' comment was made in a review for the *New York Times Book Review* of August 18, 1946, entitled "Dr. Stanton's Dilemma," pp. 3, 24. The erratic nature of the reviews of *All the King's Men* was such that Robert B. Heilman reviewed the reviewers in an essay, "Melpomene as Wallflower; or, The Reading of Tragedy," *Sewanee Review*, LV, No. 1, 154–66.

Page 111: To this day the Longs have generally stood for

the removal of racism from Louisiana politics. When Huey Long's brother, the late Earl Long, had his famous fracas with the Louisiana legislature shortly before his death, it was over the issue of Negro rights; he was seeking to prevent disfranchisement.

Page 123: Warren's remark on Faulkner and the South was made in a speech at the University of Virginia, distributed as "the First Peters Rushton Seminar in Contemporary Prose and Poetry" and dated March 13, 1951, pp. 1–15. Much of the content of this essay was later included by Warren in the essay on Faulkner in Warren's *Selected Essays* (New York: Random House, 1958, pp. 59–79). For students particularly interested in the South, however, the Charlottesville speech, entitled "William Faulkner and His South," is well worth reading in its original form.

Page 129: Harry Modean Campbell, the critic cited, discusses Warren's philosophical attitudes both in "Warren as Philosopher in *World Enough and Time*," in *Southern Renascence: The Literature of the Modern South*, edited by Robert D. Jacobs and myself (Baltimore, Md.: Johns Hopkins University Press, 1953, pp. 225–35), and in "Notes on Religion in the Southern Renascence," in *Shenandoah*, VI, No. 3, 10–18.

Page 133: Willard Thorp's *American Writing in the Twentieth Century* (Cambridge, Mass.: Harvard University Press, 1960) is otherwise a very useful survey of modern American writing.

Page 145: Robert W. Daniel's essay on Eudora Welty, subtitled "The Sense of Place," is contained in *South: Modern Southern Literature in Its Cultural Setting* (pp. 276–86).

Page 153: For some reason that I cannot understand, Jinny Love Stark of *The Golden Apples* has been described by many commentators as a lively, entirely appealing character. She seems to me, on the contrary, to be a peculiarly nasty little creature.

Page 143: Ruth Vande Kieft, in her book-length study, *Eudora Welty* (New York: Twayne Publishers, 1962), which appeared after the present essay was completed, suggests intriguingly that King MacLain's Zeus-like role in *The Golden Apples* involves fathering almost all the Morgana characters who are "terribly at large, roaming on the face of the earth." These include not only the two MacLain twins, Randall and Eugene, but also Loch Morrison, Virgie Rainey, and the orphan girl Easter.

Page 159: The fact that the Old South rested on a foundation of human slavery nowadays would seem as prohibitively marring its usefulness as the ideal agrarian society. It is difficult to realize that as late as the 1920's and 1930's, this did not seem anything more than an unfortunate historical blemish. Allen Tate, for example, declared in "The Profession of Letters in the South" (1935) that it was because *Negro* slavery was involved that Southern antebellum culture was flawed. "The distance between white master and black slave was unalterably greater than that between white master and white serf after the destruction of feudalism. The peasant *is* the soil. The Negro slave was a barrier between the ruling class and the soil." This essay appears in Tate's *On the Limits of Poetry* (New York: Swallow Press and William Morrow and Co., 1948, pp. 265–81). I cannot imagine Tate producing such an analysis today.

Page 161: The poems of Donald Davidson included herein are contained in *Lee in the Mountains and Other Poems* (New York: Charles Scribner's Sons, 1949), and are published here through courtesy of Charles Scribner's Sons. The poems of John Crowe Ransom included herein appear in his *Selected Poems* (New York: Alfred A. Knopf, 1945) and are published here through courtesy of Alfred A. Knopf, Inc. The poems of Allen Tate included herein are from his *Poems 1922–1947* (New York: Charles Scribner's Sons, 1948) and are quoted through courtesy of Charles Scribner's Sons. The poems of Robert Penn Warren included herein are taken from his *Selected Poems, 1923–1943* (New York: Harcourt, Brace, 1944) and are quoted here through courtesy of William Morris Associates.

Page 162: Warren's remarks were made at the reunion of the Nashville Fugitives at Vanderbilt University in 1956, and appear in *Fugitives' Reunion: Conversations at Vanderbilt, May 3–5, 1956,* edited by Rob Roy Purdy (Nashville, Tenn.: Vanderbilt University Press, 1959).

Page 185: An interview with Styron by David Dempsey appeared in the *New York Times Book Review* for September 9, 1951, p. 27.

Page 188: Mailer's critique of Styron in *Advertisements for Myself* (New York: G. P. Putnam's Sons, 1959, pp. 464–65) was renewed in *Esquire* magazine for July, 1963 (pp. 64–69, 105), in a polemic entitled "Norman Mailer versus Nine Writers." Mailer seems to find this sort of thing much more satisfying than writing fiction.

Page 197: Aldridge's remarks on Styron appear in his *In Search of Heresy: American Literature in an Age of Conformity* (New York: McGraw-Hill, 1956, pp. 140–48). My own review of *Lie Down in Darkness*, entitled "What To Do About Chaos," was published in the *Hopkins Review*, V, No. 1, 65–68.

Page 221: Tate's "Hart Crane," in *On the Limits of Poetry*, cited above, pp. 225–37, has been extremely influential in subsequent estimates of Crane's work.

Page 231: *Fugitives' Reunion*, cited above.

INDEX

[Italicized page numbers indicate that the principal discussion of the entry is on those pages.]

248